FROM BORDERS TO PATHWAYS

INNOVATIONS AND REGRESSIONS IN THE
MOVEMENT OF PEOPLE INTO EUROPE

FROM BORDERS TO PATHWAYS

INNOVATIONS AND REGRESSIONS IN THE MOVEMENT OF PEOPLE INTO EUROPE

EDITED BY
MATTHEW ZAGOR

Australian
National
University

ANU PRESS

PERSPECTIVES ON EUROPE

Australian
National
University

ANU PRESS

Published by ANU Press
The Australian National University
Canberra ACT 2600, Australia
Email: anupress@anu.edu.au

Available to download for free at press.anu.edu.au

ISBN (print): 9781760466596
ISBN (online): 9781760466602

WorldCat (print): 1443551939
WorldCat (online): 1443561322

DOI: 10.22459/FBP.2024

Cover design and layout by ANU Press

This book is published under the aegis of the Perspectives on Europe editorial board of ANU Press.

Contents

List of illustrations

Figures

Tables

Abbreviations

AMIF	Asylum Migration and Integration Fund
CEAS	Common European Asylum System
CJEU	Court of Justice of the European Union
EC	European Commission
ECHR	European Court of Human Rights
EU	European Union
Frontex	European Agency for the Management of Operational Cooperation at the External Borders
GCR	Global Compact on Refugees
GRF	Global Refugee Forum
NGO	nongovernmental organisation
OECD	Organisation for Economic Co-operation and Development
TFEU	*Treaty on the Functioning of the European Union*
TPD	Temporary Protection Directive
UK	United Kingdom
UN	United Nations
UNHCR	United Nations High Commissioner for Refugees
US	United States

Contributors

Nicholas Clark is Professor of Political Science at Susquehanna University in Selinsgrove, Pennsylvania. His research focuses on elections, voting behaviour and public opinion in advanced industrial democracies. His research has been published in *Political Studies*, the *Journal of Common Market Studies*, *European Union Politics* and the *Journal of Elections, Public Opinion, and Parties*.

Dr Daria Davitti is Associate Professor (docent) of Public International Law in the Faculty of Law at Lund University, Sweden, where she works on the sustainability screenings introduced by the EU Taxonomy and their implications for international human rights law and international environmental law. Her research more broadly focuses on the implementation of international human rights law in complex contexts, including situations of armed conflict, climate breakdown, forced migration and humanitarian emergencies. She examines the obligations and responsibilities of states, international organisations (including international financial institutions) and private companies operating in such contexts, especially in relation to the privatisation of migration and the relevance of impact investing in refugee responses. Before joining academia, Professor Davitti served as a human rights field officer with the United Nations and was deployed in Afghanistan from 2006 to 2009. Her research in Afghanistan on the protection of the right to water in the context of extractive-sector investment was published as *Investment and Human Rights in Armed Conflict: Charting an Elusive Intersection* (Hart Publishing, 2019).

Dr Hab. Marcin Dębicki is a Professor at the University of Wrocław, Poland, in the Department of Sociology of Borderlands, Institute of Sociology, and a member of the Centre for Regional and Borderlands Studies. He deals with the social face of Central Europe, with particular emphasis on Poland's relationships with its neighbours, including its borderlands, publishing dozens of scientific articles and several essays and journalistic pieces on related issues. Marcin is the author of four monographs: on Czech–Polish stereotypes (2010), on the attitudes of Poles towards Lithuania and Lithuanians (2016, with Julita Makaro), essays on Central Europe (2017, with Marta Cobel-Tokarska) and on the Central Europeanness of the Polish town of Cieszyn (2021, with Radosław Zenderowski). He has co-organised a series of academic conferences and co-edited seven volumes on Poland's 'neighbourships' (2011–20, with Julita Makaro).

Timothy Hellwig is Professor of Political Science at the University at Buffalo, State University of New York. His interests are in voting behaviour and political parties. He is co-editor of *Economics and Politics Revisited* (Oxford University Press, 2023) and co-author of *Democracy Under Siege? Parties, Voters, and Elections after the Great Recession* (Oxford University Press, 2020).

Clare McBride-Kelly works at a global firm and is co-founder and Director of the Refugee and Migrant Swimming Project in the Australian Capital Territory. Clare spent 2023 as an intern with the United Nations Human Rights Office of the High Commissioner South-East Asia Regional Office in Bangkok, and continues to work on the establishment of a UN Strategic Litigation Network for the region. Clare graduated from The Australian National University in 2022 with a Bachelor of Asian Studies and a Bachelor of Laws (First Class Honours). She was awarded a Tuckwell Scholarship, a New Colombo Plan Scholarship and was named ANU Student Volunteer of the Year. Her specialist interests lie in international law, human rights law, dispute resolution, constitutional law, administrative law and refugee law.

Nicholas Simoes da Silva is reading for an MPhil in Law at the University of Oxford as a Lionel Murphy Scholar. He is a research assistant at the University of Oxford Faculty of Law and has six years experience in law reform in government, working at the intersection of law, data analytics and policy. He has worked at the Australian Securities and Investments Commission and the Australian Law Reform Commission and is a Research Associate at the Centre for European Studies, The Australian National University.

Dr Zvezda Vankova is Associate Professor of EU Migration Law at the Law Faculty of Lund University, Sweden, and the principal investigator of the project 'Refugee Protection or Cherry Picking? Assessing New Admission Policies for Refugees in Europe' (2023–27) funded by the Swedish Research

Council. Her research aims to examine the interface of legal infrastructures of human mobility and how their enforcement influences the rights and trajectories of people on the move.

Matthew Zagor is an Associate Professor at the ANU College of Law and Director of The Australian National University's Law Reform and Social Justice program. His scholarship draws on his background in anthropology, religious studies and human rights activism, focusing on the cultural, geopolitical and normative contexts within which constitutional, international, refugee and human rights law operate. His recent scholarship has unpacked assumptions about safe legal pathways in Europe and the Sahel, the evolving human rights culture wars in the wake of Covid-19, the political theology underpinning refugee resettlement rhetoric and the centring of refugee voices and lived experience in judicial decision-making. He was the lead investigator on the Borders to Pathways cluster of the Policy, Politics, Culture: EU Migration and Integration (PPCEUMI) network supported by the Erasmus+ program of the European Union.

Foreword

It was in the late 1980s when I first realised that Europe is defined by borders, walls and barriers. As a child, I went with my parents for a daytrip from Poland to East Berlin. I do not remember much about the trip, why or how we managed to get on the bus, but I do remember an army of border guards searching the bus for hours and, when we finally made it to Berlin, an intense sense of approaching another, this time impassable, border. Even without coming near the Berlin Wall, I remember being filled with a deep sense of anxiety mixed with excitement that somewhere there, very close but beyond our reach, was the true and colourful 'European Europe' (as contrasted with the 'Other Europe' to which we belonged). Years later, I read Larry Wolff's *Inventing Eastern Europe*[1] to better understand my initial sense that Europe and Europe's identity are grounded in splits, divisions and borders. In fact, as many cultural theorists argue, Europe essentially defines itself along its eastern borders and against its eastern neighbours, whoever they are. This has not changed much with the expansion of the European Union and NATO, only 'the east' acquired a broader and more complex meaning, while the Berlin Wall became 'a symbol of *all* border walls'.[2] The border remained a necessary element of European 'imaginative geography'[3] and, in fact, of Europe's idea of itself, as exposed by its response to the rising number of migrants and asylum seekers.

In 2015, about 1.3 million third-country nationals came to Europe to request asylum. In response to this situation, which became known as a 'migration crisis', the EU rushed to develop a comprehensive European framework for migration and asylum management. Five years later, in 2020, the New Pact on Migration and Asylum was launched and, after

---

1   Larry Wolff, *Inventing Eastern Europe: The Map of Civilization on the Mind of the Enlightenment* (Stanford: Stanford University Press, 1994).
2   David Frye, *Walls: A History of Civilization in Blood and Brick* (London: Faber, 2018).
3   Edward Said, *Orientalism* (New York: Pantheon Books, 1978).

extended negotiation, the key regulations were agreed on by EU member states and the European Parliament in December 2023. After decades of ad hoc measures taken to cope with the increased movement of people into the EU and after years of bitter debates between EU member states, we finally witnessed what European Parliament President Roberta Metsola hailed as a 'truly historic day'. Even though the agreement is fragile and politically charged, built on questions (such as the concept of third safe countries) and uneasy compromises (such as on the system of mandatory solidarity), the new pact deal, which promises to create fairer and more sustainable pathways, is expected to be sealed before this book reaches its readers.

While for some the EU has been making slow but steady progress in various aspects of migration management, for others, its response to migration has been unceasingly focussed on borders, walls and fences, and the policies of deterrence and exclusion. The 2015 European Agenda on Migration was heavily criticised by humanitarian organisations for favouring border security over human rights. The 2020 New Pact appears to be focussed on borders as well: improving border control, strengthening external borders or externalising European borders and enhancing border procedures. In the meantime, humanitarian organisations have been calling on EU institutions and member states to put human rights at the centre of all decisions and actions, while member states have become more determined to guard their borders even if it means restricting access to international protection for those who manage to reach them.

European Commission President Ursula von der Leyen recently announced: 'Migration is a European challenge that requires European solutions.'[4] However, looking from the inside unavoidably narrows the view. For an insular Europe, greater international cooperation is driven by the 'not-in-my-backyard' approach: forming partnerships with key third countries of origin, shifting responsibility to neighbouring countries such as Libya, Tunisia or Egypt, or learning from distant Australia how to 'stop the boats'. But external perspectives and experiences could be useful to better understand the challenge: to situate the 'crisis' and 'massive influx' narratives within a broader context, to revisit a dominant security narrative and, most importantly, to focus on pathways.

---

4   'Statement by President von der Leyen on the Political Agreement on the Pact on Migration and Asylum', Press release, 20 December 2023, European Commission, Brussels, ec.europa.eu/commission/presscorner/detail/en/statement_23_6781.

This book is such an attempt: a great collaborative effort to explore and rethink the borders-to-pathways dynamic from within Europe and from the perspective of third countries. Drawing on their multidisciplinary and multinational backgrounds, the authors analyse Europe's borders-to-pathways phenomenon in its complexity, from public attitudes, visa allocation mechanisms and economic-based routes to the multidirectional nature of pathways. Matthew Zagor has put together an excellent collection of high-quality interdisciplinary academic analyses that generously contribute to one of the most important and urgent challenges of the modern world. The collection reflects his own research approach characterised by transdisciplinarity and diversity and informed by his experience working with migrants and asylum seekers.

From Borders to Pathways is the first of three edited volumes arising from the research project 'Policy, Politics, Culture: EU Migration and Integration' supported by the Erasmus+ Jean Monnet Network program of the European Union and managed by the Centre for European Studies at The Australian National University. As the project's coordinator and its series editor, I would like to wholeheartedly thank all the contributors—those who have shaped the project from its beginning and those who joined us a short time ago to comment on the most recent events—for their work, expertise, commitment and dedication. The project, examining third-country migration and integration in the EU through the lenses of politics, policy, governance and culture, offers multifaceted, multidisciplinary and cross-sectoral insights into the complexities of the movement of people across borders. Bringing together scholars from Europe and the traditionally immigrant-based states of Australia, New Zealand, the United States and Singapore, it facilitates critical and comparative exchanges on global mobility and global responsibility. *From Borders to Pathways* is a great outcome of these efforts and an invitation to an ongoing and focussed reflection on barriers, fences, borders and walls to ensure we do not lose sight of pathways and possible new detours.

Katarzyna Kwapisz Williams
December 2023

1

From borders to pathways: Innovations and regressions in the movement of people into Europe—An introduction

Matthew Zagor

The gardeners have to go to the jungle. Europeans have to be much more engaged with the rest of the world. Otherwise, the rest of the world will invade us, by different ways and means.

—Josep Borrell, High Representative of the European Union for Foreign Affairs and Security Policy, Speech to European Diplomatic Academy, 13 October 2022

Where is the humanness? This is what I want to understand. Where is the humanness in this issue? She's ten years old and you know that I'm in Europe. You have the ability to solve this. It's a paper. They speak about humanity and humanitarianism and cooperation. Okay, but where? I didn't [see] any of this. Nothing. Nothing.

—ATH2.33, a woman from Syria in Athens, waiting to be reunified with her daughter, quoted in Squire et al. (2021)

The title of this volume relies on a pervasive image in European political and legal discourse. Just as the 'wall' was often adopted as reflecting the European postwar condition, so have borders and pathways come to represent the tensions, anxieties and vulnerabilities of Europeans, as well as the frustrations and aspirations of those hoping to make Europe their new home. It may be, of course, that the cartographical metaphor from which the title borrows excludes as much as it explains. Yet, this very simplicity and selectivity are also part of its attraction—politically as well as analytically. While we struggle to define Europe as a coherent geographical, let alone cultural, political, constitutional or even historical, entity, it nonetheless remains hard to think or talk about it without reverting to lines on maps, whether internal or external. And, as has been the case since the birth of mapping, how and where we draw or imagine those lines are consequential, both for those crossing them and for those for whom they provide a sense of identity, coherence and community (Hartley 1992; Wood 2010; Pickles 2003).

An interdisciplinary approach to the border–pathways phenomenon provides a nuanced picture of Europe's current reality, with disciplines learning from and drawing on each other in an increasingly fruitful dialogue. The rich literature coming out of border studies, for instance, has provided insights into the border as a productive process, de-territorialised and performative, constructed as much by sociopolitical narratives and geopolitical imperatives as by cartographical method and legal principle, and creating relations as much as separations (see Mezzadra and Neilson 2013; Gržinić 2018). International law and political theory have similarly taken significant 'spatial' turns over the past two decades, borrowing from historians who have exposed the role of the cartographical method in the establishment of empire and the concomitant construction of Europe, as well as the development of domestic, regional and international legal principles that have given the exercise of geopolitical power an appearance of rationality and neutrality (Miles 2018). Alongside this, of course, has been increased attention to the significance of the transfer of people, products and ideas over the centuries, following lines, pathways and networks (see, for instance, Benton 2010). Meanwhile, research on postcolonialism and neo-colonialism has worked with and, on occasion, reformulated and upended the spatial image of the European metropole and periphery to describe power dynamics and structural inequalities that remain embedded in today's geopolitics. These works persuasively demonstrate how such systemic factors continue to inform the European Union's foreign policy choices and, in turn, its migration priorities (Wimmer and Glick Schiller 2002; Fassin 2011: 213; Chakrabarty 2008). After all, it is no coincidence that the term 'fortress Europe', with its myriad martial connotations and historical resonances, continues to have such currency, not least in Europe's former colonies.

In brief, the legal, normative and culturally symbolic divisions of land, seas and resources still very much dictate European attempts to define the current *nomos*—the distribution of power and resources among nations, peoples and communities[1]—as well as the European Union's specific self-projection as a coherent, relevant and potent entity. And with both internal and external borders closing during the height of the Covid-19 pandemic, the division, exclusion, preferences and privileges founded on European efforts to control borders, territories and ocean-scapes only became more pronounced. This is very much a borders-to-pathways moment.

Some of these intellectual and discursive themes have found their way into informed lay culture. Books about walls, mapping and border politics are enjoying a particular popularity, at least in English-language bookstores,[2] just as the empire's ongoing ramifications for Europe—including with respect to migration—are debated in the public sphere on all sides of an increasingly muddled political spectrum.[3] Yet, the critical insights contained therein have largely failed to influence policy approaches to the movement of people. If anything, ethical nuance and policy sophistication have become increasingly rare commodities, especially when it comes to how Europe responds to irregular arrivals. The June 2023 tragedy of the *Adriana*, which sank with the loss of more than 600 lives despite being tracked for several days by Greek authorities and the European Agency for the Management of Operational Cooperation at the External Borders (Frontex), stands as a sober example. The deaths—all too common on the Mediterranean—were met with a brief outpouring of outraged grief and political finger-pointing, followed by the arrest of Egyptian people smugglers and a recommitment to tackling the scourge of the trade in human misery. What was absent from official statements was any reflection on the complicity of Greek, Italian and EU actors for pursuing policies of deterrence, facilitating pushbacks and stoking a dehumanising narrative of illegality and advantage-seeking, let alone any consideration of the geopolitical context that led to flight in the first place.[4]

---

1   Although I hesitate to cite his work, the starting point for these ideas remains Schmitt (2006).
2   A sample of books one might find includes Dodds (2021); Walia (2021); Brotton (2016); Marshall (2016).
3   Italy's Five Star Movement, the largest party in the Italian Parliament after the 2018 elections, epitomises the ideological confusion of the populism sweeping the continent, merging anti-immigrant and anti-establishment attitudes with humanitarian and environmental concerns.
4   This complicity has not escaped informed media coverage. See, for instance, Niarchos (2023); Stevis-Gridneff and Shoumali (2023). See also the work of Kenan Malik on earlier drownings (for example, Malik 2018).

This is consistent with attitudinal surveys over time, which is the opening topic of this collection. As political scientists and legal theorists have demonstrated (including several of those featured in this volume), the European public, media and politicians view national sovereignty, identity and security as intimately tied to the capacity to control the movement of non-citizens across the physical territorial border—understood through the blunt instrument and tired imaginary of the standardised map. As importantly, survey data indicate a tendency to view the European Union itself as uniquely responsible for failing to secure Europe's external borders and for opening internal ones to unwanted European guests, despite this being a shared legal responsibility.[5] In such a context, European politicians see both their political future and the viability of the union as dependent on addressing the fears and perceptions that have brought to power— whether in government or as a viable opposition—anti-immigration parties across the continent. It is thus unsurprising that criminalisation, securitisation, externalisation and deterrence remain key policy parameters and political tropes.

Crises narratives and the rise of Frontex: An invidious starting point

Identifying the myriad themes, trends and trajectories that inform and frame European responses to borders and pathways is an invidious task. A common starting point for those in the academy or civil society working on the movement of people is the dominant and uncomfortable narrative of the crisis. Seminar discussions and papers invariably start with contesting the label. It is standard procedure to remind an audience that the perceived criticality of any 'crisis' moment, whether in 2015 or since, is more a product of febrile European anxieties, institutional pathologies and historical hangovers of empire than any empirical challenge to the bloc's absorptive capacities, cultural integrity or general security. Indeed, the swift and largely effective response to 6.8 million Ukrainians fleeing the Russian invasion appears to prove the point and informs the discussion in at least two chapters in this collection.

5   See the regular surveys by Eurobarometer (europa.eu/eurobarometer/) and the Pew Research Center (www.pewresearch.org/), available online.

Yet, while we attempt to reframe 2015 discursively as a crisis point for Europe's constitutional order (Byrne et al. 2020: 871) or for 'solidarity' (Takle 2018; ECRE 2023a), capitalism, structural racism (Gržinić 2018: 'Introduction'), 'hospitality'[6] or European identity,[7] the popular and political narrative of a border or migrant crisis remains potent, pervasive and invasive, its ubiquity evident in the language of EU politicians and the popular media. Indeed, there are even dedicated draft regulations on 'crisis and *force majeure*' and 'situations of instrumentalisation' of migration that propose derogations from international and regional norms when the going gets tough (EC 2020)—consistent with the green light provided to Poland, Lithuania and Latvia in 2022 when faced with the conduct of Belarus. Lost in the debate, of course, are the voices of those whose movement along routes and pathways is 'instrumentalised' or characterised as threatening. The crisis narrative, moreover, continues to feed a broader justificatory discourse for policies and even institutional nomenclature (who can forget Ursula von der Leyen's 'Protecting Our European Way of Life' migration portfolio?) that until relatively recently would instead have been considered incompatible with European values and law. These values may make an appearance in relevant EU instruments, but such assurances seem increasingly empty alongside manifestly antagonistic policy formulations and rhetoric.

In this context, the fact that Frontex is rapidly becoming Europe's best-resourced agency should come as little surprise (European Parliament and European Council 2019).[8] Now a truly independent entity with expanded operational powers and its own personnel and standing corps,[9] Frontex is the most visible symbol of the EU's presence and potency, attempting to do what opinion polling repeatedly says the EU is expected—and failing—to do: control and secure the external border.[10] When EU commissioners

---

6   Some of these themes were apparent in the insightful comments of Catherine Woollard, Heaven Crawley, Masooma Torfa and Lucy Mayblin at the LSE European Institute and 89 Initiative public lecture, 'Europe's Refugee "Crisis": Where Are We Now?', London, 16 June 2021.

7   Woollard, in ibid.

8   This regulation, adopted in 2019, significantly expanded Frontex's mandate and reinforced its role as the European Border and Coast Guard Agency. It granted Frontex more operational powers, such as the ability to deploy its personnel and equipment in member states without their explicit consent, conduct joint operations and provide technical and operational assistance.

9   The European Border and Coast Guard standing corps, comprising border and coastguard officers from member states as well as Frontex staff, aims to provide a rapid response to border management needs and can be deployed at short notice to assist member states facing challenges at their external borders.

10   'Europeans increasingly associate the EU with not enough control at external borders, though far less so than with freedom of movement. At the same time, major Southern host countries must contend with persistently critical domestic attitudes towards the hosted displaced populations of concern' (Dennison and Dražanová 2018).

talk about breaking the people-smuggling business model while saving lives at sea or coordinate interceptions with Libya while purportedly training its coastguard in human rights protection—tempering the bloc's muscular approach to border control with its well-rehearsed humanitarian rhetoric—it is Frontex that is expected to achieve this delicate balancing act, making us feel simultaneously virtuous and safe. The language of official Frontex reports reflects this palpable sense of a continent at siege (Hage 2016: 38), with its *Strategic Risk Analysis 2022* presenting a set of drivers, all of which are disappointingly if predictably external to the EU and decontextualised from the foreign policy intrigues and economic interventions of European powers (Frontex 2022).[11] According to its authors, these drivers will result in increasing migration pressures over the coming decade and beyond. Europe's border concerns, in other words, are not going away. And, despite coming under deserved scrutiny for potential complicity in pushbacks that breach international law, it is Frontex with its burgeoning budget and expanding mandate that shapes the EU's view of the border and those seeking to cross it.[12] It is an agency of crisis, and 'crisis management', as Frontex itself explains, is now 'a permanent feature of EU border management'.

Faced with the dominance and ubiquity of this narrative of the permanent border crisis, compounded by the regular proclamation of existential threats from population implosions and endemic debt distress to the spread of xenophobic nativism and Viktor Orbán–style 'illiberal democracy',[13] scholars understandably look for theories that will explain the phenomena. A popular starting point is the work of Giorgio Agamben (2005: 1.2), whose prescient description of modernity as characterised by the 'voluntary creation of a permanent state of emergency' has left such a lasting impression on academic (if not policy) borders-to-pathways debates.[14] For Agamben, the Schmittian 'state of exception' in which law is suspended

---

11   The report singles out six 'megatrends'—security, demographics, climate change, inequalities, health challenges and governance systems—alongside the 'instrumentalisation of migration by non-EU countries', arguing, interestingly, that '[c]ompetition between global powers affects international cooperation and leads to a deglobalisation trend in which strategic autonomy is the dominant tendency'.

12   The budget of €6 million in 2005 had increased to €543 million in 2021. It is scheduled to receive €900 million in 2027, with the number of staff growing from 1,400 in 2005 to 10,000 today.

13   Viktor Orbán's 2014 speech calling for the creation of 'an illiberal new state based on national values', which he also labelled as 'Christian democracy', has become a favourite far-right trope in the United States and Europe. See Tjalve (2021: 332).

14   '[T]he state of exception has today reached its maximum worldwide deployment. The normative aspect of law can thus be obliterated and contradicted with impunity by a governmental violence that—while ignoring international law externally and producing a permanent state of exception internally—nevertheless still claims to be applying the law' (Agamben 2005: 6.10).

by the sovereign to deal with an emergency, whether real or manufactured, reduces to bare life those thereby excluded from the protection of the law. Importantly, those thereby excluded *from* the law *by* the sovereign (usually using the law itself) are nonetheless foundational to the social order and the formation, consolidation and extension of political power. Moreover, for Agamben, this dynamic takes its prototypical form in the state's treatment of the refugee and in the peculiar logic of the refugee camp[15] and, *mutatis mutandis*, the border whose structure I would argue is increasingly 'camp-like'. As Daria Davitti, a contributor to this volume, has said elsewhere, the physical, legal and biopolitical infrastructures that have converged around the crisis framing to push out borders and exclude non-citizens are the very embodiment of Agamben's state of exception: conduct enabled rather than hindered by international legal argumentation.[16]

Indeed, that the law operates to provide 'objective' criteria for the exercise of state violence comes up in chapters by Davitti and Zvezda Vankova, Clare McBride-Kelly and myself in this collection. This much is apparent in many of the policy developments and strategic postures that characterise Europe's approach to the border today. Many of these operate at or beyond the border—for instance: the externalising and outsourcing of coercive migration practices to third countries and private actors through non-binding (and thus largely unreviewable) arrangements,[17] paying non-European coastguards to intercept vessels before they reach European waters, adopting Australian-style offshore processing regimes,[18] conditioning receipt of aid or signing of pre-accession agreements on the criminalisation and detention of Europe-bound migrants (Akkerman 2022) and, under the New Pact for Migration, promoting European detention centres in border areas for expedited assessments. For human rights lawyers, the reinterpretation of international law to support such measures is a peculiarly concerning development. Indeed, the fact that some member states are currently arguing that persons held in border camps under the proposed Asylum Procedures Regulation

---

15   For development of these themes in the European refugee context, see Davitti (2018: 1173).
16   Ibid.
17   The General Court of the Court of Justice of the European Union declared that it lacked jurisdiction to determine actions brought by asylum seekers against the EU–Turkey Statement for being incompatible with EU fundamental rights, concluding that the statement was not an 'agreement' that could be reviewed under art. 263 of the *Treaty on the Functioning of the European Union*. See Orders of the General Court in *Cases T-192/16, T-193/16 and T-257/16, NF, NG and NM v European Council*. For the Danish proposals to introduce Australian-style offshore processing, see Tan (2022).
18   It is worth noting that these were rejected as inconsistent with European obligations to protect rights under both EU law and the *European Convention on Human Rights* when first proposed by Tony Blair's UK Government in 2003.

would not be on the state's territory—a manifestly untenable proposition in international law—only heightens the 'exceptional' nature of the proposal, normalising the practice of employing legal method effectively to suspend the protection of the law to marginalised communities (ECRE 2023b).[19] In this sense, juristic walls are alive and well in the new European Union.

Walls, pathways and the technological violence at Europe's borders

Nor have actual physical 'walls' disappeared. If anything, they are enjoying something of a renaissance, with more than 1,700 kilometres of migrant-unfriendly infrastructure built over the past eight years along the borders of Greece, Hungary, Poland, Lithuania, Latvia and Spain—a list to which we may soon be able to add Finland (Martín et al. 2023; Kauranen 2023). As the United Kingdom's *Telegraph* newspaper noted in a feature piece on the subject in December 2021: 'The European Union says that it builds bridges, not walls. Yet all around Europe, tall walls and fences, bristling with sophisticated technology, are being erected' (Rigby and Crisp 2021). While it is true that the EU, for now at least,[20] does not fund barriers of cement, steel and razor wire, this does not appear to apply to radars, drones, cameras and heat sensors, let alone the equipping and empowering of Frontex as Europe's border guard. In this context, the humanitarian sentiment that frowns on the building of walls looks increasingly performative.

This touches on another theme relevant to any work on borders and pathways: the increasingly technological nature of their creation and regulation and the close linkages between industry, science and border violence facilitated by the adoption of such technology. As noted, the EU's specific involvement in border technology to date is largely financial, but no less significant for being so. Take, for instance, those projects with tech-clever names such as ROBORDER and iBorderCtrl, which have received millions of euros from the EU to pilot often experimental technologies for use in state-based border control and immigration enforcement. A recent *Euronews* article listed an impressive array of such border-zone gadgets, including '[m]ixed reality glasses, unmanned underwater vehicles, 3D

---

19   It would also fall foul of the *European Convention on Human Rights*. See *Amuur v France*, Application No. 19776/92 (25 June 1996).
20   The tide may be turning on this issue. See Nielsen (2021); and European Council (2023: paras 23[d], [e]).

radars, radio frequency analysers, and 360[-degree] cameras … thermal imaging cameras, night-vision goggles, special sensors for detecting mobile phones, tracking devices and surveillance towers'—all designed to stop undocumented migrants crossing the many routes into Europe (Askew 2023). Nor are these being rolled out exclusively at the physical and oceanic borders. Drone flyovers of vessels carrying 'irregular' migrants on the high seas are now ubiquitous—a surveillance activity ill-coordinated with rescue obligations, as the recent tragedy of the *Adriana* grotesquely highlights. Some technology brings the border inwards, such as that now being used in refugee status determinations[21] or in migrant detention centres (Amnesty International 2020); other technology pushes the border outwards, as I argue in my contribution in this collection documenting the export of technology to police in the Sahel as part of conditional aid packages aimed at disrupting traditional migration routes across the Sahara.

Criticisms of the 'new digital borders of Europe' (Broeders 2007: 71; also Molnar 2020) and the proliferation of surveillance technologies have focussed on their potential to adversely impact the enjoyment of basic rights. Human Rights Watch, for instance, has documented the use of drones to facilitate illegal pushbacks between Türkiye and Greece and, when information is distributed to coastguards in Libya, to prevent the departure of those escaping abuse, thereby deflecting legal responsibility for the violations that often follow (Sunderland and Pezzani 2022). In her capacity as UN Special Rapporteur on contemporary forms of racism, racial discrimination, xenophobia and related intolerance, Professor E. Tendayi Achiume dedicated her 2020 General Assembly report to 'the xenophobic and racially discriminatory impacts of emerging digital technologies on migrants, stateless persons, refugees and other non-citizens, as well as nomadic and other peoples for whom migratory traditions are central'. Noting, *inter alia*, that in using digital technologies states are 'extracting large quantities of data … on exploitative terms that strip these groups of fundamental human agency and dignity', Achiume observed that they also advance and perpetuate 'the xenophobic and racially discriminatory ideologies that have become so prevalent, in part due to widespread perceptions of refugees and migrants as *per se* threats to national security' (OHCHR 2020: [3]). Other scholars such as Hashmi and Chander have reached similar conclusions that the use of artificial intelligence (AI) and other automated systems in Europe

---

21 See, for instance, the chapters in Olwig et al. (2019); also Molnar (2018; 2019: 7).

'contribute[s] to an increasingly racialised regime of surveillance of people on the move, often exacerbating violent and punitive border practices' (Hashmi and Chander 2022: 23).

The use of these technologies by border enforcement agencies is only likely to increase in the 'militarised technological regime of border spaces' (OHCHR 2020: [14], citing Csernatoni 2018: 175). This marries with the strong biopolitical element long evident in border control, but provides a disturbing twist: technology such as facial and emotional recognition tools now being used by Greece, Hungary and Latvia as part of their 'decision support systems' effectively treats the migrant's body as a site for border experimentation, which is justified by the twin objectives of scientific advancement and national security. Again, externalisation facilitates this conduct by removing the activity from obvious jurisdictional scrutiny, with the 'lawlessness' of the high seas the laboratory for testing new border technology.[22] The mapping of borders and bodies and the invasion of even the emotional life of the precarious migrant by the state are new frontiers for cartography not captured on the geopolitical map.

'Borders to pathways' as a composite phrase

So far, this introduction may appear somewhat imbalanced in its focus on the border rather than the pathway. There is, however, a deliberate double entendre in the composite phrase 'borders-to-pathways'. At first blush, it can be read as a progressive policy trajectory, whether descriptive, prescriptive or aspirational, from the exclusive to the inclusive. There is, after all, an oft-stated EU policy imperative to create safe and complementary pathways into Europe for 'legal' migrants, whether as part of labour, humanitarian or family-based migration streams. The original title of our research program, 'From Walls to Pathways', better captured such a dynamic, normative narrative.[23]

---

22   As Caterina Rodelli of Access Now has been quoted as saying: '[T]he relatively lawless international waters of the Med[iterranean] have served as a perfect laboratory for trialling and refining state-of-the-art technologies.' See Askew (2023).

23   The research program was funded by Erasmus+. See the Policy, Politics, Culture: EU Migration and Integration (PPCEUMI) network, at: ces.cass.anu.edu.au/research/projects/jean-monnet/policy-politics-culture-eu-migration-integration/about.

What has become clear while working on the project, however, is the extent to which borders and pathways are part of a conjoined, interdependent narrative, each calling the other into existence. How a state or supranational bloc envisages, regulates, depicts and monitors its physical and metaphorical borders determines and is determined by the movement of people across them, whether on legally sanctioned routes or those created and managed by migrants themselves and other non-state actors. The European concern with irregular arrivals is, after all, frequently framed as a matter of closing 'illegal' smuggling and trafficking 'routes' into Europe—pathways in their own right—and replacing them with safe alternative, 'legal' ones, regulated and controlled by state and supranational actors in partnership with third countries. This is consistent with international policy developments, with both the UN Global Compact on Migration and the Global Compact on Refugees stressing such complementary routes as necessary (if not sufficient) policy responses to the problems of large-scale and often dangerous irregular migration. In the field of refugee policy, Canadian norm entrepreneurs have long promoted the export of their private–public resettlement sponsorship programs, assisted by enthusiastic elements in civil society in Europe, not least faith-based organisations. The development of labour mobility programs and the growth in national resettlement regimes are testament to the efforts of these groups. For the most part, however, Europe is in the very early stages of policy development on such regulated migration 'pathways'—a theme that comes out in several of the contributions.

In this sense, both border and pathway operate to create relations *between* rather than merely to *separate* or *exclude*. Even when in tension or opposition, the border-to-pathway composite connotes connection and interdependence, generated by public discourses, opinions and categorisations. This might be between communities within Europe itself defined in part by their historical movement across borders or their self-definition as 'native' born; or it may be between states, between migrant communities or even between corporations vying for geopolitical, economic and normative influence in our increasingly interconnected world. In this sense, as has happened with the border, the pathway is an entity worth rethinking as part of a multidirectional, normatively fluid network or web—a type of border entity in itself and thus a description of a process, dynamic or relation as much as a line on a two-dimensional map.

An overview of the volume

Although necessarily abbreviated, the above conceptual depiction of the current moment sets the backdrop for the case studies chosen in this volume for exploring the borders-to-pathways dynamic.

Consistent with the model adopted in the original research proposal, this is undertaken under three thematically linked parts, which in turn complement the approach to third-country migration and integration in the EU through the lenses of politics, policy, governance and culture covered in the other two volumes of this collection. These three themes collectively encapsulate the complex dynamics shaping Europe's migration border movement narratives. First, understanding societal attitudes is foundational, as public opinion directly affects policy direction and the integration of migrants. Europe's changing demographics and the influence of populist narratives make this a critical area of study. Second, as both European attitudes and migration patterns evolve, so too must our frameworks for understanding migration control. The introduction of financial mechanisms and policy innovations in Part 2 therefore highlights the adaptability, complexity and normative tensions within contemporary migration management strategies. Last, grounding these current realities in the context of Europe's colonial past, as Part 3 does, underscores the continuity and sometimes contradictory nature of migration policies. By weaving these themes together, the text emphasises that Europe's border-to-pathways problem is a symbiosis of past legacies, present sentiments and future innovations, underscoring the importance of a holistic understanding of this crucial issue.

Pitched within the research project's objective of examining the impact of popular narratives of the border-crossing migrant, Part 1, 'European border attitudes: People, politics and populism', opens with a study by Timothy Hellwig and Nick Clark of the attitudes across Europe of different social groups towards migrants and refugees, and how they are influenced by exposure to mass media. Hellwig and Clark home in on four categories of 'cultural outsiders'—first and second-generation migrants, ethnic minorities and linguistic minorities—and show, by reference to interviews conducted in 27 European states over eight months, how the media facilitates a convergence of thinking about migration. This in turn sheds light on 'how public preferences may solidify both in favour of and against welcoming immigration policies'. Their analysis engages with a voluminous literature that has identified various sources informing public opinion, including perceptions of threats to security, economic wellbeing and the cultural integrity of nativist groups, the last building on identity theory, and all founded on a certain zero-sum thinking. Hellwig and Clark's approach is to look instead at the grey zone between insider and outsider, identifying a tendency for the media to play a homogenising role by creating or deepening a sense of community across different social groups. While work on the relationship between media representation and public attitudes tends to confirm suspicions of a regressive, race-to-the-bottom orientation towards the journey of the migrant, Hellwig and Clark's chapter aims to improve our understanding—and potential policy responses—of the socially constructed narratives about the movement both across the physical border and within the cultural and temporal borders that structure lives in the years and decades after arrival.

Marcin Dębicki's chapter takes the theme of border attitudes into the specificity of Poland—a state that in many ways has moved from the periphery to the heart of Europe since 2015, especially in the wake of the Russian invasion of Ukraine and the arrival of more than 7 million Ukrainian displaced persons, most of whom crossed into the EU at the Polish border. The dominance, until recently, of the Law and Justice (PiS) party with its agenda of prioritising so-called traditional values and national identity and its implementation of policies aimed at consolidating power, including its controversial judicial reforms—an increasingly popular strategy in 'anti-liberal democracies'—has left a legacy of ongoing tensions with EU institutions concerned about the erosion of democratic principles and the rule of law (see Sadurski 2019; Coakley 2021; Kość 2023).[24]

This is the backdrop of Dębicki's study of the attitudes of Poles towards the reception of different categories of migrants, both in the abstract and in the face of real phenomena. Put in the context of the diverse factors influencing population movements globally, the chapter highlights several key themes related to the reception of migrants in Poland. This includes theoretical declarations of help for migrants, the influx of approximately 1.5 million Ukrainian labour migrants between 2014 and 2021, the migration crisis on the Poland–Belarus border starting in 2021 and the mass flight of Ukrainians after Russia's invasion in February 2022. Dębicki uses surveys, data, reports, articles, observations from everyday life, and historical and civilisational concepts to provide a comprehensive understanding of

---

24 For the popularity of judicial reforms as a means of consolidating power, see Dixon and Landau (2021).

Poles' attitudes towards refugee reception in recent years and the factors that influence them. However, his key concern is to understand the difference in the reception of Syrian or Iraqi refugees to the scale of declarations made about Ukrainians.

Breaking the analysis into ethical, economic, demographic, strategic and socio-cultural questions, and focussing on the popular image of the 'deserving' migrant, Dębicki builds a sophisticated analytical frame to demonstrate how the Polish border has been theoretically constructed as sacralised, racialised, historicised, gendered and geopoliticised. While his conclusion about the lack of acceptance of refugees from 'distant cultures' is blunt, the picture he presents is far from simple. Indeed, the hypothesis that a degree of 'guilt' about Polish passivity towards migrants from Africa and Asia might be at play is presented with sensitivity to the data, media coverage and attitudinal surveys. This is complemented by theories such as Monika Bobako's notion of a 'cognitive freeze-over which flattens social reality', as well as the political psychology literature on peer group attitudinal formation. While not defending the deep resentment and lack of empathy, Dębicki calls for greater attention to the complexity of the factors at play and, in so doing, provides an element of hope.

Part 2 of the collection, 'Paradigm shifts and market mechanisms in migration control', features two chapters that pick up on the theme of 'pathways' by critically examining evolving strategies employed to manage and regulate migration into Europe. In Chapter 4, Daria Davitti and Zvezda Vankova discuss the emergence of refugee finance as a response to the decline in aid from traditional bilateral and multilateral donors. 'Refugee finance' in this context refers to the utilisation of new financial instruments, such as refugee bonds and technical assistance funds, to mobilise private capital to achieve social impact objectives, particularly in the realm of refugee protection. According to the authors, the appeal of refugee finance lies in its ability to bridge the gap between short-term humanitarian assistance and long-term development programming. Crucially, it also plays a growing role in the implementation of EU policies focussed on containment, externalisation and selective acceptance of refugees by prioritising solutions in the region of origin and purporting to enhance 'active refugee admission policies' for international protection. Placing itself within the broader critical literature on externalisation and containment, the chapter highlights a broader paradigmatic shift in the conceptualisation of international protection with the emergence of a new spectrum of refugeehood, which ranges from the hyper-vulnerable refugee to the 'refugee entrepreneur', illustrating the diversity and complexity within refugee populations. For Davitti and Vankova, the narrative promoting refugee finance justifies itself by the purported need to transition 'from funding to financing', suggesting private capital can complement public sector funding of refugee responses and support of host countries that face fiscal stress from hosting refugees. This approach seeks to address the challenges associated with the changing landscape of refugee assistance and adapt to the evolving needs of both refugees and host communities.

Davitti and Vankova unpack this rationalisation, highlighting the challenges faced by refugees across the emerging spectrum of refugeehood as they confront issues of precarity and the non-durability of protection. For refugee entrepreneurs, achieving durable solutions depends on their qualifications, skills and opportunities to access permanent residence in the host EU member state. Meanwhile, hyper-vulnerable refugees who benefited from resettlement options or obtained refugee protection are increasingly at risk of being returned to their country of origin due to the adoption of cessation of refugee status provisions, particularly in Nordic countries. In this context of enforced cessation, involuntary returns and temporary protection, refugee finance emerges as a set of financial instruments to expedite short-term protection measures by scaling up and mobilising private capital. And while humanitarian organisations have demonstrated an eagerness to embrace refugee finance, there is a need to critically assess how this could reshape international protection at a broader level. As the authors conclude, while 'complementary pathways' can offer viable solutions for refugees in protracted situations who do not qualify for limited resettlement places, questions arise about the impact of a focus on sustainable investors, policies that promote self-reliance and whether an international (and EU) system built around such norms can genuinely protect those in need when it is so dependent on private investors as enablers and co-providers of protection.

Nicholas Simoes da Silva's Chapter 5 moves the discussion from the general trend towards economic-based pathways to an analysis of the allocation of visas through migration lotteries. While noting that there is, as he puts it, 'something deeply discomforting about the notion that luck should determine a person's outcomes', da Silva demonstrates that deliberately designed social lotteries can also be understood as a just, or perhaps a *more* just, way of allocating certain burdens or benefits, increasing equality of opportunity among those who are eligible for family, labour or humanitarian visas.

Building on the work of justice theorists such as Neil Duxbury, Jon Elster, Joseph Carens, Barbara Goodwin and Aveek Bhattacharya (to name just a few of the thinkers with whom he engages), da Silva suggests that while achieving substantive equality of opportunity or equality of outcomes may require a revolutionary change in migration policy, a more immediately achievable goal is to distribute the opportunity to migrate as equally as possible among those with equal claims. This thesis is executed in the context of an analysis of the social lottery as a tool for allocating benefits in situations where multiple individuals have equal or indeterminate entitlements. A lottery is seen as fair because it eliminates the need for decision-makers to make arbitrary choices—a constant justice problem in discretionary migration programs. It may also provide equality of opportunity by giving everyone within the pool an equal chance of accessing the benefit. While weighted lotteries, in which some individuals have a higher chance of winning due to multiple entries, deviate from the pure notion of equality of opportunity, they still provide a degree of equality compared with other mechanisms like adjudication or market-based approaches, which often reward privilege and wealth. In situations such as this, lotteries can enhance equality of opportunity 'in situations where demand among people with equal claims is significant, while also preserving many of the normative benefits of "first-come, first-served"'.

The final part of the collection, 'Recolonisation, siege mentalities and the myth of difference', looks at two significant developments in European policy approaches to the regulation of border movements: the triggering of the Temporary Protection Directive (TPD) in 2022 for those fleeing Ukraine, and the new European enthusiasm, in rhetoric if not yet in reality, for 'safe, legal pathways' as alternatives to 'unsafe, illegal' movements of refugees into Europe.

While a fair bit of commentary has critiqued the public response to and differential treatment of Ukrainians in 2022 compared with Syrian, Iraqi and other (mostly Muslim) refugees in 2015, Clare McBride-Kelly's Chapter 6 provides the first robust doctrinal analysis of the myriad ways in which the activation and implementation of the TPD fall foul of EU non-discrimination law. Her approach, however, is to focus not solely on the EU's seemingly discriminatory conduct in failing to trigger the directive for 'non-European' refugees in 2015—a theme also taken up in Marcin Dębricki's Chapter 3—but on the ways in which the directive's language differentiates unreasonably and illegally between different categories of refugees leaving Ukraine itself—further reflected in its implementation in

Poland and Hungary. Again, these categories of refugees are distinguishable on racial or religious grounds. Her analysis thus provides a strong basis for strategic litigation advocating for the protection of non-Ukrainian displaced persons in compliance with EU law.

This doctrinal analysis is followed by a critique using the tools of 'Third-World approaches to international law' (TWAIL) as articulated by B.S. Chimni. McBride-Kelly adopts Chimni's depiction of a 'myth of difference' as a dominant theme in the post–Cold War rhetoric of refugee law and politics and his discussion of the 'refugee' as bearer of symbolic geopolitical value as a means of understanding responses to refugee arrivals in both 2015 and 2022, including the different categories covered by the TPD. Assuming Frontex's identification of push factors is correct and Europe will continue over the coming decades to face further 'waves' of arrivals (to adopt an unfortunate water metaphor), these are legal and ethical arguments that should inform future responses to irregular border arrivals.

To conclude the collection, my own Chapter 7 returns the volume to the border-to-pathways problem. I examine Europe's enthusiasm for the adoption of 'safe, legal pathways' as a policy tool to address the 'unsafe, illegal' routes into the continent. Using concepts drawn from the neo-colonial literature, necro-politics, border studies and international legal history, I explore the function, structure and importance of the pathway as a normative and geopolitical concept in migration law and policy and its consistency with Europe's adoption of deterrence, securitisation and externalisation as central elements of border practice. As an international lawyer, my concern is also with how the legal/illegal pathway binary works to consolidate the trope of 'civilisation' (or international law's 'civilising mission') in contemporary international legal argumentation, facilitating European interventions in regions such as the Sahel, which sits at the heart of the network of pathways along which flow people, finance, ideas and technologies. This leads to an analysis of the multidirectional nature and multifunctional purposes of pathways and, as with the technological violence depicted above, their tendency to facilitate neo-colonial policing practices of communities both within and outside Europe. The chapter concludes by highlighting the propensity of the pathway trope to shore up a European border mindset, its susceptibility to being leveraged for the commodification, extraction and transformation of non-European bodies, and its place in the creation of differentiated, suspended and anomalous legal zones for the transfer and manipulation of global norms. Although I present a hypercritical depiction of the European border-to-pathway discourse, my analysis is an attempt to reveal flaws in the normative reasoning to build fairer models for the movement of people.

Together, these three parts form a cohesive exploration of the complexities surrounding migration, offering readers a nuanced understanding of the multifaceted nature of border control, societal attitudes and impacts on individual lives. It challenges preconceived notions, invites empathy and ultimately advocates for a shift towards pathways that prioritise inclusivity, cooperation and shared global responsibility.

References

Agamben, G. 2005. *State of Exception*. Translated by K. Attrell. Chicago: University of Chicago Press.

Akkerman, M. 2022. *Outsourcing Oppression: How Europe Externalises Migrant Detention Beyond Its Shores*. Policy Briefing. Amsterdam: Transnational Institute and Stop Wapenhandel.

Amnesty International. 2020. *Out of Control: Failing EU Laws for Digital Surveillance Export*. 21 September, Index No. EUR 01/2556/2020. London: Amnesty International.

Askew, J. 2023. '"Mass Surveillance, Automated Suspicion, Extreme Power": How Tech is Shaping EU Borders.' *Euronews*, [Brussels], 6 April. www.euronews.com/next/2023/04/06/mass-surveillance-automated-suspicion-extreme-power-how-tech-is-shaping-the-eus-borders.

Benton, L. 2010. *A Search for Sovereignty: Law and Geography in European Empires, 1400–1900*. Cambridge: Cambridge University Press. doi.org/10.1017/CBO9780511988905.

Broeders, D. 2007. 'The New Digital Borders of Europe: EU Databases and the Surveillance of Irregular Migrants.' *International Sociology* 22, no. 1: 71–92. doi.org/10.1177/0268580907070126.

Brotton, J. 2016. *A History of the World in 12 Maps*. New York: Viking.

Byrne, R., G. Noll, and J. Vedsted-Hansen. 2020. 'Understanding the Crisis of Refugee Law: Legal Scholarship and the EU Asylum System.' *Leiden Journal of International Law* 33, no. 4: 871–92. doi.org/10.1017/S0922156520000382.

Chakrabarty, D. 2008. *Provincializing Europe: Postcolonial Thought and Historical Difference*. Princeton: Princeton University Press. doi.org/10.1515/9781400 828654.

Coakley, A. 2021. 'Poland Fights EU Over Rule of Law, Courts EU Over Immigration Crisis.' *Foreign Policy*, 1 December. foreignpolicy.com/2021/12/01/poland-crisis-european-union-immigration-democracy-law/.

Csernatoni, R. 2018. 'Constructing the EU's High-Tech Borders: FRONTEX and Dual-Use Drones for Border Management.' *European Security* 27, no. 2: 175–200. doi.org/10.1080/09662839.2018.1481396.

Davitti, D. 2018. 'Biopolitical Borders and the State of Exception in the European Migration "Crisis".' *European Journal of International Law* 29, no. 4 (November): 1173–96. doi.org/10.1093/ejil/chy065.

Dennison, J., and L. Dražanová. 2018. *Public Attitudes on Migration: Rethinking How People Perceive Migration*. Florence: Migration Policy Centre, European University Institute.

Dixon, R., and D. Landau. 2021. *Abusive Constitutional Borrowing: Legal Globalization and the Subversion of Liberal Democracy*. Oxford: Oxford University Press. doi.org/10.1093/oso/9780192893765.001.0001.

Dodds, K. 2021. *The New Border Wars: The Conflicts That Will Define Our Future*. New York: Diversion Publishing Corporation.

European Agency for the Management of Operational Cooperation at the External Borders (Frontex). 2022. *Strategic Risk Analysis 2022*. July, SAMD/RAU/ SFALEM/7782/202. Warsaw: Risk Analysis Unit, Frontex.

European Commission (EC). 2020. *Proposal for a Regulation of the European Parliament and of the Council Addressing Situations of Crisis and Force Majeure in the Field of Migration and Asylum*. COM/2020/613 final. Brussels: EC. eur-lex. europa.eu/legal-content/EN/TXT/?uri=CELEX%3A52020PC0613.

European Council. 2023. *Special Meeting of the European Council (9 February 2023): Conclusions*. EUCO 1/23. Brussels: General Secretariat of the Council of the European Union. data.consilium.europa.eu/doc/document/ST-1-2023-INIT/ en/pdf.

European Council on Refugees and Exiles (ECRE). 2023a. *Solidarity: The Eternal Problem—Recent Developments on Solidarity in EU Asylum Policies*. Policy Paper, 26 January. Brussels: ECRE.

European Council on Refugees and Exiles (ECRE). 2023b. 'A Possible Agreement on the Reform of the CEAS at the Council in June: What Is at Stake?' *News*, 6 June. Brussels: ECRE.

European Parliament and European Council. 2019. *Regulation (EU) 2019/1896 of the European Parliament and of the Council of 13 November 2019 on the European Border and Coast Guard and Repealing Regulations (EU) No 1052/2013 and (EU) 2016/1624*. Strasbourg: European Parliament and Council of the European Union. eur-lex.europa.eu/legal-content/EN/TXT/?uri=CELEX%3A 32019R1896.

Fassin, D. 2011. 'Policing Borders, Producing Boundaries: The Governmentality of Immigration in Dark Times.' *Annual Review of Anthropology* 40: 213–26. doi.org/10.1146/annurev-anthro-081309-145847.

Gržinić, M., ed. 2018. *Border Thinking: Disassembling Histories of Racialized Violence*. New York: Sternberg Press.

Hage, G. 2016. 'État de siège: A Dying Domesticating Colonialism?' *American Ethnologist* 43, no. 1: 38–49. doi.org/10.1111/amet.12261.

Hartley, J.B. 1992. *Deconstructing the Map*. Ann Arbor: University of Michigan Press.

Hashmi, M., and S. Chander. 2022. *Ending Fortress Europe: Recommendations for a Racial Justice Approach to EU Migration Policy*. Paper, March. Brussels: Equinox. www.equinox-eu.com/wp-content/uploads/2022/06/Ending-Fortress-Europe.pdf.

Kauranen, A. 2023. 'Finland Starts Fence on Russian Border Amid Migration, Security Concerns.' *Reuters*, 14 April.

Kość, W. 2023. 'Crunch Time in Poland for Tackling EU Rule of Law Dispute', *Politico*, [Washington, DC], 7 February. www.politico.eu/article/andrzej-duda-poland-nationalism-tackling-eu-rule-of-law-dispute-morawiecki/.

Malik, K. 2018. 'How We All Colluded in Fortress Europe.' *The Guardian*, 10 June. www.theguardian.com/commentisfree/2018/jun/10/sunday-essay-how-we-colluded-in-fortress-europe-immigration.

Marshall, T. 2016. *Prisoners of Geography: Ten Maps that Explain Everything*. London: Elliott & Thompson.

Martín, M., S. Ayuso, and Y. Clemente. 2023. 'Migration: The Fences Dividing Europe: How the EU Uses Walls to Contain Irregular Migration.' *El País English*, [Madrid], 8 April. english.elpais.com/international/2023-04-08/the-fences-dividing-europe-how-the-eu-uses-walls-to-contain-irregular-migration.html.

Mezzadra, S., and B. Neilson. 2013. *Border as Method, or, the Multiplication of Labor*. Durham: Duke University Press. doi.org/10.2307/j.ctv1131cvw.

Miles, K. 2018. 'Insulae Moluccae: Map of the Spice Islands, 1594.' In *International Law's Objects*, edited by J. Hohmann and D. Joyce. Oxford: Oxford University Press. doi.org/10.1093/oso/9780198798200.003.0021.

Molnar, P. 2018. *Bots at the Gate: A Human Rights Analysis of Automated Decision-Making in Canada's Immigration and Refugee System*. Toronto: The Citizen Lab, University of Toronto.

Molnar, P. 2019. 'New Technologies in Migration: Human Rights Impacts.' *Forced Migration Review* 61 (June).

Molnar, P. 2020. *Technological Testing Grounds: Migration Management Experiments and Reflections from the Ground Up*. Brussels: EDRi and Refugee Law Lab.

Niarchos, N. 2023. 'Why Hundreds Drowned Off the Coast of Greece: The Tragedy of the Adriana Comes Amid Renewed Anti-Immigrant Sentiment in Europe.' *The New Yorker*, 26 June. www.newyorker.com/news/daily-comment/why-hundreds-drowned-off-the-coast-of-greece.

Nielsen, N. 2021. 'Dozen Ministers Want EU to Finance Border Walls.' *EU Observer*, 8 October. euobserver.com/migration/153169.

Office of the High Commissioner for Human Rights (OHCHR). 2020. *Report of the Special Rapporteur on Contemporary Forms of Racism, Racial Discrimination, Xenophobia and Related Intolerance*. A/75/590, 10 November. Geneva: OHCHR. www.ohchr.org/en/newyork/Documents/A-75-590-AUV.docx.

Olwig, K.F., K. Grünenberg, P. Møhl, and A. Simonsen. 2019. *The Biometric Border World: Technology, Bodies and Identities on the Move*. London: Routledge. doi.org/10.4324/9780367808464.

Pickles, J. 2003. *A History of Spaces: Cartographic Reason, Mapping and the Geo-Coded World*. Abingdon: Taylor & Francis.

Rigby, J., and J. Crisp. 2021. 'Fortress Europe: How 1,800km of Walls and Fences Are Keeping Desperate Migrants Out.' *Telegraph*, [London], 16 December.

Sadurski, W. 2019. *Poland's Constitutional Breakdown*. Oxford: Oxford University Press. doi.org/10.1093/oso/9780198840503.001.0001.

Schmitt, C. 2006 [1950]. *The Nomos of the Earth in the International Law of the Jus Publicum Europaeum*. Translated by G.L. Ulmen. Candor: Telos Press Publishing.

Squire, V., N. Perkowski, D. Stevens, and N. Vaughan-Williams. 2021. *Reclaiming Migration: Voices from Europe's 'Migrant Crisis'*. Manchester: Manchester University Press. doi.org/10.7765/9781526144829.

Stevis-Gridneff, M., and K. Shoumali. 2023. 'Everyone Knew the Migrant Ship Was Doomed. No One Helped.' *New York Times*, 1 July. www.nytimes.com/2023/07/01/world/europe/greece-migrant-ship.html.

Sunderland, J., and L. Pezzani. 2022. *Airborne Complicity: Frontex Aerial Surveillance Enables Abuse*. Report, 8 December. New York: Human Rights Watch.

Takle, M. 2018. 'Is the Migration Crisis a Solidarity Crisis?' In *The Crisis of the European Union: Challenges, Analyses, Solutions*, edited by A. Grimmel. London: Routledge. doi.org/10.4324/9781315443683-9.

Tan, N.F. 2022. *Denmark's Extraterritorial Asylum Vision*. Refugee Law Initiative Blog, 19 April. London: School of Advanced Study, University of London. rli.blogs.sas.ac.uk/2021/04/19/denmarks-extraterritorial-asylum-vision/.

Tjalve, V.S. 2021. 'Judeo-Christian Democracy and the Transatlantic Right: Travels of a Contested Civilizational Imaginary.' *New Perspectives* 29, no. 4: 332–48. doi.org/10.1177/2336825X211052979.

Walia, H. 2021. *Border and Rule: Global Migration, Capitalism, and the Rise of Racist Nationalism*. Chicago: Haymarket Books.

Wimmer, A., and N. Glick Schiller. 2002. 'Methodological Nationalism and Beyond: Nation-State Building, Migration and the Social Sciences.' *Global Networks* 2, no. 4: 301–34. doi.org/10.1111/1471-0374.00043.

Wood, D. 2010. *Rethinking the Power of Maps*. New York: Guilford Press.

Part 1.
European border attitudes:
People, politics and populism

2

Cultural outsiders, the media and views of migrants in Europe

Nicholas Clark and Timothy Hellwig

An objective of this volume is to advance our understanding of the popular narratives about the journey of the irregular migrant from their country of origin to their destination. These narratives are shaped in critical ways by the perspectives of the mass public in the destination countries. Why do some people welcome newcomers with open arms while others remain hostile? The question of immigration has long structured public discourse in European societies and has assumed even greater prominence over the past decade. The migrant crisis of 2015 brought waves of new residents into Europe and placed the issue at the forefront of governing agendas across the continent. Spikes in the influx of foreigners, both real and imagined, coincided with increasing support for populist leaders and parties across Europe. These nationalist movements have ensured that issues surrounding the acceptance and integration of migrants remain prominent within national political arenas.

Often lost among these discussions are questions about how different, often overlapping social groups react to the issue of immigration and how the mass media, as a primary source of information, can—or cannot— bring these groups together. These questions strike at the heart of this volume's theme of borders, pathways and the division between them. As highlighted in Chapter 1, Europe's efforts to control its borders through 'division, exclusion, preference and privilege' have a long history and, we submit, will not be ending anytime soon. Much of this control is exercised through physical borders, as indicated by the rise of the European Agency for the Management of Operational Cooperation at the External Borders (Frontex). But exclusion and division are not based on cartography alone; rather, divisions within 'Europe' are drawn by value-based and cultural distinctions, not to mention differences in access to power and resources.

To contribute to these discussions, we raise two related possibilities concerning public opinion about recent migrants. First, we expect that what we call 'cultural outsiders'—individuals who were not born in the country of their residence or who belong to an ethnic or racial minority—are more likely to be receptive to and welcoming of migrants. These individuals are more likely to appreciate the value of cultural diversity and to empathise with the plight of many recent migrants. As such, this group should express stronger support for admitting migrants into their country of residence. Second, we expect that socialisation through the consumption of national media could prompt the public to consider different ways of looking at migrants and, in turn, shift mass opinion on these issues. More specifically, the mass media, as a homogenising force, can play a formidable role in bridging the gaps in attitudes between natives and recent arrivals.

Studies show that the media influences opinion on specific issues, particularly those with a cross-border dimension, at the national and European levels (de Vreese and Semetko 2004; de Vreese and Boomgaarden 2006). When exposed to common issue frames (Merolla et al. 2013), individuals from different social groups may start to think about migrants in similar ways. Given exposure to the same cues and messages within the media, the positions of native-born residents and cultural outsiders may converge. We contribute to the collective understanding of the conditions that influence public opinion towards migrants and asylum seekers. The existing research tends to focus on the socioeconomic profile (Citrin et al. 1997; Kehrberg 2007) or the strength of national identity among national publics (Givens and Luedtke 2005). More recently, researchers have examined how the immigrants' area of origin, economic status and religion shape popular attitudes (for example, Brader et al. 2008; Strabac and Listhaug 2008; Ford 2011; Hainmueller and Hopkins 2015; Hellwig and Sinno 2017). We build on this strand of scholarship to examine the cultural background of different social groups, investigating whether cultural outsiders are more receptive to and supportive of immigrants. Moreover, while some studies examine the media's influence on immigration positions (Dunaway et al. 2010), none has considered the role of the media in facilitating a convergence of thinking about the issue of immigration. The results shed light on how public preferences may solidify both in favour of and against welcoming immigration policies.

We first review existing research on the predictors of public opinion towards migrants and the effects of media coverage on public opinion. We then advance a set of claims about how people's status relative to the dominant in-group shapes attitudes towards immigrants. Analysis of survey data from across Europe shows that while first and second-generation residents hold more accommodating views, ethnic and linguistic minorities appear no different from national publics overall. Addressing the puzzle of these null effects, we show how media consumption matters. Results from multivariate analyses show that increased media exposure leads to a convergence of views of migrants, boosting support for migrants among natives and diminishing support among cultural outsiders. The conclusion discusses the implications of the media's homogenising role.

Natives' attitudes towards immigrants

Motivated by a need to understand the foundations of persistent anti-foreigner backlash across Europe, a spate of research on public opinion towards immigrants has appeared in recent years. Researchers have identified a wide range of sources, many of which address perceptions of threat to the security, economic wellbeing and cultural integrity of nativist groups. With respect to economic factors, theories of labour market competition predict that individuals will oppose accepting migrant workers with skills similar to their own but support the immigration of workers with different skill levels (Mayda 2006). Regarding security concerns, studies find that perceptions associating immigrant groups with terrorists produce psychological distress that increases feelings of threat from minorities and, consequently, predicts exclusionist attitudes towards them (Canetti-Nisim et al. 2009; Lahav and Courtemanche 2012).

Studies that emphasise the cultural bases of anti-foreigner sentiment build in part on identity theory (Tajfel 2010). Such analyses emphasise feelings of threat to national identity (Sniderman et al. 2004), religious values (McDaniel et al. 2011), cultural values and religious beliefs (Hainmueller and Hiscox 2007; Poynting and Mason 2007), ethnic differences (Brader et al. 2008) and conservative social attitudes (Ford 2011). Views towards immigrants are thus conditioned by natives' beliefs in cultural differences, which, in turn, feed into perceptions of social status. Since social status is based on a rank ordering, it serves as a positional good: '[W]hen many others acquire more status, the value of one's own status may decline' (Gidron and Hall 2017: 66). Such zero-sum thinking means that if people perceive there to be gains from some groups, they will tend to perceive there to be losses from others (Bobo and Hutchings 1996; Norton and Sommers 2011).

Social dominance theory predicts that people have preferences for group-based hierarchies, such that citizens who identify with dominant groups prefer systems that reinforce the oppression of low-status groups and attendant group-based inequalities through existing ideologies and social policies (Sidanius and Pratto 1999; Ho et al. 2012; Mutz and Kim 2017). Social dominance orientation increases when people feel threatened (Morrison and Ybarra 2008). Over time, perceptions about the direction of gains and losses between groups imply a potential threat to social status and thus evoke feelings of hostility towards out-groups (Tajfel 1978).

We explore the effects of in-group and out-group differences as an explanation for attitudes towards immigrants. On the face of it, immigrants are seen as members of cultural out-groups, particularly people of a different racial, ethnic or linguistic backgrounds than most members of society. In practice, however, identification with the in-group or out-group may not be straightforward. We identify three groups that fit in this grey area between insider and outsider. The first are the children of immigrants. Second-generation immigrants tend to have higher incomes, are better educated and are less likely to live in poverty than their predecessors. They tend to resemble the nativist population more than first-generation individuals (Pew Research Center 2013). Thus, their social attitudes, including on immigration, may align more closely with those of the general population. A second group is those born in the country but whose ethnic background places them in the minority. Particularly in small, homogeneous societies, members of these groups tend to identify most closely with their ethnicity or nation of ancestry rather than as members of their country of residence. A third group is citizens who communicate with family and friends in a language that differs from that of the majority in that nation.[1] This leads to

---

1   Additional bases of cultural outsider-ness may also be considered, such as race or religion. However, since the survey data we use do not provide sufficient leverage to explore these differences, we leave these for future research.

our first hypothesis, *H1: Compared with cultural insiders, members of cultural out-groups—second-generation immigrants, ethnic minorities and linguistic minorities—are more likely to hold favourable views towards migrants.*

The role of the media

Even in the age of social media, national broadcast and print media remain a homogenising force (Anderson 1983). Apart from group identities, exposure to culturally homogenising environmental conditions serve to diminish differences between groups. Coverage of immigration by national media outlets is one such environmental condition. While prominent media studies in the United States have found a null effect on public opinion (Zaller 1996; Bennett and Iyengar 2008), the media appears to have a more pronounced role in Europe (Boomgaarden et al. 2013). Most Europeans lack direct experience with these issues and are thus more likely to be influenced by media coverage (Walgrave and De Swert 2007; Maier and Rittberger 2008; Azrout et al. 2012). As such, the frequency and tone of media coverage influence perceptions of and support for the European Union (Semetko et al. 2003; de Vreese and Boomgaarden 2006). Similarly, more frequent discussion of immigration policy appears to increase the salience of that issue for European voters (Walgrave and de Swert 2004; Burscher et al. 2015).

How does media consumption shape views of immigration? Immigration is often presented as an inherent threat to the wellbeing of native-born residents; migrants are portrayed as taking native jobs and creating potential security risks for the country (Dinas and van Spanje 2011; Caviedes 2015; van der Linden and Jacobs 2016). Such coverage appears to promote anti-immigrant biases among the native population (van Klingeren et al. 2014; Atwell and Seate 2016). Moreover, frequent media coverage of this issue improves the electoral fortunes of anti-immigrant parties by promoting the salience of their core concerns (Damstra et al. 2019).

However, the media does not always present immigration in a negative light. First, ideology matters. Right-leaning media outlets are more likely than left-leaning outlets to offer negative stories about immigrants (Kaye 2001). Second, stories that focus on the implications of immigration for crime and/or the economy are more likely to engender negative feelings than those framing immigration from the point of view of the migrant or covering immigration more abstractly (Burscher et al. 2015; McLaren et al. 2018).

Of note, these studies largely focus on aggregate levels of public opinion about immigration or support for anti-immigrant parties and do not parse media effects on different social groups within the broader electorate.

We argue that the media plays a homogenising role: depending on the editorial slant of the coverage, the media can create or deepen a sense of community across different social groups. And to the extent that media markets overlap with or are nested within nation-states, they have the potential to shift, narrow or break down the boundaries between insider and outsider. One implication of this possibility is that media consumption narrows the gap between insiders and outsiders with respect to views on immigration. We, therefore, expect that the views of insiders and outsiders differ most when the media influence is weakest; this is the case where socialisation and knowledge networks remain on a more familial level. Under greater media exposure, in contrast, the impact of cultural identities on social attitudes matters less. *H2: Increasing media coverage of immigration reduces differences in public opinion over immigration between natives and cultural outsiders.*

Data and measures

We assess these expectations using data from the European Social Survey (ESS), a cross-national survey that has been conducted across Europe every two years since 2001. For an up-to-date reading of perceptions, we used data from Round 9, which included surveys conducted across 27 countries. Most fieldwork was done in early 2019—a time between the shocks of the 2015 migrant crisis and Covid-19–induced uncertainty.[2]

We create three sets of measures to test our expectations. The first is respondents' attitudes towards immigrants. Since our focus is on the views towards cultural outsiders, we rely on responses to the following question: 'To what extent do you think [country of residence] should allow people of a different race or ethnic group from [country] to come and live here?' Respondents were asked to select among 'allow many to come and live here', 'allow some', 'allow a few' and 'allow none'. Examining this item is not only theoretically germane but also puts us in conversation with previous cross-

---

2   Interviews were conducted from September 2018 to May 2019, though most were in March 2019. The dataset includes respondents from Austria, Belgium, Bulgaria, Croatia, Cyprus, Czechia, Estonia, Finland, France, Germany, Hungary, Ireland, Italy, Latvia, Lithuania, Montenegro, Netherlands, Norway, Poland, Portugal, Romania, Slovenia, Slovakia, Spain, Sweden, Switzerland and the United Kingdom.

national studies that have relied on ESS data to examine the determinants of anti-immigrant sentiment (for example, Dancygier and Donnelly 2013; Hainmueller and Hiscox 2007).

The second set of measures classify respondents into cultural in-groups and out-groups. First-generation immigrants are those born outside their country of residence; we identify second-generation immigrants as individuals whose father and mother were born outside the country. Ethnic minorities are those who self-identify as such. Linguistic minorities are those who mainly speak at home a language other than the official language(s) or dominant language of the country of residence. Table 2.1 reports the size of these groups relative to the overall sample.

Table 2.1 Immigrants and minorities as share of total survey sample (per cent)

	Share of total (N=44,615)	Share of first gen. (N=4,353)	Share of second gen. (N=3,411)	Share of ethnic minority (N=2,796)	Share of linguistic minority (N=3,430)
First-generation immigrant	9.8	–	0.0	37.9	49.4
Second generation	7.6	0.0	–	16.7	14.3
Ethnic minority	6.3	24.4	13.7	–	37.3
Linguistic minority	7.7	38.9	14.4	45.7	–

Note: Cells report percentage responses.
Source: ESS (2019).

Figure 2.1 provides a first-cut assessment of how views of immigrants differ across these groups. For ease of presentation, graphs present attitudes averaged by countries. Figure 2.1A charts the share of respondents in each country who would allow 'many' or 'some' people of a different race or ethnic group to come to live in their country (y-axis) against the percentage of members of the group in question. We observe a positive relationship, suggesting that in places with more immigrants, the population is more accommodating, while those residing in places with fewer immigrants tend to have more restrictive views.[3] Figure 2.1B shows a similar relationship among respondents who are of the second generation in the country. Figures 2.1C and 2.1D, however, suggest that views among national publics about foreigners are unaffected by the share of ethnic or linguistic minorities present in the country—a point to which we will return.

---

3   Switzerland is an outlier.

A. Immigrants

B. Second Generation

C. Ethnic Minorities

D. Linguistic Minorities

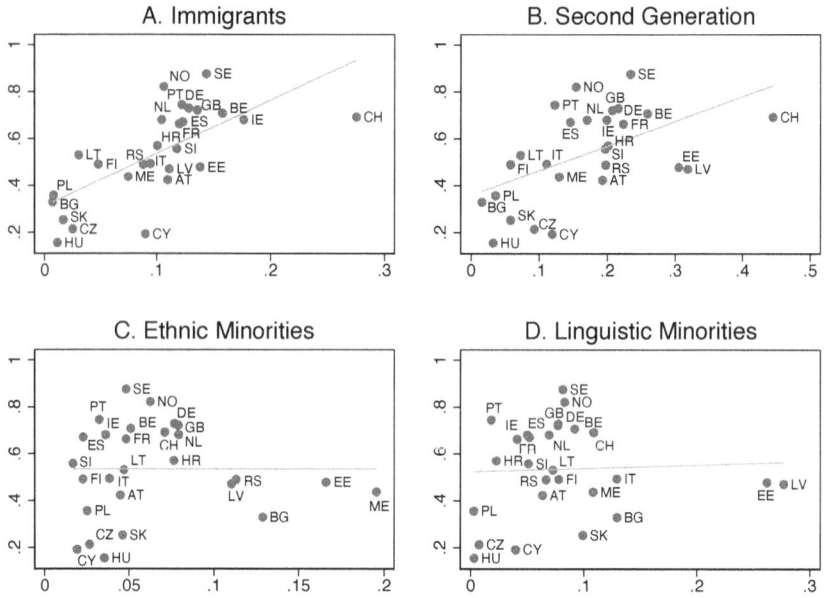

Figure 2.1 Country support for immigration and share of respondents in different cultural outsider groups

Note: Graphs plot the share of respondents by country with the given attribute (x-axis) against the share of respondents who would 'allow many' or 'allow some' people of a different race or ethnic group 'to come and live' in their country, by country (y-axis).

Source: ESS (2019).

Figure 2.2 compares mean averages across different groups. Figure 2.2A shows that those born in-country ('natives') are roughly equally divided between those who support immigration of people of a different race or ethnic group, thus measured, and those who oppose it (52 per cent versus 48 per cent). This contrasts sharply with first-generation residents, 70 per cent of whom favour more inward migration to the country. This division in views between natives and immigrants is not surprising, but what about other recent arrivals and so-called cultural outsiders? Figure 2.2B shows that support for immigrants remains at 52 per cent among those whose family members have lived in the country for three or more generations. As expected, later arrivals—those with parents born elsewhere—hold views more in line with those of immigrants themselves, with 63 per cent holding accommodating views. The same, however, cannot be said for the views of ethnic or linguistic minorities. Among those born in the country, individuals belonging to minority ethnic and linguistic communities are no more likely to support increased migration of ethnic and racial outsiders than those belonging to the majority groupings (Figures 2.2C and 2.2D).[4]

Our third measure of theoretical interest is media exposure. The ESS questionnaire asks respondents: 'On a typical day, about how much time do you spend watching, reading or listening to news about politics and current affairs?' The responses range from zero to 1,440 minutes per day. We recode the measure to provide 18 hours (1,080 minutes) as the maximum allowable time spent consuming news. Since the measure is right-skewed (with few respondents consuming exorbitantly high levels), we transform the measure by adding one minute and taking the natural log.

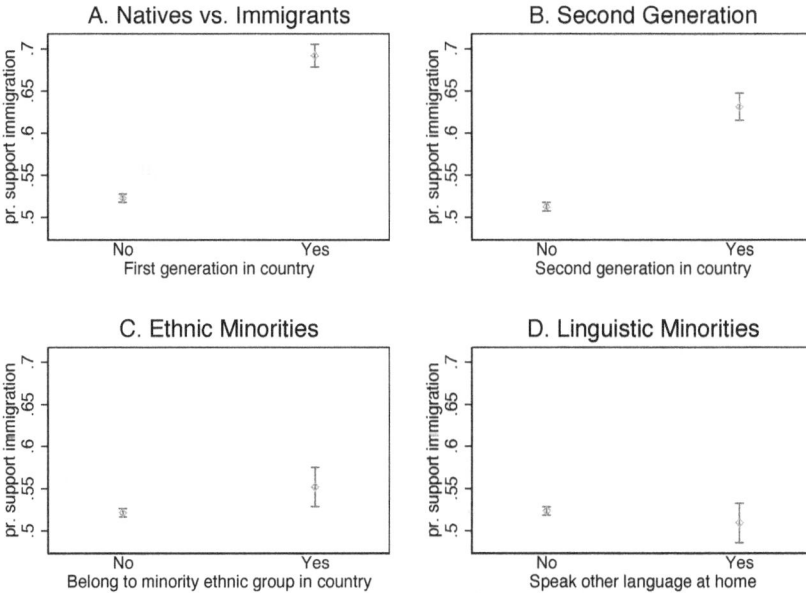

Figure 2.2 Probability of support for immigration by group
Notes: Graphs report the share of respondents with the given attributes who would 'allow many' or 'allow some' people of a different race or ethnic group 'to come and live' in their country. 'Natives' refers to all respondents except first-generation migrants.
Source: ESS (2019).

---

4   We classify individuals as ethnic minorities based on responses to the question, 'Do you belong to a minority ethnic group in [country]?' We identify people as members of minority-language communities by responses to 'What language or languages do you speak most often at home?'. Individuals whose first response to the question is with a language other than the country's official language (or, in the absence of official language designation, a majority language) are classified as a 'linguistic minority'.

Analysis

As anticipated, first and second-generation residents are more accepting than others of immigration. These differences are evident from comparing both country publics (Figure 2.1) and individuals (Figure 2.2). Less anticipated, however, is the apparent absence of differences in the opinions of ethnic and linguistic minorities vis-a-vis the general population. Is it not the case that cultural outsider-ness unites groups? Why are ethnic and linguistic minorities no more likely to hold accommodating, pro-immigration views than members of the majority groupings?

We explore these questions by performing multivariate analyses. Following previous analyses of the ESS data, we collapse the response set for the immigration attitude item such that 'allow many/some' is coded 1 and 'allow a few/none' is coded 0 (Hellwig and Kweon 2016). We model these responses as a function of one's status as a first or second-generation resident in-country and as a member of an ethnic or linguistic minority. Multivariate analysis allows us to control for other factors that shape public opinion, including education, age, income, gender and urban/rural location.[5]

Table 2.2 reports estimates using logistic regression with country-fixed effects. The first column confirms what we saw above: immigrants and second-generation residents are more likely than the population overall to support immigration to the country. The analysis also reveals a positive influence of ethnic-minority identity on attitudes towards ethnic immigrants, though language differences continue to exert no effect (the coefficient carries a negative sign and is imprecisely estimated). Demographic variables for education, age, income, gender and residence all register their expected effects. These results are broadly consistent with H1: members of cultural out-groups, particularly second-generation immigrants and ethnic minorities, are more likely to hold favourable views of migrants than are native-born cultural insiders.

---

5   Education is measured using the seven-category International Standard Classification of Education (ISCED). Age is age in years, divided into deciles. For income, we use a subjective measure that asks respondents to identify the description that comes closest to how they feel about their household's income: 'Living comfortably on present income' (coded 1), 'Coping on present income' (coded 0) or '(Very) difficult on present income' (−1). Gender and urban/rural residence are measured using dummy variables.

The remaining models condition these effects on media consumption. Model 2 examines the conditioning effect of media consumption on the views of first-generation immigrants, Model 3 for second-generation residents, Model 4 for those of ethnic minorities and Model 5 for those of linguistic minorities. In each case, the sign on the interaction terms is negative, indicating that their views of immigrants become less exceptional (that is, accommodating) and more typical of the general population (that is, restrictive) as media consumption increases.

Figure 2.3 provides a more substantive interpretation of these results in terms of predicted probabilities. The graphs display the differences produced in probabilities of favouring immigration by comparing an individual who is not a member of the given group with one who is. In Figure 2.3A, we use estimates from Model 2 in Table 2.2 to assess the influence on support for immigrants of being a native-born cultural insider.[6] Among these members of the in-group, media exposure serves to moderate anti-immigrant views. Figure 2.3B unveils a *declining difference in support probabilities* between second-generation residents and the general (native) population as media exposure increases. Figure 2.3C shows a similar conditional effect of media for ethnic minorities. The largest decrease in immigration support occurs among those who speak a different language at home. Figure 2.3D indicates that at the rates of highest media exposure, those whose vernacular is different from the nation's majority are *less* supportive of immigration than the general population.

Each of these results taken in isolation is notable: the media prompts majority groups to become more supportive and minority groups to become less supportive of immigrants. Taken together though, it becomes clear how the media shapes and produces a national consensus on this issue. Consistent with H2, the results show that differences between natives and cultural outsiders in public opinions on immigration are reduced due to the homogenising influence of exposure to the mass media.[7]

---

6   Specifically, we estimate the change in the probability of having favourable views of immigrants for an individual who is not an immigrant, not a second-generation resident and neither an ethnic nor a linguistic minority.
7   Additional analyses show the results reported above are robust to considerations of subjective feelings of belonging in/identity with the country of residence.

Table 2.2 Modelling attitudes towards immigrants

	(1) Baseline	(2) Media: 1st gen	(3) Media: 2nd gen	(4) Media: Ethnic minority	(5) Media: Linguistic minority
First generation	0.386***	0.665***	0.387***	0.389***	0.385***
	(0.049)	(0.120)	(0.049)	(0.049)	(0.049)
Second generation	0.253***	0.254***	0.528***	0.255***	0.251***
	(0.048)	(0.048)	(0.128)	(0.048)	(0.048)
Ethnic minority	0.316***	0.317***	0.319***	0.673***	0.315***
	(0.059)	(0.059)	(0.059)	(0.137)	(0.059)
Linguistic minority	−0.022	−0.025	−0.024	−0.022	0.371**
	(0.055)	(0.055)	(0.055)	(0.055)	(0.126)
Education	0.159***	0.159***	0.159***	0.159***	0.159***
	(0.007)	(0.007)	(0.007)	(0.007)	(0.007)
Age	−0.150***	−0.150***	−0.150***	−0.150***	−0.150***
	(0.007)	(0.007)	(0.007)	(0.007)	(0.007)
Subjective income	0.280***	0.280***	0.280***	0.281***	0.280***
	(0.019)	(0.019)	(0.019)	(0.019)	(0.019)
Female	0.080***	0.080***	0.080**	0.080**	0.080***
	(0.024)	(0.024)	(0.024)	(0.024)	(0.024)
Rural	−0.185***	−0.185***	−0.185***	−0.184***	−0.184***
	(0.025)	(0.026)	(0.025)	(0.026)	(0.026)
Media	0.058***	0.067***	0.065***	0.067***	0.069***
	(0.009)	(0.010)	(0.010)	(0.010)	(0.010)
First generation × media		−0.077**			
		(0.030)			
Second generation × media			−0.078*		
			(0.033)		
Ethnic minority × media				−0.101**	
				(0.035)	
Linguistic minority × media					−0.108***
					(0.031)
Constant	−0.257***	−0.289***	−0.282***	−0.290***	−0.295***
	(0.077)	(0.078)	(0.078)	(0.078)	(0.078)
Log likelihood	−25,950	−25,945	−25,945	−25,943	−25,940
N	44,149	44,149	44,149	44,149	44,149

* $p < 0.05$

** $p < 0.01$

*** $p < 0.001$

Notes: Cells report logit model estimates with standard errors in parentheses. Estimates based on post-stratification design weights. All models include country-fixed effects (not shown).

Source: ESS (2019).

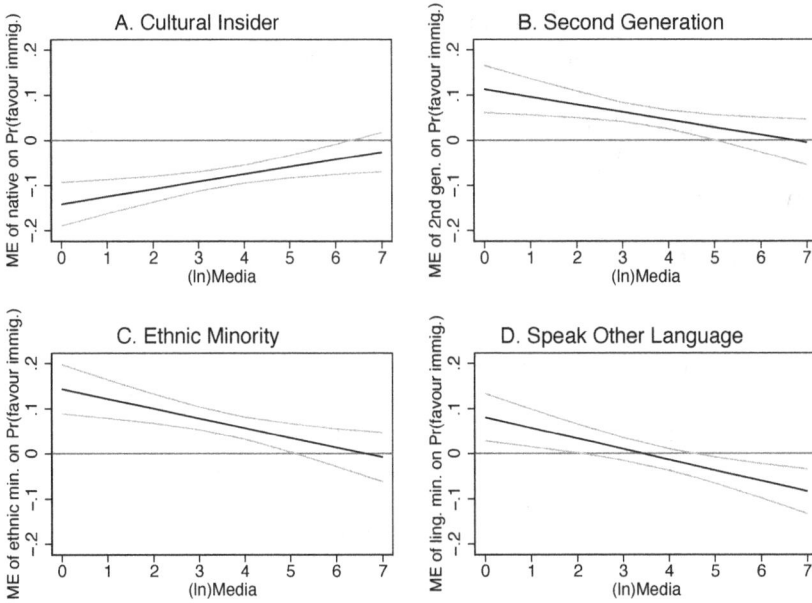

Figure 2.3 Predicted probabilities of favouring immigrants, first differences

Notes: Graphs produced using estimates from Table 2.2, Models 2–5. The black line reports the difference in the expected probability of favouring immigrants produced by the shift from the general public to the group indicated in the title. Grey lines report 95 per cent confidence intervals.

Source: ESS (2019).

Discussion

European societies have long been divided into haves and have-nots, the deserving and undeserving, and insiders and outsiders. The hardening of these divisions has stood in the way of creating more inclusive societies. As contributions to this volume show, few issues better illustrate these barriers to inclusivity than the politics of immigration and refugees. Analyses of survey data from 27 European countries suggest that while views of immigrants are rooted in one's identity, differences in views can be ameliorated by culturally and nationally homogenising communications through media environments. This study thus sheds new light on the possibilities of creating societies more accepting of cultural outsiders and, in so doing, of deepening our understanding of the socially constructed narratives about the journey of the migrant from their country of origin. Our chapter thus contributes to the broader theme of this volume on the differences between outsider groups—a theme that reappears in Marcin Dębicki's chapter on Poland's reception of refugees from Ukraine compared with those from Syria and Iraq (Chapter 3) and Clare McBride-Kelly's chapter on how the EU's Temporary Protection Directive differentiates between categories of refugees (Chapter 6).

The results of our analyses suggest that some social groups are indeed more supportive of immigration—specifically, those who may have lived similar experiences to immigrants, such as those in the second generation or ethnic minorities. However, the media serves to diminish differences in public opinion about immigrants between these groups and the dominant majority, bringing about more of a national consensus on this issue. Interestingly, under conditions of greater media exposure, support for immigrants increases among some groups and decreases among others. This finding carries implications for the likely effects of media narratives on public opinion.

Prior research on the media and immigration suggests a largely unidirectional effect: media coverage either frames immigrants as threatening, thus depressing support, *or* depicts immigration in a more neutral tone and either increases support or has a null effect. These findings suggest a more nuanced role for the media in constructing narratives about immigrants. That narrative may include both positive and negative elements, the effects of which may depend on the frame of reference for different groups. If the majority groupings in society already fear immigration and the baseline media coverage either notes some potential benefits to immigration or presents the issue from an immigrant's point of view, one can imagine how it increases support within the majority group. If that same coverage also highlights the potential economic costs of immigration, one can imagine how groups who begin more supportive of immigrants, such as second-generation residents and ethnic minorities, might grow slightly more sceptical. In other words, the possibility of balanced coverage, especially after aggregating across multiple media sources, has the potential to bring different groups together on the issue.

The resulting national narrative is one that likely includes both positive and negative reactions to immigrants and does not lead simply to complete opposition to or unwavering support for more open immigration policies. Some elements may include assumptions that immigrants represent a threat to the community. Other elements of this narrative may adopt a more positive or sympathetic view of immigrants. The most fervent consumers of media coverage within each social group will likely be exposed to the same elements of this national narrative, bringing about a convergence in opinion on the issue among these individuals.

The broader political and economic contexts matter for the likely effects of media exposure. The media's homogenising effect may be diminished during periods of perceived threat to national wellbeing or high economic stress. At these moments, support for immigration may decline across all groups (rather than converge at a midpoint) or even diverge more as minority groups resist the urge to blame immigrants for the country's problems. Future efforts could seek to better examine the effects of media coverage on different groups under different levels of national anxiety.

Ultimately, our study affirms the idea that different narratives matter. The minority groups examined here likely began in a position of greater support because they had experienced very different narratives than the majority groups. The media appears to shift opinions among all groups by presenting different narratives. Based on these findings, efforts to build greater support for immigrants could focus on disseminating positive or neutral narratives as widely as possible.

References

Anderson, B. 1983. *Imagined Communities*. London: Verso.

Atwell Seate, A., and D. Mastro. 2016. 'Media's Influence on Immigration Attitudes: An Intergroup Threat Theory Approach.' *Communication Monographs* 83, no. 2: 194–213. doi.org/10.1080/03637751.2015.1068433.

Azrout, R., J. van Spanje, and C. de Vreese. 2012. 'When News Matters: Media Effects on Public Support for European Union Enlargement in 21 Countries.' *Journal of Common Market Studies* 50, no. 5: 691–708. doi.org/10.1111/j.1468-5965.2012.02255.x.

Bennett, W.L., and S. Iyengar. 2008. 'A New Era of Minimal Effects? The Changing Foundations of Political Communication.' *Journal of Communication* 58, no. 4: 707–31. doi.org/10.1111/j.1460-2466.2008.00410.x.

Bobo, L., and V.L. Hutchings. 1996. 'Perceptions of Racial Group Competition: Extending Blumer's Theory of Group Position to a Multiracial Social Context.' *American Sociological Review* 61, no. 6: 951–72. doi.org/10.2307/2096302.

Boomgaarden, H.G., C.H. de Vreese, A.R. Schuck, R. Azrout, M. Elenbaas, J.H. van Spanje, and R. Vliegenthart. 2013. 'Across Time and Space: Explaining Variation in News Coverage of the European Union.' *European Journal of Political Research* 52, no. 5: 608–29. doi.org/10.1111/1475-6765.12009.

Brader, T., N.A. Valentino, and E. Suhay. 2008. 'What Triggers Public Opposition to Immigration? Anxiety, Group Cues, and Immigration Threat.' *American Journal of Political Science* 52, no. 4: 959–78. doi.org/10.1111/j.1540-5907.2008.00353.x.

Burscher, B., J. van Spanje, and C.H. de Vreese. 2015. 'Owning the Issues of Crime and Immigration: The Relation Between Immigration and Crime News and Anti-Immigrant Voting in 11 Countries.' *Electoral Studies* 38: 59–69. doi.org/10.1016/j.electstud.2015.03.001.

Canetti-Nisim, D., E. Halperin, K. Sharvit, and S.E. Hobfoll. 2009. 'A New Stress-Based Model of Political Extremism: Personal Exposure to Terrorism, Psychological Distress, and Exclusionist Political Attitudes.' *Journal of Conflict Resolution* 53, no. 3: 363–89. doi.org/10.1177/0022002709333296.

Caviedes, A. 2015. 'An Emerging "European" News Portrayal of Immigration?' *Journal of Ethnic and Migration Studies* 41, no. 6: 897–917. doi.org/10.1080/1369183X.2014.1002199.

Citrin, J., D.P. Green, C. Muste, and C. Wong. 1997. 'Public Opinion Toward Immigration Reform: The Role of Economic Motivations.' *The Journal of Politics* 59, no. 3: 858–81. doi.org/10.2307/2998640.

Damstra, A., L. Jacobs, M. Boukes, and E. Vliegenthart. 2019. 'The Impact of Immigration News on Anti-Immigrant Party Support: Unpacking Agenda-Setting and Issue Ownership Effects Over Time.' *Journal of Elections, Public Opinion and Parties* 31, no. 1: 97–118. doi.org/10.1080/17457289.2019.1607863.

Dancygier, R.M., and M.J. Donnelly. 2013. 'Sectoral Economies, Economic Contexts, and Attitudes Toward Immigration.' *The Journal of Politics* 75, no. 1: 17–35. doi.org/10.1017/S0022381612000849.

de Vreese, C.H., and H.G. Boomgaarden. 2006. 'Media Effects on Public Opinion about the Enlargement of the European Union.' *Journal of Common Market Studies* 44, no. 2: 419–36. doi.org/10.1111/j.1468-5965.2006.00629.x.

de Vreese, C.H., and H.A. Semetko. 2004. 'News Matters: Influences on the Vote in the Danish 2000 Euro Referendum Campaign.' *European Journal of Political Research* 43, no. 5: 699–722. doi.org/10.1111/j.0304-4130.2004.00171.x.

Dinas, E., and J. van Spanje. 2011. 'Crime Story: The Role of Crime and Immigration in the Anti-Immigration Vote.' *Electoral Studies* 30, no. 4: 658–71. doi.org/10.1016/j.electstud.2011.06.010.

Dunaway, J., R.P. Branton, and M.A. Abrajano. 2010. 'Agenda Setting, Public Opinion, and the Issue of Immigration Reform.' *Social Science Quarterly* 91, no. 2: 359–78. doi.org/10.1111/j.1540-6237.2010.00697.x.

European Social Survey (ESS). 2019. *ESS9: Integrated File, Edition 3.2.* ESS Data Portal. [Online.] London: European Social Survey European Research Infrastructure Consortium. Ess.sikt.no/en/datafile/b2b0bf39-176b-4eca-8d26-3c05ea83d2cb/266?tab=0.

Ford, R. 2011. 'Acceptable and Unacceptable Immigrants: How Opposition to Immigration in Britain is Affected by Migrants' Region of Origin.' *Journal of Ethnic and Migration Studies* 37, no. 7: 1017–37. doi.org/10.1080/1369183X.2011.572423.

Gidron, N., and P.A. Hall. 2017. 'The Politics of Social Status: Economic and Cultural Roots of the Populist Right.' *The British Journal of Sociology* 68: S57–S84. doi.org/10.1111/1468-4446.12319.

Givens, T., and A. Luedtke. 2005. 'European Immigration Policies in Comparative Perspective: Issue Salience, Partisanship and Immigrant Rights.' *Comparative European Politics* 3, no. 1: 1–22. doi.org/10.1057/palgrave.cep.6110051.

Hainmueller, J., and M.J. Hiscox. 2007. 'Educated Preferences: Explaining Attitudes Toward Immigration in Europe.' *International Organization* 61, no. 2: 399–442. doi.org/10.1017/S0020818307070142.

Hainmueller, J., and D.J. Hopkins. 2015. 'The Hidden American Immigration Consensus: A Conjoint Analysis of Attitudes Toward Immigrants.' *American Journal of Political Science* 59, no. 3: 529–48. doi.org/10.1111/ajps.12138.

Hellwig, T., and Y. Kweon. 2016. 'Taking Cues on Multidimensional Issues: The Case of Attitudes Toward Immigration.' *West European Politics* 39, no. 4: 710–30. doi.org/10.1080/01402382.2015.1136491.

Hellwig, T., and A. Sinno. 2017. 'Different Groups, Different Threats: Public Attitudes Toward Immigrants.' *Journal of Ethnic and Migration Studies* 43, no. 3: 339–58. doi.org/10.1080/1369183X.2016.1202749.

Ho, A.K., J. Sidanius, F. Pratto, S. Levin, L. Thomsen, N. Kteily, and J. Sheehy-Skeffington. 2012. 'Social Dominance Orientation: Revisiting the Structure and Function of a Variable Predicting Social and Political Attitudes.' *Personality and Social Psychology Bulletin* 38: 583–606. doi.org/10.1177/0146167211432765.

Kaye, R. 2001. 'An Analysis of Press Representation of Refugees and Asylum-Seekers in the United Kingdom.' *Media and Migration: Constructions of Mobility and Difference* 8: 53.

Kehrberg, J. 2007. 'Public Opinion on Immigration in Western Europe: Economics, Tolerance, and Exposure.' *Comparative European Politics* 5, no. 3: 264–81. doi.org/10.1057/palgrave.cep.6110099.

Lahav, G., and M. Courtemanche. 2012. 'The Ideological Effects of Framing Threat on Immigration and Civil Liberties.' *Political Behavior* 34: 477–505. doi.org/10.1007/s11109-011-9171-z.

Maier, J., and B. Rittberger. 2008. 'Shifting Europe's Boundaries: Mass Media, Public Opinion and the Enlargement of the EU.' *European Union Politics* 9, no. 2: 243–67. doi.org/10.1177/1465116508089087.

Mayda, A.M. 2006. 'Who is Against Immigration? A Cross-Country Investigation of Individual Attitudes Toward Immigrants.' *Review of Economics & Statistics* 88, no. 3: 510–30. doi.org/10.1162/rest.88.3.510.

McDaniel, E.L., I. Nooruddin, and A.F. Shortle. 2011. 'Divine Boundaries: How Religion Shapes Citizens' Attitudes Toward Immigrants.' *American Politics Research* 39, no. 1: 205–33. doi.org/10.1177/1532673X10371300.

McLaren, L., H. Boomgaarden, and R. Vliegenthart. 2018. 'News Coverage and Public Concern about Immigration in Britain.' *International Journal of Public Opinion Research* 30, no. 2: 173–93. doi.org/10.1093/ijpor/edw033.

Merolla, J., S. Karthick Ramakrishnan, and C. Haynes. 2013. '"Illegal", "Undocumented" or "Unauthorized": Equivalency Frames, Issue Frames and Public Opinion on Immigration.' *Perspectives on Politics* 11, no. 3: 789–807. doi.org/10.1017/S1537592713002077.

Morrison, K.R., and O. Ybarra. 2008. 'The Effects of Realistic Threat and Group Identification on Social Dominance Orientation.' *Journal of Experimental Social Psychology* 44, no. 1: 156–63. doi.org/10.1016/j.jesp.2006.12.006.

Mutz, D.C., and E. Kim. 2017. 'The Impact of In-Group Favoritism on Trade Preferences.' *International Organization* 71, no. 4: 827–50. doi.org/10.1017/S0020818317000327.

Norton, M.I., and S.R. Sommers. 2011. 'Whites See Racism as a Zero-Sum Game That They Are Now Losing.' *Perspectives on Psychological Science* 6, no. 3: 215–18. doi.org/10.1177/1745691611406922.

Pew Research Center. 2013. *Second-Generation Americans: A Portrait of the Adult Children of Immigrants*. Washington, DC: Pew.

Poynting, S., and V. Mason. 2007. 'The Resistible Rise of Islamophobia: Anti-Muslim Racism in the UK and Australia Before 11 September 2001.' *Journal of Sociology* 43, no. 1: 61–86. doi.org/10.1177/1440783307073935.

Semetko, H.A., W. van der Brug, and P.M. Valkenburg. 2003. 'The Influence of Political Events on Attitudes Towards the European Union.' *British Journal of Political Science* 33, no. 4: 621–34. doi.org/10.1017/S0007123403000280.

Sidanius, J., and F. Pratto. 1999. *Social Dominance: An Intergroup Theory of Social Hierarchy and Oppression*. New York: Cambridge University Press. doi.org/10.1017/CBO9781139175043.

Sniderman, P.M., L. Hagendoorn, and M. Prior. 2004. 'Predisposing Factors and Situational Triggers: Exclusionary Reactions to Immigrant Minorities.' *American Political Science Review* 98, no. 1 (February): 35–49. doi.org/10.1017/S000305540400098X.

Soroka, S.N. 2002. 'Issue Attributes and Agenda-Setting by Media, the Public, and Policymakers in Canada.' *International Journal of Public Opinion Research* 14, no. 3: 264–85. doi.org/10.1093/ijpor/14.3.264.

Strabac, Z., and O. Listhaug. 2008. 'Anti-Muslim Prejudice in Europe: A Multilevel Analysis of Survey Data from 30 Countries.' *Social Science Research* 37, no. 1: 268–86. doi.org/10.1016/j.ssresearch.2007.02.004.

Tajfel, H. 1978. 'The Achievement of Inter-Group Differentiation.' In *Differentiation between Social Groups*, edited by H. Tajfel, 77–100. London: Academic Press.

Tajfel, H., ed. 2010. *Social Identity and Intergroup Relations. Volume 7*. Cambridge: Cambridge University Press.

Tajfel, H., and J.C. Turner. 1979. 'An Integrative Theory of Intergroup Conflict.' In *The Social Psychology of Intergroup Relations*, edited by W.G. Austin and S. Worchel, 33–47. Monterey: Brooks/Cole.

van der Linden, M., and L. Jacobs. 2016. 'The Impact of Cultural, Economic, and Safety Issues in Flemish Television News Coverage (2003–13) of North African Immigrants on Perceptions of Intergroup Threat.' *Journal of Ethnic and Racial Studies* 40, no. 15: 2823–41. doi.org/10.1080/01419870.2016.1229492.

van Klingeren, M., H.G. Boomgaarden, R. Vliegenthart, and C.H. de Vreese. 2015. 'Real World is Not Enough: The Media as an Additional Source of Negative Attitudes Toward Immigration, Comparing Denmark and the Netherlands.' *European Sociological Review* 31, no. 3: 268–83. doi.org/10.1093/esr/jcu089.

Walgrave, S., and K. De Swert. 2004. 'The Making of the (Issues of the) Vlaams Blok.' *Political Communication* 21, no. 4: 479–500. doi.org/10.1080/105846 00490522743.

Walgrave, S., and K. De Swert. 2007. 'Where Does Issue Ownership Come From? From the Party or From the Media? Issue–Party Identifications in Belgium, 1991–2005.' *Harvard International Journal of Press/Politics* 12, no. 1: 37–67. doi.org/10.1177/1081180X06297572.

Zaller, J. 1996. 'The Myth of Massive Media Impact Revived: New Support for a Discredited Idea.' *Political Persuasion and Attitude Change* 17: 17–78.

Zucker, H.G. 1978. 'The Variable Nature of News Media Influence.' *Annals of the International Communication Association* 2, no. 1: 225–40. doi.org/10.1080/23808985.1978.11923728.

3

Immigrants unwelcome in Poland? Facts, figures and their broader sociocultural contexts

Marcin Dębicki

Population displacements is, in principle, an eternal phenomenon, the course of which is conditioned by a range of variables. In different parts of the globe, it is experienced at different historical moments, with varying intensity, runs in different directions (emigration versus immigration) and its subjects are communities that are more or less culturally different from the host society and undertake their activities for different reasons (although fleeing from armed conflicts, persecution, lack of life prospects or even hunger seem to be the most frequent ones). All these factors also play an important role in the context of the migration challenges that have been affecting Poland since at least mid-2015. These challenges strongly shape public debate, raising several vital questions for Poland and its inhabitants. Therefore, shining light on the events in Poland in recent years, as well as outlining their broader social, cultural and historical contexts, will constitute the main focus of this reflection.

In this chapter,[1] these issues will be linked to several key thematic bundles, with the common denominator being the attitudes of Poles towards the reception of different categories of migrants. The first bundle relates to declarations made in terms of helping migrants: at the beginning of 2015, strongly 'theoretical' and abstract, but in the following months, verified by a real phenomenon—the massive wave of refugees that reached Europe. The second theme concerns the reception of the approximately 1.5 million newcomers from Ukraine (almost exclusively labour migrants) who arrived in Poland between 2014 and 2021. The third theme focusses on the migration crisis that was playing out on the Poland–Belarus border for a year, starting in the summer of 2021. Fourth, we will turn to the most recent problem facing Poland (but also Europe): the mass flight of Ukrainians from the war triggered by Russia in February 2022. Finally, within the framework of the fifth part of the chapter, a reflection oriented towards the specificity of Poles' attitudes to the reception of both categories of immigrants will be undertaken, together with an attempt to show the broader context. For it should be remembered that the phenomena discussed, although occurring in contemporary Poland and with their own local colouring and conditions, partly reflect trends and cultural patterns observed more broadly—in Central Europe, as a peculiar cultural circle, and Europe as a whole, developing over the years, decades or even centuries. By taking this broader context into account, we obtain an appropriately wide-ranging perspective, which is necessary for a better understanding of the problem presented here: the attitudes of Poles towards the reception of refugees in recent years and the conditions that create them.

These points will be discussed based on four strongly differentiated types of sources. First, there will be the results of surveys conducted in Poland between 2015 and 2022 showing the social reception of the phenomena described. Second, we will refer to basic facts and figures that outline a more objective picture of reality. Third—and especially in relation to the most recent events—we will turn to reports, press articles, observations and intuitions provided by everyday life (the presence of which will make the chapter less scientific and more essayistic in places). And fourth, more broadly drawn concepts of a historical and civilisational nature will prove useful; this applies mainly to the last of the above five thematic bundles, which would be difficult to capture with current empirical data alone.

---

1   The central themes of this chapter were first presented to a seminar held by the B/orders In Motion Centre at the European University Viadrina Frankfurt (Oder) in June 2022. The data and political context are current as of early October 2022.

Attitudes of Poles towards the reception of refugees, 2015–2018

This section focusses on the attitudes of Poles towards the reception of refugees that were diagnosed before the main wave reached Europe in the summer of 2015 (and thus refugees were a 'theoretical' or abstract phenomenon for respondents). It compares these results with the attitudes towards the migrants already present close to Poland's borders (in Germany or Hungary) and looks at the evolution of these attitudes through the 2015 migrant wave. The analysis is based on the results of opinion surveys, particularly those carried out by the Public Opinion Research Centre (in Polish, Centrum Badania Opinii Społecznej, or CBOS)[2] in 2015–18— that is, at a time when this issue was prominent in Polish public debate.

An interesting piece of introductory information about Poles' attitudes towards Muslims is offered by Public Opinion Research Centre's March 2015 survey, the results of which indicated that most Poles (88 per cent) did not personally know a Muslim and it is legitimate to suppose that those who did may have established such contacts mostly during travel abroad. Moreover, those who knew a Muslim tended to be better educated, had higher income per capita, refrained from religious practices and were politically left-oriented. According to the survey, 44 per cent of Poles had negative attitudes towards Muslims, 23 per cent had a positive attitude and 33 per cent were indifferent. Although the survey was conducted a few weeks after the terrorist attack on the French weekly *Charlie Hebdo*, more than half of respondents did not have negative feelings towards Muslims at that time; what is more, the results were more or less the same as those obtained a decade earlier (CBOS 2015a: 1; Feliksiak 2015: 1).[3]

In mid-May 2015, when the first information about the influx of migrants into southern Europe appeared, most Poles agreed that people affected by a military conflict, regardless of where they were from, should be allowed to find shelter in Poland. A closer analysis shows that 58 per cent of respondents claimed Poland ought to receive such migrants until they could return to their country of origin and 14 per cent believed they should be allowed to settle

---

2   The Public Opinion Research Centre is one of the most important centres of its kind in Poland. Established in 1982, it is directly supervised by the Polish Prime Minister. Surveys are usually conducted on a representative random sample of approximately 1,000 adult Poles by face-to-face interviews.
3   Generally, the surveys are presented in Polish; some, however, are also in English, yet in a much shorter version, so both sources are used.

in Poland. Altogether, 72 per cent of respondents approved of the presence of refugees in some form in Poland (with 21 per cent against). However, the answers to other questions revealed that, in fact, Poles distinguished between refugees according to their place of origin. Respondents were more eager to grant international protection (refugee status) to Ukrainians fleeing the armed conflict in their homeland (moderate and strong support shared by 46 per cent; 36 per cent against) than to refugees from the Middle East and Africa (33 per cent in support; 53 per cent against).[4] Moreover, most respondents expressed moderate rather than strong support for the idea of taking in refugees from both regions (CBOS 2015b: 1–2; Kowalczuk 2015a: 2–3), which should have served as a warning that in many cases this acceptance was declarative only.

It is noteworthy that much the same results held true for immigrants (that is, not refugees). As the June 2015 survey showed, generally speaking, there was approval of the presence of migrants in the Polish labour market, although more than half of respondents wanted American and Western European migrants, followed by those wanting Ukrainians (38 per cent) and representatives of other nations that had long been present in Poland doing poorly paid jobs: Vietnamese, Belarusians and Russians (30–32 per cent); Africans (26 per cent); Turks (20 per cent); and Arabs (14 per cent). At the same time, most Poles (52–62 per cent) found the presence of Turks and Arabs disadvantageous (CBOS 2015c: 1–2; Kowalczuk 2015b: 7).

Returning to refugees themselves, the May 2015 survey recorded a relatively high level of acceptance of refugees coming to Poland. After this time, as the immigration crisis in Europe unfolded, Poles grew reluctant to accept newcomers, with most subsequent surveys showing a decline in support and an increase in unwillingness to accept refugees settling in Poland (for detailed data, see Table 3.1). At the same time, it is difficult to say to what extent the respondents associated refugees with those from Asia and Africa only (these kinds of data are included in Table 3.2) or whether that included Ukrainians. Looking at the data for 'Ukrainian refugees' from 2016 to 2018, the level of acceptance of these people coming to Poland is much higher than for other groups, yet slowly decreasing.[5] Table 3.2 also differs from Table 3.1 in that in the former the respondents were informed that

---

4   Interestingly, former Polish prime minister Beata Szydło suggested such a strategy—unjustifiably treating Ukrainians who were needed in the Polish labour market as refugees.

5   At the beginning of 2016, 61 per cent of Poles supported receiving Ukrainian refugees in Poland and 31 per cent were against; in April 2017, this ratio was 55:40 and, in mid-2018, 56:35 (with the rest undecided).

these refugees had already arrived in an EU country, thus the investigation was also about the degree of solidarity Poles had with other European states. It appears, however, that this factor did not play a crucial role here: in all the cases analysed the percentage of respondents ready to give refugees (temporary) shelter in Poland without knowing where they were at the time (Table 3.1) outnumbered those for whom solidarity was implied (Table 3.2). It is therefore tempting to say the results are not so much about solidarity as about the African or Asian origin of these migrants.

Table 3.1 Poles' attitudes to receiving refugees in Poland, 2015–18 (per cent)

Attitude	May 2015	Aug. 2015	Dec. 2015	Apr. 2016	Sept. 2016	Dec. 2016	Oct. 2017	June 2018
Allow settlement	14	6	5	3	4	4	4	5
Allow temporary stay	58	50	37	30	40	40	29	29
No refugees	21	38	53	61	52	52	63	60
Unsure	7	6	5	6	4	4	4	6

Source: Author's elaboration based on data from Public Opinion Research Center (CBOS, 2015–18).

Table 3.2 Poles' attitudes to receiving refugees from Africa or the Middle East via EU countries, 2015–18 (per cent)

Attitude	May 2015	Oct. 2015	Dec. 2015	Apr. 2016	Sept. 2016	Dec. 2016	Oct. 2017	June 2018
Strongly supportive	3	7	5	2	3	3	4	5
Moderately supportive	30	36	25	23	25	25	16	17
Moderately opposed	32	21	30	28	28	27	23	26
Strongly opposed	21	30	34	43	39	40	52	46
Unsure	14	6	6	4	5	5	5	6

Source: Author's elaboration based on data from Public Opinion Research Center (CBOS, 2015–18).

As we can see, certain events (such as acts of violence) in Western Europe provoke respondents to express stronger reluctance to help refugees—as was the case, for example, in the December 2015 survey, carried out soon after the terrorist attacks in Paris. Compared with the data gathered two months earlier, the percentage of those supportive of accepting refugees in Poland dropped rapidly from 43 per cent to 30 per cent, along with a simultaneous sharp increase in respondents opposing this idea (from 51 per cent to 64 per cent). This was a turning point: since that moment, the percentage of those who are 'definitely against' receiving refugees in Poland has consistently been higher than the aggregated percentage of those moderately and strongly supportive of this idea (Głowacki 2017: 1).

From the second half of 2018, fewer surveys were conducted about refugees. Yet, it is not difficult to observe that Poles' attitudes to them continued to harden, with the October 2017 survey showing that as many as three-quarters of respondents opposed receiving refugees in Poland and only 20 per cent were supportive (most of whom showed only moderate support). At the same time, two surveys carried out by a different research centre[6] revealed an interesting indicator of how solid respondents' opinions were, as they were asked whether Poland should receive refugees if there was a threat of losing EU funding if they did not. In mid-2018 the percentage of those who would be against having newcomers in Poland even with this hypothetical loss was 75 per cent. This attitude received confirmation of sorts in another survey, which found that as many as 51 per cent of Poles would rather leave the EU than receive refugees. To grasp the full significance of this result, one needs to know that Poles were then (and still are) among the greatest supporters of the EU; in December 2017, 83 per cent wanted Poland to remain within the union and only 11 per cent were opposed. As noted, this issue was not included in the CBOS surveys after June 2018, returning only in September 2021—at the same time as the growing crisis at the Poland–Belarus border.

Leaving aside scepticism or even aversion on the part of Poles towards the reception of refugees from Africa or Asia—which, after all, are the regions identified by respondents from which people movements have negative consequences—it is worth emphasising the serious divergence among respondents depending on whether refugees were an imagined or a real entity, heading towards the European Union or already within its borders. Not for the first time, it appears that the phenomenon presented in the abstract leads to more positive declarations from respondents than when refugees are at the border and identified with real, including personal, costs.

---

6   Both surveys were conducted by the Kantar Millward Brown Agency, part of the international Kantar network, based in London.

Ukrainian labour migrants in Poland since 2014

Since the annexation of Crimea and the start of the war in Donbas by the Russian Federation in 2014, as well as Ukraine's steadily deteriorating economic situation, there has been an increased influx of Ukrainians in Poland. Despite the military context, almost all those who arrived in Poland between 2014 and 2021 did so for economic reasons, usually without taking steps to obtain refugee status. The intense rate of growth in the number of Ukrainians in Poland in the first years of Russian aggression saw Poland become a global leader in the inflow of seasonal, short-term workers in 2017 (OECD 2018: 26–27). For Poland, traditionally an emigrant country, this was an unusual phenomenon, which was explained by an expert from the Polish think tank the Centre for Eastern Studies as follows:

> The current influx of short-term migrants has been possible due to the specific confluence of 'pull' factors (a very liberal system for the employment of foreigners in Poland geared to one geographical direction—the Eastern Partnership countries) with 'push' factors: the situation of shock in Ukraine after the outbreak of war and economic collapse in 2014–15. In addition, many Ukrainian migrants left Russia for Poland due to the Russian aggression. Other important factors attracting Ukrainian citizens to Poland are the low travel costs, the ability to maintain family ties in Ukraine, extensive migration networks, and similarities of language and cultural closeness. For this reason, one of the terms given to the current wave of migration from Ukraine to Poland is 'local mobility', meaning a specific system of frequent short-term journeys to Poland, and where at the same time spending within the country of residence is limited, and living activities are concentrated in Ukraine, as opposed to migration in the classical sense, which assumes a permanent change of the centre of life activities. This conglomerate of factors has resulted in a noticeable worldwide boom in the short-term migration sector.
>
> (Jaroszewicz 2018: 6)

This 'local mobility' has made it difficult to estimate the number of Ukrainians working in Poland. In 2020–21, calculations were made more difficult by the outbreak of the Covid-19 pandemic, which forced some migrants to return to Ukraine. At the beginning of February 2022—that is, shortly before Russia's invasion of Ukraine—the number of Ukrainians in Poland was estimated at 1.5 million (Wojdat and Cywinski 2022: 50).

It is worth mentioning that the EU dimension was present here, too, as Ukrainians qualified for visa-free entry and travel for three months within the Schengen Area. In the demographic structure of this stage of migration, there was a noticeable predominance of men, often working in construction.[7] Over time, some migrants began to bring their families to Poland, which translated into, among other things, changes in the ethnic structure of school classes: within a few years, the percentage of Ukrainian children and youths studying in Polish schools reached the level of a few or even a dozen per cent. This could signal that some families were considering settling in Poland permanently. Women arriving in Poland most often worked as domestic helpers, carers of the elderly, in orchards and in minor public services. Mention should also be made of tertiary students, who in some institutions constituted a noticeable proportion of those gaining an education in the country.

It is important to note that Poles and Ukrainians generally coexisted happily, although of course there were a number of incidents, including misdemeanours and crimes: fraud against Ukrainian workers, various forms of exploitation of their difficult social and economic situation, and sometimes abuse and assaults of Ukrainians based on their nationality (sometimes relating to the difficult history between the two countries).[8] Overall, however, until February 2022, when the more intense influx of Ukrainians began, the initial stages of the Ukrainians' integration were successful. It is important to keep in mind the broader context of this population movement: a rapid, large influx of labour migrants into a society long untamed by ethnic diversity.[9] At the same time, Ukrainians tend to assess the situation through the prism of a different set of variables to Poles. On the one hand, they place greater emphasis on the financial advantages of staying in Poland (which are mutual as the Polish economy also benefits

---

7   After 24 February 2022, some returned to Ukraine to enlist in the territorial defence forces or join the army, which had an immediate impact on the Polish construction industry, as they were then replaced almost exclusively with women and children.

8   Perhaps the most important event in this regard is the antagonism relating to the so-called Volhynian massacres of 1943–45, when up to 100,000 Poles were (often brutally) murdered by Ukrainian nationalists. The problem here is not only the memory of these events, which is still alive in some places and maintained through intergenerational transmission, but also the perception of this crime by contemporary Ukrainians, which differs from that of the Poles.

9   A phenomenon that may have further hindered the course of this familiarisation in many Polish cities is the tendency—active in the past dozen or so years—to emphasise their alleged, rather than real, multiculturalism as an element of urban marketing strategies. This phenomenon was neatly captured in the title of a book on one Polish city: *On the Multiculturalism of Monocultural Wrocław* (Dolińska and Makaro 2013).

from the Ukrainians' presence in the labour market), while on the other, they pay more attention to Polish behaviour affecting individual Ukrainians—their fellow nationals. A report by the Association of Ukrainians in Poland, for example, draws attention to acts such as the negative campaign against migrants, targeted attacks and beatings (Tyma 2019: 27–33). In other words, acts of resentment or violence on the part of Poles towards Ukrainians, even if few in number, affect individuals, whose testimonies (for example, on the internet) can influence their own and other Ukrainians' sense of security.

Migration crisis at the Poland–Belarus border, since summer 2021

Another challenge Poland faced was the so-called migration crisis at its border with Belarus. The widespread use of the term should be understood as an attempt by Belarus to destabilise the social and political situation in Poland, Lithuania and Latvia, and—as a consequence—in the countries of Western Europe, by directing there in the summer of 2021 a stream of migrants from Asia and Africa (particularly, from Syria, Iraq, Afghanistan and Congo). Belarusian President Alexander Lukashenko is directly responsible for this, but at least tacit approval must have been given by his political patron, Russian President Vladimir Putin. The plan was initially carried out under the pretext of these migrants spontaneously making tourist visits to Belarus, but relatively quickly, Polish authorities discovered the real intention: the deliberate importation of large numbers of migrants, who, for a high fee, were promised passage to the borders of the European Union. The essence of this crisis can be described on several interrelated levels.

First, there is the international context—that is, the attempt to destabilise the countries of the European Union and the growing tension between it and Belarus (with Russia in the background). This was driven by the EU's refusal to recognise Lukashenko's fraudulent re-election as President of Belarus and, therefore, the lack of prospects for political and financial support for his regime, combined with the help the EU offered to the Belarusian opposition, creating an artificial (and geographically odd) migration route from the Middle East to Western Europe.

Second, the challenge was thrown down to Poland (and Lithuania and Latvia) to protect the EU's external borders. The involvement of Belarusian services—initially offering all kinds of support to the 'tourists' and later acting as a barrier to those who decided to abandon their plan to enter the EU and tried to return to Belarus—created a peculiar situation: migrants were pushed (often even physically shunted) by officers from both countries between the Polish and the Belarusian sides of the border. Further context is provided here by Poland's multifaceted dispute with EU institutions over several years: tensions with the European Council over the way it went about deciding which countries would accept migrants under the relocation regime, challenges in the Court of Justice of the European Union, along with concerns about the rule of law and the Polish judiciary expressed by some EU bodies. This translated into the reluctance of Polish authorities to seek assistance from the relevant EU entity, Frontex, even though it is based in Warsaw. Poland's refusal to accept refugees during the 2015 migration crisis also has significance here.

The third, and most important, point is the serious humanitarian crisis created at the Poland–Belarus border. Poor weather, difficult (forest and marshy) terrain and chronic shortages of food, water, medicines, warm clothing and cleaning products led to at least a dozen deaths among the migrants, not to mention the physical and mental health costs paid by an incalculable number of people for their journey to Western Europe. The enormity of the cruelty meted out to migrants by the services of both countries has been documented in reports by various organisations, including Amnesty International (2022). Significantly, many of these costs would have been avoided if the Polish Government had not banned nongovernmental organisations (NGOs), medical services, volunteers and journalists from entering 183 villages along the Poland–Belarus border where the refugee drama unfolded (and where a state of emergency was in place from 2 September 2021 to 30 June 2022). Those who wanted to deliver food or medicines to the migrants faced harassment from officials, as well as the possibility of being charged with aiding and abetting the crime of illegally crossing the border. At some point, it became clear that Warsaw's plan for resolving this crisis boiled down to making life difficult for migrants to serve as a deterrent and minimise illegal crossings until a wall could be completed along a considerable part of the border in July 2022. Interestingly, it has become clear that this barrier cannot stop the illegal crossings; all it can do is limit their number and make the whole process more technically complicated.

This strategy had its origins not only in the tensions between Warsaw and Brussels, but also—and this is the fourth point—in the attitudes of the Polish public towards accepting refugees. According to a survey from

September 2021, when the crisis on the border was already several months old but still far from its peak, 9 per cent of respondents agreed that Poland should accept refugees from countries experiencing armed conflict and allow them to settle and 33 per cent declared their readiness to accept such people until they could return to their country of origin. Meanwhile, 48 per cent did not support this scenario under any formula (10 per cent were 'unsure'). Moreover, support for refugees from the border being able to apply for asylum in Poland was expressed by 33 per cent of respondents, with 52 per cent opposed (15 per cent of respondents had no opinion on this issue) (CBOS 2021: 1).

Finally, the crisis revealed the limitations of the European Union when it comes to its potential to influence Poland, as well as its willingness to provide institutional assistance to migrants (cf. Kwapisz 2021). As with the 2015 migration crisis, deeper questions were again raised among the general public, experts and academia about the functioning of EU border mechanisms (de-bordering versus re-bordering processes), the effectiveness of the protection they provided and the price the EU's authoritarian neighbours demanded to help in solving a problem—including one that, as in the case of Belarus, they had themselves created. Also highlighted was the contrast in the attitudes of the Polish authorities and society, as well as of other EU countries and the EU itself, towards migrants from Asia and Africa compared with the reception of refugees from Ukraine, to whom EU borders have been widely opened. This theme will be discussed in the next section.

Ukrainian refugees in Poland since 24 February 2022

On 24 February 2022, Russia's aggression against Ukraine began—or, rather, intensified—creating a new geopolitical reality, part of which was the arrival in many countries on the European continent of people fleeing Ukraine. It is worth mentioning that, as far as its genesis is concerned, this crisis is different from those experienced in recent decades when refugees from the former Yugoslavia, Afghanistan, Iraq, Libya and Syria were arriving in Western Europe, escaping wars involving or even provoked by states of the prosperous Global North. A difficult political and economic situation also prevailed in places where the West replaced colonial practices with neo-colonial ones (Becker and Becker 2018: 4–7). As for the war in Ukraine, although Western and Global North states are involved there, too, it is difficult to suggest they caused the conflict (even though there are plenty who believe that NATO, which has supported Ukraine, is partly to blame for Russian aggression) or the underlying (neo-)colonial practices.

With the start of hostilities, the first refugees began to appear on the Poland–Ukraine border; from the very beginning, they were met with great kindness from Polish society. Particularly noteworthy was the spontaneous mobilisation of ordinary people who went to the border, offering food, clothing and sometimes a room in their own homes to the newcomers. Many collections of money, food, cleaning products and first-aid items for refugees, as well as for those who remained in Ukraine, were organised throughout the country. A great deal of work was done by a multitude of volunteers (including foreigners) who were active at railway stations or reception points. Private entrepreneurs, companies, churches and various public institutions such as kindergartens, schools and universities also showed generosity. Local municipal authorities launched assistance programs and small-town and village communities provided various forms of support. Of great importance was the introduction of a simplified procedure for refugees to cross the Polish border, the enactment by the parliament in mid-March 2022 of a special law regulating the stay of refugees in Poland (early implementation of the EU's Temporary Protection Directive), as well as other actions addressing the needs of newcomers (the right to free travel on public transport, financial allowances for registered persons with children under 18 and so on). However, many felt that the involvement of the Polish Government was, at least in the initial stage of the crisis, less than was expected (Kwapisz and Dębicki 2022); most of the work was done by local governments and NGOs (both of whom, for political reasons, had long been deprived of financial support by the central administration) or by activists and individual volunteers. It should be noted that considerable assistance was also provided by Ukrainians, approximately 1.5 million of whom were already living in Poland, who often provided the newcomers with accommodation and food and helped them take their first steps on Polish soil, deal with formalities or find work.[10] All of this meant there was no need to set up refugee camps in Poland (as of the beginning of October 2022).

---

10   For example, in a survey conducted at the end of April 2022, 23 per cent of refugees admitted that they lived with acquaintances or family from Ukraine; 46 per cent of respondents found accommodation with the help of Ukrainian friends living in Poland (Union of Polish Metropolises 2022b: 18–19).

It is difficult to present here statistics showing the scale of Ukrainian migration to Poland, as the situation remains dynamic and various institutions employ differing methodologies to collect data. However, it can be said that, at the beginning of October 2022—that is, seven months after the start of the regular war—almost 6.75 million Ukrainian refugees had arrived in Poland. Some 4.96 million of these people would manage to return to Ukraine[11] or move on to other countries, so the number of refugees remaining in Poland by the end of May was about 1.5 to 2 million.[12] The extent of the relocation, which significantly hampers estimations, is evident, for example, in the fact that on 15 June 2022, 24,300 people arrived in Poland from Ukraine, while 25,000 went in the opposite direction.[13] In contrast, at the end of February and the beginning of March 2022, more than 100,000 people were arriving in Poland daily from Ukraine (sometimes up to 125,000), with very few going in the opposite direction. According to Ukrainian migration researcher Natalia Kovalisko (2022), more than 150,000 refugees a day were leaving Ukraine at the time.

An interesting source of data on the location of refugees was an April 2022 study by experts at the Paweł Adamowicz Centre for Analysis and Research of the Union of Polish Metropolises (in Polish: Centrum Badań i Analiz, Unia Metropolii Polskich im. Pawła Adamowicza), who, based on the geo-trapping method, established the most important quantitative indicators, such as how much the population of the largest Polish cities had increased in the previous weeks. Their report said that some Polish metropolises had experienced a significant increase in population—for example, Rzeszów (by 53 per cent), Gdańsk, Katowice and Wrocław (23–25 per cent), and Kraków and Warsaw (18–19 per cent). Thus, the percentage of Ukrainians in the population of many Polish cities had increased to 20–25 per cent (in Rzeszów, to 35 per cent), meaning they now made up about 8 per cent of the country's population (Wojdat and Cywiński 2022)[14]—a result that had been achieved in just eight years.

---

11   Both figures (for 2 October 2022) are from the Polish Border Guard.

12   This figure was taken from other findings: that there were about 3.37 million Ukrainians in Poland at the end of May (Union of Polish Metropolises 2022a: 8), yet an estimated 1.5 million of these had arrived before 24 February 2022.

13   By 2 October 2022, for example, the respective numbers were 24,800 and 30,400 people (according to the Polish Border Guard).

14   As an update to this report suggests, at the end of May, the cities with the highest percentages of Ukrainians (before and after 24 February) were: Rzeszów (37 per cent), Wrocław (28 per cent) and Gdańsk (24 per cent). In absolute numbers, Warsaw dominated (about 343,000 people), followed by Wrocław (250,000) and Gdańsk (ca. 150,000). Generally, the update shows that the highest number of Ukrainians (3.85 million) and their highest percentage of the population (9 per cent) were recorded in April 2022 (Union of Polish Metropolises 2022a: 8, 15).

From the very first involvement of so many Poles in helping refugees, the question was repeatedly raised of how long such mobilisation and generosity would last. This was based on the assumption that such gestures, driven by fear or compassion, would eventually fade and meet fatigue-induced resistance. There were also questions about the long-term prospects for such coexistence—particularly in terms of the care and benefits provided to refugees by the Polish State. There was no shortage of voices saying that, in time, Poles would become indifferent to events in Ukraine and the fate of the migrants and become more concerned with the challenges in their own lives. In view of this, it is worth tracing the attitudes of Poles towards the war in Ukraine and the refugees arriving from there over recent months.

Just a few days after the start of hostilities by Russia (between 28 February and 10 March), CBOS pollsters asked Poles whether Poland should accept Ukrainian refugees from conflict areas. To this question, 57 per cent of respondents answered strongly in the affirmative and a further 37 per cent offered moderate support, giving a total of 94 per cent support (3 per cent answered 'unsure'). The survey release notes reported that, since August 2015—that is, since CBOS began to monitor the issue—the attitude of Poles to asylum seekers from Ukraine had never been so unambiguously positive. By March 2022, support for the acceptance of Ukrainian refugees reached a maximum of just 60–62 per cent, of whom only a minority expressed strong support (CBOS 2022a: 2; Felisiak and Roguska 2022: 8). Importantly, a very high level of support for accepting refugees (91 per cent of respondents) was recorded two months later, at a time when it would be expected that openness motivated by the freshness of a given experience would be waning. In addition, 63 per cent of respondents declared that they or someone from their household had helped refugees; most often this was material and financial assistance (CBOS 2022b: 1; Feliksiak 2022: 4, 7). The survey in early July showed that Poles maintained their support: 34 per cent of respondents strongly believed Poland should receive Ukrainian refugees and 50 per cent declared moderate support (CBOS 2022c: 3; Scovil 2022: 5). Similar results were obtained in the early September survey, with a slight decline in support compared with the first survey measurements. A different perspective was provided by a Kantar[15] survey, to which 52 per cent of respondents believed war refugees from Ukraine should stay in Poland as long as necessary. Another 26 per cent thought they should be

---

15   The survey was conducted on 3–6 June 2022 by computer-assisted telephone interviews on a representative sample of 1,000 adult Poles.

temporarily hosted in Poland and then relocated to other EU countries (Janicki 2022). It is worth interpreting this indicator through the prism of the 2015 migration crisis, when 50–70 per cent of respondents believed Poland should not receive refugees who had come to EU member states from Africa or the Middle East (see Table 3.2).

Some issues, however, have already emerged that could lead to tensions between Poles and refugees—related to the burden on the welfare system, competition in the labour market (including the 'Ukrainisation' and 'de-Polonisation' of some sectors), changes in the demographic structure of the population towards its feminisation (as the majority of newcomers are women), deterioration in the quality of primary and secondary schools (already overpopulated before February 2022), proposals to give Ukrainians the right to vote in local elections or grant them citizenship, unsettled historical issues, and so on. In October 2022—that is, after seven months of Ukrainian refugees in Poland—there were serious signs of indifference (clearly visible, for example, in a decline in donations to Ukrainian charities) and even boredom with the issue. Additionally, increasing numbers of Poles were asking why their state should continue to support the refugees financially, especially when—it has sometimes been claimed—some of them were displaying a high standard of living. The situation is further complicated by the continuing rise in inflation, as well as expected increases in the price of energy, which together are not a good omen for the migrants. This assumption is confirmed empirically: in July 2022, 38 per cent of respondents strongly or moderately believed that accepting refugees from Ukraine in Poland would be economically beneficial for the country in the long run, with 46 per cent disagreeing (CBOS 2022c: 3; Scovil 2022: 7). This suggests support for refugees is based on humanitarian rather than economic grounds, which is borne out by other results: 78 per cent of those surveyed would like Ukrainians to return home when the war is over, with only 6 per cent wishing them to stay in Poland permanently (Scovil 2022: 8). To grasp the scale of possible antagonisms in the future, one must juxtapose these figures with the results of a UN study conducted between mid-May and mid-June 2022, which found that as many as 79 per cent of Ukrainian refugees living in Poland planned to stay there in the near future (UNHCR 2022: 16). Clearly, these responses are based on the present situation—Ukraine still engulfed in war—yet one must ask: How many of these people would like to settle in Poland permanently, especially if the war drags on? And will they continue to be welcome there?

For the time being, however, the evidence cited so far shows the level of involvement of ordinary Poles in helping Ukrainians, even if it is not as massive as the sometimes almost euphoric media reports might suggest. This picture contrasts with the scale of declarations of support that were offered to Syrians or Iraqis stuck on the border with Belarus, leading us to the next point of consideration: the reasons for this clear preference for refugees from Ukraine.

Two sorts of refugees

Countries receiving refugees cannot ignore the fact that some of them will want to tie their lives to their new place of residence. The issue of the two sorts of refugees that appeared at the Polish border raises several questions. The first, ethical question is: is it fair to allow countries that have been invaded or engulfed in war to be drained of their population? The second, economic question relates to the receiving state's budget: will it benefit or lose from the influx of refugees? The third question is related to demographics and whether depopulation in the receiving state (due to emigration and/ or a falling birthrate) can be counteracted by the newcomers. The fourth, strategic question asks: is it to the receiving country's advantage that a given state (Ukraine, Iraq, Somalia, etc.) will lose some of its human potential— so important when the time for reconstruction comes?[16] These dilemmas have been approached in various ways, yet the discussion always ends with a fifth question (of a sociocultural nature)—about the course, pace and depth of refugee integration into the receiving population. This has been heightened by the warm welcome given to refugees from Ukraine—which has proved to be more lasting than expected—in contrast with the reception of those stuck on the border with Belarus, who are, apparently, considered less deserving.

This thesis was confirmed by the results of a survey carried out at the beginning of May 2022. To the question 'Do migrants and refugees attempting to enter Poland via the border with Belarus deserve the same assistance as refugees from Ukraine?', 35 per cent of respondents answered 'definitely

---

16 Observations so far suggest that for Ukrainians in Poland, the following are unlikely to return to Ukraine even when the war is over: families with children attending school or university abroad, those who have received higher education, who speak a foreign language, have high incomes and are more mobile (Kovalisko 2022)—that is, the types of people who have extraordinary potential for helping reconstruct the postwar state.

not' and a further 25 per cent answered 'possibly not'; 14 per cent answered 'definitely yes', with 21 per cent offering moderate support (Danielewski 2022). Given the considerable real and symbolic support offered to Ukrainians, questions about these responses inevitably arise. Debates in the Polish media and academia have offered a number of explanations but, in the absence of empirical research, such claims must remain hypotheses— although they do seem to have quite strong foundations in many years of observation of everyday interethnic relations in Poland. The claims of several authors outlined below also fulfil several theoretically constructed attributes of state borders today: sacralised, racialised, historicised, gendered and geopoliticised (Dębicki et al. 2022: 13–16).

The first of these attributes is important because we are dealing (it is presumed) with predominantly Muslim people on the Poland–Belarus border. The Islamophobia violently provoked by some Polish politicians in 2015 and since successively strengthened has reached a high level in Poland (Bobako 2017)—so much so that this issue could in principle close the case. Meanwhile, in the context of Ukrainians, it need not be said that most are nominally Christian, nor does it matter much that they are generally Ukrainian Orthodox or (much less frequently) Greek Catholic; the fact that they are not Muslim is implicitly sufficient. Thus, the importance of this factor seems to be revealed primarily on cultural grounds, in the form of expectations about difficult daily interethnic coexistence, conditioned by the assumed norms of social life formulated by Christianity and Islam, rather than on strictly religious grounds.

Second—and strongly connected to the previous point—the borders are racialised. Syrians, Afghans and citizens of many other countries are representatives of cultures and civilisations other than those with which the statistical Pole is familiar. Indeed, based on some of the dehumanising statements made about Muslims in the domestic public sphere, the Polish authorities could be accused of racist attitudes. According to Legut and Pędziwiatr (2018), there is a discursive construction of cultural otherness of the migrant-Muslim-terrorist-jihadist-rapist, which is presented as the antithesis of Europeanness, confirming the coherence of European identity in tension with its Stranger. Meanwhile, Ukrainians are Slavs, culturally close to Poles, with whom they have been learning to live for several years, with some success.

Third, in terms of the historicisation of borders, somewhere deep in the collective Polish psyche lies the concept of *Kresy*. Sometimes inadequately translated as 'Borderlands', *Kresy* these days refers to primarily an area that was part of interwar Poland, taken over by the Soviets in 1945 and, after the collapse of the USSR, divided between independent Lithuania, Belarus and Ukraine. This is by no means a matter of territorial revisionism inspired by Russian aggression, but a conviction that, by helping Ukrainians, the Poles are engaging in a cause that is in a sense also 'theirs'. This point was inadvertently and metaphorically touched on by Ukrainian President Volodymyr Zelenskyy when, at the beginning of the war and in the context of Polish hospitality, he told the Sejm (lower house) of the Republic of Poland that between the two nations 'there are no more borders' (Zelenskyy 2022).[17] The persistence of this feeling may also be fostered by common references to Ukraine as the 'brotherly nation' (which, incidentally, is not unintentional in the context of the nature of Polish–Russian/Ukrainian coexistence in the *Kresy*). Needless to say, there is no equivalent feeling in the context of those refugees on the Poland–Belarus border.[18]

Another point related to the previous thoughts is that borders are gendered. Indeed, in the case of refugees on the Belarusian border, their demographic structure is also important, with young men making up the highest proportion. Situating them in the context of 'male vitality' seems to be one of the more important stereotypes here, which, moreover, among Polish men often transforms into images of Muslim (read: African or Asian) immigrants gaining 'easy access' to Polish women. It is worth noting that this theme has also been exploited in Germany, following numerous assaults (including sexual ones) on women around New Year's Eve 2015 in many cities there (Kosnick 2019: 172–73). Meanwhile, almost all the Ukrainian victims of the Kremlin's aggression who have fled to Poland are women and children (about 95 per cent).

The fourth factor has a clear geopolitical face. Ukrainians are fleeing an aggressor which, in the Polish experience and in projections of the country's future, occupies a particularly prominent place on the scale of hostility. It is

---

17   The crucial part of the President's speech was: 'Just in one day, on the first day of the war, it became clear to me and to all Ukrainians, and, I am sure, to all Poles that there are no more borders between us, between our nations. No physical ones. No historical ones. No personal ones' (Zelenskyy 2022).

18   However, while treating the borders as 'nationalised', it should be remembered that there is serious historical antagonism between Poles and Ukrainians relating to the Volhynian massacres of 1943–45 (see Note 8). It is difficult to make far-reaching predictions here, but four months after the influx of Ukrainian refugees to Poland, it appeared that these events were not influencing mass public opinion in Poland.

therefore worth recalling that today's aid is a continuation of the political, material and symbolic support Poland gave to Kiev during the Ukrainian revolution in 2004–05 and 2013–14. In this sense, the Ukrainians fighting a war against Russia are Poland's allies, fighting 'for our freedom and yours'—that is, affirming a romantic ideal strongly inscribed in the native tradition, and marking their European aspirations with blood.[19] Meanwhile, the oppressor from whom Africans and Asians are fleeing is drawn from a high continental–civilisational level of generality and, therefore, as good as undefined. The oppressor is some amorphous figure, located thousands of kilometres away, in parts of the world where 'something evil happens all the time anyway'.

The geopolitical element is difficult to separate from the institutional; nevertheless, as a separate, fifth argument, it is important to point out several places where the two overlap. While the functioning of borders is institutionally regulated, the European Union

> appeared to be unprepared for the migration challenge, and its asylum system failed to guarantee the access to verify the legal claims. Both the governments and the EU representatives introduced or supported a variety of tools to prevent migrants coming from Belarus to enter the EU, and, in fact, made them 'stuck' in a so-called no-man's land: from implementation of states of emergency, 'legalisation' of pushbacks, to building new fences at the border.
>
> (Dębicki et al. 2022: 14)

While the European Union was rather restrained, seemingly lacking deep conviction about the rigorous Polish measures on the Belarusian border, the Ukrainian refugees were met with goodwill, including by the inhabitants of many other European countries. Refugees from Asia and Africa were not helped by the fact that they became inadvertently a tool in the game played against the EU by President Lukashenko and his Russian counterpart and promoter, Putin. By organising the transfer of people in an attempt to destabilise the EU, they blurred the significance of the human tragedy taking place on the border, reducing it to a geopolitical game. Finally, in the eyes of some Poles, it is not insignificant that Africans and Asians, unlike

---

19   At the same time, it is not only Poland that looks at Ukrainians 'through Russian glasses', seeing the threat coming from Moscow as real. As Kira Kosnick (2022) argues, the dominant political discourse in Germany sees Russia's current political course as a threat not just to Ukraine, but also to the EU and therefore Germany. Consequently, Ukraine and Ukrainians gain much more European support than might have been expected before the war—in social, economic and political terms.

Ukrainians, are trying to cross the border without authorisation (although the deeper reasons for this are not always known or understood by the wider public).

Reflecting more deeply on the reasons for the dissimilarity in the reactions of Poland (the state and its officials) and Poles to the two groups of migrants—those on the border with Belarus and people fleeing Ukraine—it is worth adopting a much longer and broader perspective. One could recall two important concepts: Fernand Braudel's 'history of different lengths' (Braudel and Wallerstein 2009) and the migration model proposed by Stephen Castles and Mark J. Miller (2009), both of which provide theoretical tools for knowing and understanding the position inherent in other Central European countries as well. In so doing, it should be emphasised that it is a matter of knowing and understanding the reasons for, and not seeking to justify, the way migrants have been treated at the Poland–Belarus border.

The first of these views directs our attention to stories stretched across three different time lines: the 'traditional' (short-term) history, oriented to 'brief time spans' and thus concentrating on individuals and certain events; the 'new economic and social history', referring to 'cyclical shifts' encapsulated in one or a few decade(s) and therefore known as medium-term history; and a 'history of even more sustained breadth' (long-term history), which spans centuries (Braudel and Wallerstein 2009: 173–74). Following this three-element model, Central European countries, including Poland, have reproduced significantly different paths to Western Europe and other important centres of the West in terms of perceptions of civilisation over the past few years, decades and centuries.

Taking a long-term perspective, these states were never subjected to colonialism—an experience that, on at least two levels, fosters familiarisation with the 'ethnic Other': first, through many years of multigenerational contact with it in private and public spaces, which gives rise to sentiments such as the one described by French historian Daniel Beauvois (2006: 47) as 'nostalgeria', which disguises a kind of longing for the 'idyllic' world of colonised Algeria. This made it possible to look at the presence of people from the Maghreb in French social spaces in a broader, less homogeneous perspective, even though it, obviously, is not a remedy for all the ills of interethnic coexistence there. Second, familiarisation is fostered by the awareness that the 'Other', having long occupied a position of subordination to the coloniser, was intensely exploited by them—a fact that sometimes gives rise to a need for expiation, promoting an increased level of acceptance, forbearance or tolerance. It should be stressed again that these factors do not, by default, provide a suitable environment for peaceful coexistence, but their absence certainly makes it more difficult to achieve such a state.

A medium-term perspective directs our attention towards the half-century after World War II, when Central European countries were part of the communist bloc. Unlike Western European societies, they did not benefit from the kind of support offered by Turks, Moroccans, Libyans and others in the postwar reconstruction of Germany, France and Italy. The representatives of these nations—sometimes referred to as guest workers— thus became co-creators of the European 'economic miracle' and bearers of the fruits of growth for indigenous Europeans (who thus incurred a debt from their 'guests'), while at the same time contributing to the creation of common social spaces, even though they led largely parallel private lives. Moreover, going beyond the economic context, we can see that the absence of these experiences reinforced the far-reaching ethnic homogeneity of several Central European states, including Poland. Indeed, it is worth remembering that because of World War II, postwar population transfers and the Kremlin-imposed policy of internationalism ('we are all brothers in socialism'), these states became (almost) mono-ethnic in theory (speaking of one's adherence to minority groups was forbidden) and sometimes in practice, too (due to real homogeneity in a given society).

Finally, in terms of recent history, there are three issues to consider. The first is the 'transformation pains' that are said to have originated from, among other things, the too-rapid, too-violent, too far-reaching and insufficiently amortised transformations that took place in Eastern Europe after 1989 and the skilful exploitation by some local political elites of the resentments that arose. Therefore, a right-wing populist turn from insufficiently internalised cultural (and economic) liberalism to conservatism has taken place in some Central European countries, which preys on resentfulness towards people who are markedly different ethnically, religiously or culturally. Second, it is again worth mentioning the inadequacy of refugee mechanisms within the European Union itself, which lacked the will and conviction to become more decisively involved in the Poland–Belarus border crisis. In addition, it had already lost considerable moral legitimacy through its previous 'trade' in refugees with various regimes such as Recep Tayyip Erdoğan's Turkey and Muammar Gaddafi's Libya. Third, a series of negative experiences with multiculturalism (particularly assassinations) in Western countries in the past two decades played a huge role in discouraging the acceptance of immigrants from distant cultures.

One could argue that these events derived from inadequate policymaking—often erroneously called 'multiculturalism'—that tended to ghettoise newcomers and was driven by a desire for assimilation, ignoring the fundamental differences in attitudes towards the host country by successive generations of migrants (see Scheffer 2010: 37–49). Yet, it is difficult to expect Central European societies, lacking basic experience of interethnic coexistence, to apply EU solutions to, for example, asylum procedures when they see the dramatic reports coming from Madrid, Paris or Berlin in suitably crafted media propaganda. The West's migration problems have been cynically, simplistically but effectively presented as a fate that will also befall Eastern Europe unless its states resist the invasion of *multiculti* and the associated 'political correctness'. To try to understand Central Europe, one must remember that it has been less than two decades since the European Union's eastern enlargement in 2004—insufficient time for these societies to internalise values that Western EU member states have been wrestling with and learning to implement since World War II.

A framework that could prove instructive in the context of the limited openness to migration in Central Europe is Castles and Miller's classification of immigration types, which connects (though not explicitly) with elements contained in the Braudel approach. The first (classical) type refers to the realities of countries such as Australia, the United States and Canada (that is, settler–colonial states), in which everyone who is not a member of the relatively small Indigenous populations is a newcomer. Under the second (colonial) type, immigration is seen as a result of previous colonialism, as seen, for example, in France and the United Kingdom. The third type, known from Germany, Switzerland and Belgium, among others, grows from a policy of inviting migrants ('guest workers'). Importantly, none of these models fits the specificities of contemporary migration, which is essentially amorphous and illegal, thus forming the fourth (hybrid) type (Castles and Miller 2009).[20] Its qualitative distinctiveness significantly limits the possibilities of drawing on previous experiences (not all of which are suitable anyway), thus posing a further challenge to Central European countries' ability to develop appropriate solutions to this matter.

These explanations are intended not to justify the rather frequent attitudes in these countries of aversion to newcomers from Asia or Africa, but to place these behaviours in a broader context of the long history of migration

---

20 Interestingly, the comments about the amorphous and illegal nature of contemporary migration do not apply to the current movements from Ukraine.

across other parts of Europe. Also crucial to the whole debate, however, is that Central European societies and their elites turned a blind eye to the issue of migration until they began to articulate their aspirations for EU membership. And, although the countries of the region are still far less attractive to migrants from Africa or Asia than Germany, the United Kingdom or Scandinavia, the major changes to civilisation—including those already being caused by climate change—show that Central European states cannot imagine themselves as migrant-free. The region is only beginning to think about embracing ethnically diverse societies and still has much work to do in this regard. And, although only three decades have passed since the wave of democratic change across the region, it is not clear whether these states and their societies will be given enough time to catch up.

The research leaves no doubt: most Poles do not want to accept refugees from distant cultures. Moreover, with regard to refugees from their neighbour Ukraine, Polish support increased once hostilities were no longer confined to irregular skirmishes in a relatively small area of eastern Ukraine and the risk of war became a real and geographically proximate threat to their own lives. In contrast, in the case of migrants from Asia and Africa—an analogous circumstance—their imminent arrival in Poland had a demotivating effect on respondents.

The contrast between the attitude of Poles towards refugees from Syria or Iraq and towards those from Ukraine is even more surprising given something that a cynical mind would expect to increase support for more humane treatment of the newcomers: the fact that most of the former would not qualify for international protection in Poland anyway. Moreover, those who managed to cross the Poland–Belarus border continued their journey to Germany, as was their original intention—unlike the majority of Ukrainian migrants. At the same time, many individual Poles wanted to be actively involved in helping migrants at the Belarusian border—especially once it became clear how high a price they were paying for their decision to go to Western Europe—but were prevented from doing so by repressive regulations introduced by the Polish state.[21] Therefore, when considering

---

21 Many organisations, institutions and individuals, including professionals such as lawyers, doctors, translators and others, have been involved in helping refugees on the Poland–Belarus border. However, their activities have been hampered by Polish authorities, who, for example, declared this borderland a restricted zone (with no entry therein), which certainly deterred other potential helpers. One social movement particularly involved in helping refugees (in cooperation with several other social actors) is The Border Group (Polish: Grupa Granica), whose report documents many of the events and actions that took place on the border with Belarus (see Grupa Granica 2021).

the reasons some Poles became so heavily involved in helping Ukrainians, it is worth bearing in mind the hypothesis that they wished to redeem at least some of the guilt related to their passivity towards the migrants from Asia and Africa.

For the findings of the 2015–18 surveys to be of any usefulness for us in understanding events in Poland, there are two powerful circumstances to consider. First, few Poles have had direct contact with a Muslim person and for those who have, it was most likely with a wealthy, well-educated tourist, the sort of person towards whom they would probably have a more positive attitude anyway. Second, even a cursory analysis of television coverage[22] reveals that the TV stations most often criticising Poland's right-wing government and supporting the country's deeper integration with the EU based on a set of common values are the same stations that provide detailed coverage of Islamist terrorist attacks in Paris, Brussels and London and everyday crime involving migrants, rather than highlighting the numerous examples of Muslims' successful integration into and coexistence in Europe (including Poland itself). And even when broadcasters do not exploit the failed integration of Muslims with the same devotion as the right-wing media, programs can still generate fear, hostility or anger, leading to what Monika Bobako (2017: 13) calls 'cognitive freeze-over which flattens social reality and turns it into a playground for the most primitive political forces'. Additionally, from about 2015, refugees began to be regarded as people to be laughed at or whose condition could be used to offend others.[23] (I am thinking of the phenomenon of Polish teenagers, who, as the immigration crisis of 2015 unfolded, began to insult one another by saying 'You refugee!', meaning someone alien, poor or worse.)

So, these three factors—lack of direct experience; media reports presenting violence and crime as consequences of Muslims' presence in Europe; and the lack of sympathy exhibited by certain peer groups—seemed sufficient to create an extremely negative image among Poles of Asian and African refugees. Consequently, survey respondents did not want Poland to

---

22 A separate issue is the kind of materials one can find on the internet, which is beyond the scope of this analysis.

23 There is another linguistic trend among those who have articulated their deep dislike of refugees by calling them *nachodźcy*—a neologism that is difficult to translate. Its essence, however, reverses the direction of refugees' mobility: they do not escape from (their) place but haunt or invade someone else's. The attractiveness of the term may derive from the similarity of its word formation with *uchodźcy* ('refugees'), with the prefix 'u-' simply replaced with 'na-'. Finally, there exists a vast set of offensive expressions that various age or social groups use to refer to people who are not welcome, no matter what are the reasons for their coming.

welcome people who, as one may hear in informal, everyday conversations, 'are going to rape or blow themselves up in terrorist attacks'; and many are deeply convinced that their anti-immigrant stance—although immoral and politically expensive—is the only one that is legitimate. They believe that attempts at integration of people from such different cultural backgrounds are doomed, mostly (and this tends to be explicitly declared) because of their alleged unwillingness to adjust (although implicitly, this belief also questions the competence of Polish authorities and society to carry out this process).

There are some—including various Polish liberal/leftist publications in recent years—who criticise those who are reluctant to express positive opinions of or welcome non-Ukrainian refugees out of fear of their negative impacts, claiming such fears are unfounded because there are so far no immigrants in Poland. Such criticism seems pointless, however, as the counterargument would be that 'we don't need migrants here to imagine what will happen once we have them; the reports from Western Europe are enough'. Muslims are not only in Poland but also—thanks to news reports of assaults, rapes and stabbings—in Polish homes. Consumers of such media are not inclined to verify this information; direct experience is redundant or undesired; the very possibility of such things happening in Poland seems to be enough for these people. If these acts can happen in Madrid, London, Paris, Brussels or Berlin, who can guarantee they will not happen in Poland as well?

Even further from the mark is the effectiveness of arguments in favour of accepting refugees from Africa and Asia put forward by some left-wing circles at the time to break down the homogeneity of Polish culture, which will become more diverse thanks to the newcomers. In the face of real fear among a substantial part of the Polish population about the shape of interethnic coexistence, this argument appears overly idealistic, ignoring the potentially significant social and political costs of accepting migrants from culturally distant countries, thus losing credibility in the eyes of opponents (see also Scheffer 2010: 33).

Let there be no misunderstanding: the civilisational and historical circumstances responsible for the deep resentment among most Poles towards newcomers from cultures perceived as significantly different do not justify the lack of empathy and its practical manifestations towards those fleeing war or persecution. The problem is all the greater because this resentment is sometimes exploited (even sanctified) by those in authority who claim they are merely expressing popular opinion, although, in truth, it is sometimes difficult to tell who is inspiring whom. Neither the (non-colonial) history of attitudes towards people coming to Europe from distant cultures nor the assistance offered by Poles to Ukrainians in 2022 can be treated as an excuse for Poles' passivity towards Asian and African migrants. Repeating the claims of some Central European countries that they were not the ones who practised colonisation or who invited migrants after World War II is politically frivolous and harmful. At the same time, ignoring or downplaying the specific Central European experience—as happens in Western Europe—is unwise and dishonest. Thus, the discussion in this chapter—apart from its ambition to provide the reader with facts and figures—shows that determining whether or not refugees are welcome in Poland is a more complex matter than the construction of simple survey questions suggests.

References

Amnesty International. 2022. 'Poland: Cruelty Not Compassion, at Europe's Other Borders.' Public statement, 11 April, EUR 37/5460/2022. London: Amnesty International. www.amnesty.org/en/wp-content/uploads/2022/04/EUR375460 2022ENGLISH.pdf.

Beauvois, D. 2006. 'Trójkąt ukraiński 1793–1914. Szlachta, carat i lud na Podolu, Wołyniu i Kijowszczyźnie [The Ukrainian Triangle 1793–1914. Nobility, Tsarism and People in Podolia, Volhynia and Kiev Region].' In *Dziedzictwo Kresów: Nasze wspólne dziedzictwo?* [*Is the Heritage of the Borderlands Our Common Heritage?*], edited by J. Purchla. Kraków: Międzynarodowe Centrum Kultury [International Cultural Centre].

Becker, J.M., and K. Becker. 2018. 'Causes and Triggers of Escape and Forced Migration to Europe.' In *How to Deal with Refugees? Europe as a Continent of Dreams*, edited by G. Besier and K. Stokłosa. Berlin: LIT Verlag.

Bobako, M. 2017. *Islamofobia jako technologia władzy. Studium z antropologii politycznej* [*Islamophobia as a Technology of Power. A Study in Political Anthropology*]. Kraków: UNIVERSITAS.

Braudel, F., and I. Wallerstein. 2009. 'History and the Social Sciences: The Longue Durée.' *Review (Fernand Braudel Centre)* 32, no. 2: 171–203. www.jstor.org/stable/40647704.

Castles, S., and M.J. Miller. 2009. *The Age of Migration: International Population Movements in the Modern World*. London: Palgrave Macmillan.

Danielewski, M. 2022. 'Uchodźcy gorszego sortu: Chcemy pomagać Ukraińcom, ludziom na granicy z Białorusią już nie (SONDAŻ) [Refugees of the Worst Kind: We Want to Help Ukrainians, But Not People on the Border with Belarus (SURVEY).' *OKO Press*, 12 May. oko.press/uchodzcy-gorszego-sortu/.

Dębicki, M., J. Kajta, L. Moll, N. Niedźwiecka-Iwańczak, and E. Opiłowska. 2022. 'Borders of (In)solidarity.' *Borders & Regional Studies*, no. 1.

Dolińska, K., and J. Makaro. 2013. *O wielokulturowości monokulturowego Wrocławia* [*On the Multiculturalism of Monocultural Wrocław*]. Wrocław: Wydawnictwo Uniwersytetu Wrocławskiego [University of Wrocław Press].

Feliksiak, M., ed. 2015. 'Postawy wobec islamu i muzułmanów [Attitudes towards Islam and Muslims].' *Research Note*, no. 37 (March). Warsaw: Public Opinion Research Centre. www.cbos.pl/SPISKOM.POL/2015/K_037_15.PDF.

Feliksiak, M., ed. 2022. 'Polacy wobec uchodźców z Ukrainy [Poles Against Refugees from Ukraine].' *Research Note*, no. 62 (April). Warsaw: Public Opinion Research Centre. cbos.pl/SPISKOM.POL/2022/K_062_22.PDF.

Felisiak, M., and B. Roguska, eds. 2022. 'Polacy wobec rosyjskiej inwazji na Ukrainę [Poles Against Russian Invasion of Ukraine].' *Research Note*, no. 38 (March). Warsaw: Public Opinion Research Centre. cbos.pl/SPISKOM.POL/2022/K_038_22.PDF.

Głowacki, A., ed. 2017. 'Stosunek do przyjmowania uchodźców [Attitudes Towards Receiving Refugees].' *Research Note*, no. 44 (April). Warsaw: Public Opinion Research Centre. cbos.pl/SPISKOM.POL/2017/K_044_17.PDF.

Grupa Granica. 2021. *Humanitarian Crisis at the Polish–Belarusian Border*. Report, 10 December. Poland: Grupa Granica. konsorcjum.org.pl/storage/2023/10/Grupa-Granica-Report-Humanitarian-crisis-at-the-Polish-Belarusian-border.pdf.

Janicki, M. 2022. 'Sondaż: Wojna i polityka [Poll: War and Politics].' *Polityka*, no. 25.

Jaroszewicz, M. 2018. *Migration from Ukraine to Poland: The Trend Stabilizes*. Warsaw: Centre for Eastern Studies.

Kosnick, K. 2019. 'New Year's Eve, Sexual Violence and Moral Panics.' In *Refugees Welcome? Difference and Diversity in a Changing Germany*, edited by J.-J. Bock and S. Macdonald. New York: Berghahn Books. doi.org/10.2307/j.ctv12pns28.12.

Kosnick, K. 2022. 'The Shifting Moral Terrains of German Refugee Discourses in Light of Russia's War Against Ukraine.' Speech delivered to European Borderland as Hot Spots of Crises in the 21st Century workshop, Centre for Regional and Borderlands Studies, University of Wrocław, 13–14 June.

Kovalisko, N. 2022. *Virtual Bridge Wrocław–Lviv 7*. [Online.] University of Wrocław. uwr.edu.pl/en/virtual-bridge-wroclaw-lviv-7/.

Kowalczuk, K., ed. 2015a. 'Polacy wobec Problem uchodźstwa [Poles Face the Refugee Problem].' *Research Note*, no. 81 (June). Warsaw: Public Opinion Research Centre. www.cbos.pl/SPISKOM.POL/2015/K_081_15.PDF.

Kowalczuk, K., ed. 2015b. 'Przybysze z bliska i z daleka, czyli o imigrantach w Polsce [Newcomers from Near and Far, or About Immigrants in Poland].' *Research Note*, no. 93 (June). Warsaw: Public Opinion Research Centre. www.cbos.pl/SPISKOM.POL/2015/K_093_15.PDF.

Kwapisz, W.K. 2021. 'The Belarus–EU Migrant Crisis.' *Australian Outlook*, 21 October.

Kwapisz, W.K., and M. Dębicki. 2022. 'Ukrainian Refugees in Poland: First Impressions.' *Australian Outlook*, 28 March.

Legut, A., and K. Pędziwiatr. 2018. 'Sekurytyzacja migracji w polityce a zmiana postaw Polaków wobec uchodźców [Securitisation of Migration in Politics and Changing Poles' Attitudes Towards Refugees].' In *Sami swoi? Wielokulturowość we współczesnej Europie [Our Own? Multiculturalism in Contemporary Europe]*, edited by R. Jończy. Warsaw: Dom Współpracy Polsko-Niemieckiej [Foundation for German–Polish Cooperation].

Organisation for Economic Co-operation and Development (OECD). 2018. *International Migration Outlook 2018*. Paris: OECD Publishing. read.oecd-ilibrary.org/social-issues-migration-health/international-migration-outlook-2018_migr_outlook-2018-en#page1.

Public Opinion Research Centre (CBOS). 2015a. 'Attitude to Islam and Muslims.' *Polish Public Opinion*, March. Warsaw: Public Opinion Research Centre. www.cbos.pl/PL/publikacje/public_opinion/2015/03_2015.pdf.

Public Opinion Research Centre (CBOS). 2015b. 'Opinions about Refugee Crisis.' *Polish Public Opinion*, June. Warsaw: Public Opinion Research Centre. www.cbos.pl/PL/publikacje/public_opinion/2015/06_2015.pdf.

Public Opinion Research Centre (CBOS). 2015c. 'Immigrants in Poland.' *Polish Public Opinion*, July. Warsaw: Public Opinion Research Centre. www.cbos.pl/PL/publikacje/public_opinion/2015/07_2015.pdf.

Public Opinion Research Centre (CBOS). 2021. 'Attitude to Refugees and the Situation of Migrants at the Border.' *Polish Public Opinion*, September. Warsaw: Public Opinion Research Centre. cbos.pl/PL/publikacje/public_opinion/2021/09_2021.pdf.

Public Opinion Research Centre (CBOS). 2022a. 'Opinions about the Russian Invasion of Ukraine.' *Polish Public Opinion*, March. Warsaw: Public Opinion Research Centre. cbos.pl/PL/publikacje/public_opinion/2022/03_2022.pdf.

Public Opinion Research Centre (CBOS). 2022b. 'Opinions about the War in Ukraine.' *Polish Public Opinion*, May. Warsaw: Public Opinion Research Centre. cbos.pl/PL/publikacje/public_opinion/2022/05_2022.pdf.

Public Opinion Research Centre (CBOS). 2022c. 'Opinions on EU Integration and Policies.' *Polish Public Opinion*, July–August. Warsaw: Public Opinion Research Centre. cbos.pl/PL/publikacje/public_opinion/2022/07_08_2022.pdf.

Scheffer, P. 2010. 'The Open Society and its Immigrants. The Story of Avoidance, Conflict and Accommodation.' PhD diss., Tilburg University, Netherlands.

Scovil, J., ed. 2022. 'Polacy wobec wojny na Ukrainie i ukraińskich uchodźców [Poles' (Attitudes) Towards the War in Ukraine and Ukrainian Refugees].' *Research Note*, no. 101 (August). Warsaw: Public Opinion Research Centre. cbos.pl/SPISKOM. POL/2022/K_101_22.PDF.

Tyma, P., ed. 2019. *Raport 2. Mniejszość ukraińska i migranci z Ukrainy w Polsce. Analiza dyskursu* [*Report 2. Ukrainian Minority and Migrants from Ukraine in Poland. Discourse Analysis*]. Warsaw: Związek Ukraińców w Polsce [Union of Ukrainians in Poland].

Union of Polish Metropolises. 2022a. *Urban Hospitality. Estimation of the Number of Ukrainian Nationals in the UMP Cities, March, April, May 2022: An Update to the Report, Urban Hospitality: Unprecedented Growth, Challenges, and Opportunities. A Report on Ukrainian Refugees in the Largest Polish Cities (April 2022)*. Warsaw: Union of Polish Metropolises. metropolie.pl/fileadmin/news/2022/07/Urban_hospitality_update.pdf.

Union of Polish Metropolises. 2022b. *Nowy dom czy chwilowy azyl? Sytuacja uchodźców z Ukrainy wnioskujących o numer PESEL w 12 największych polskich miastach pod koniec kwietnia 2022 r.* [*A New Home or a Temporary Refuge? The Situation of Refugees from Ukraine Applying for a PESEL Number in the 12 Largest Polish Cities at the End of April 2022*]. Report, September. Warsaw: Unia Metropolii Polskich [Union of Polish Metropolises]. metropolie.pl/fileadmin/news/2022/09/Nowy_dom_czy_chwilowy_azyl_raport_z_badania.pdf.

United Nations High Commissioner for Refugees (UNHCR). 2022. *Lives On Hold: Profiles and Intentions of Refugees from Ukraine #1*. July. Geneva: UNHCR Regional Bureau for Europe. data.unhcr.org/en/documents/details/94176.

Wojdat, M., and P. Cywiński. 2022. *Urban Hospitality: Unprecedented Growth, Challenges and Opportunities. A Report on Ukrainian Refugees in the Largest Polish Cities*. Warsaw: Union of Polish Metropolises.

Zelenskyy, V. 2022. 'Speech by President of Ukraine Volodymyr Zelenskyy in the Sejm of the Republic of Poland.' 11 March. www.president.gov.ua/en/news/vistup-prezidenta-ukrayini-volodimira-zelenskogo-v-sejmi-res-73497.

Part 2.
Paradigm shifts and market mechanisms in migration control

4

Active refugee admission policies and refugee finance: Towards a new spectrum of refugeehood?

Daria Davitti and Zvezda Vankova[1]

The European long summer of migration of 2015 (Yurdakul et al. 2017: 345; Davitti 2018: 1173) highlighted the difficulties faced by asylum seekers when attempting to reach Europe. The growing externalisation of migration controls and deterrence measures introduced by EU member states continues to severely limit spontaneous refugee arrivals. Carrier sanctions, visa requirements and offshore processing attempts by countries such as Denmark and the United Kingdom (Tan 2022a, 2022b) are only some examples of existing deterrence measures pursued across the European continent (Moreno-Lax and Vavoula 2022; Moreno-Lax 2017; Gammeltoft-Hansen and Hathaway 2015: 235). Attempts to restrict territorial access to spontaneous arrivals, however, are not limited to EU countries nor are they an entirely new phenomenon, since they can be traced back to the end of the Cold War (Chimni 1998: 350). They build on a fundamental flaw of the global refugee regime—namely, the absence of consistent state practice in providing access to protection in a state party to the 1951 Refugee Convention (Goodwin-Gill et al. 2021:

1   The authors wish to thank Albert Kraler for his comments on some parts of this chapter. This work has been partially supported by a Swedish Research Council Grant (VR, 2022-02380).

298–99). This uncertainty about how protection should be accessed is worsened by the sharp global decrease in protection opportunities provided through third-country resettlement, leading to 'a resettlement gap' (Solf and Rehberg 2021). The Covid-19 pandemic and the responses to it[2] have further exacerbated the mismatch of protection needs and opportunities (Ghezelbash and Tan 2020).

In response to increasing restrictions on spontaneous arrivals and accessible protection opportunities, there has been growing attention to the development of new legal pathways to protection. Simultaneously, over the past decade, we have also seen a change in the way multilateral actors fund humanitarian responses to refugee movements. As a result of the decline in aid from traditional bilateral and multilateral donors, refugee finance delineates itself as an emerging funding paradigm. The term 'refugee finance' refers to new financial instruments, from refugee bonds to technical assistance funds, aimed at mobilising private capital to achieve social impact objectives—in this case, refugee protection. The appeal of refugee finance revolves around the need to put in place funding modalities capable of bridging the shift from short-term humanitarian assistance to longer-term development programming (Zetter 2021).

Yet, the changes triggered by refugee finance go well beyond mere financing modalities. Looking at recent developments at the EU level, we argue that with its focus on solutions in the region of origin and on enhancing 'active refugee admission policies' for international protection—such as resettlement and complementary pathways—refugee finance plays a key role in the implementation of EU policies of containment, externalisation and 'cherry-picking' of refugees (Westerby 2020). The broader paradigmatic shift that we trace, therefore, is in the conceptualisation of international protection and the emergence of a new spectrum of refugeehood, with hyper-vulnerable refugees at one end of the continuum and refugee entrepreneurs at the other. This new conceptualisation of refugeehood, as we examine in this chapter, is de facto accelerating the end of spontaneous arrivals and closing the door to territorial asylum.

---

2   Such as border closures and halting of refugee admission.

The emergence of 'active refugee admission policies' in the EU

Devising innovative ways to protect refugees has long been part of the attempts by the international community to improve access to asylum and global refugee responsibility-sharing (Hashimoto 2021; Martin et al. 2019). The events of 2015 gave further impetus to promoting what has been conceptualised as 'active refugee admission policies' (Welfens et al. 2019). This umbrella term covers different types of admission policies and programs, targeting persons in need of protection, including traditional instruments for transferring vulnerable refugees from first countries of asylum to host countries, such as resettlement programs managed by the United Nations High Commissioner for Refugees (UNHCR) or state-led humanitarian admission programs. They also extend to a plethora of allegedly new instruments—referred to as complementary pathways to protection—based, among others, on labour migration, education and family reunification, as well as community sponsorship for refugees.[3] The last, for instance, relies on the support of members of host-country communities to act as guarantors of the settlement of refugees (Tan 2021a; see also Labman 2016).

The development of these complementary pathways has been actively promoted by several UN policy frameworks, including the 2030 Agenda for Sustainable Development (UNHCR 2020), the 2016 *New York Declaration for Refugees and Migrants* (UNGA 2016: paras 77, 79) and its Comprehensive Refugee Response Framework (Annex I, para. 14), as well as the 2018 Global Compact on Refugees (GCR 2023: paras 47, 94–96). Furthermore, complementary pathways have become priorities of the European Union Pact on Migration and Asylum (EU Pact), which outlines the future direction of European migration policy, and are portrayed as a means to offer protection to those in need by removing the incentives to embark on dangerous journeys to reach Europe (EC 2020). The recommendation on legal pathways (C [2020] 6467) accompanying the EU Pact promotes investment in the resettlement and facilitation of complementary pathways in line with the GCR. It shows the ambition to finalise the EU resettlement

---

3   The equivalent policy term is 'third-country solutions', as contained in the GCR and its policy documents, and encompassing the full range of legal pathways for admission of refugees, including resettlement and complementary pathways.

framework and encourages the development of an EU model of community sponsorship. To incentivise member states, the EU has provided technical assistance through feasibility studies,[4] expert meetings and funding.[5]

The conflict in Syria, which triggered large-scale refugee arrivals, has led to increased, but still limited, resettlement efforts by EU member states (Fratzke et al. 2021). At the time of writing, 15 member states are engaged in the resettlement of refugees from different countries. Of these, Finland, Iceland, Norway, Sweden,[6] Belgium, Croatia, France, Germany, Ireland, Portugal and Romania have demonstrated 'strong political will to resettling refugees' (Fratzke et al. 2021). Several EU member states have also engaged in the development of complementary pathways. For instance, community sponsorship programs have been piloted or established in Germany, Ireland and Spain (Tan 2021a). Belgium, Malta and Portugal pledged at the 2019 Global Refugee Forum[7] to explore pilot community sponsorship models and Sweden has a pilot. Italy and France have been frontrunners in the development of humanitarian corridors (Ricci 2020) and, since 2013, refugee student scholarship programs have been developed in at least eight EU countries: Czechia, France, Germany, Italy, Lithuania, Portugal, Slovakia and Spain (Fratzke et al. 2021). When it comes to labour migration pathways, pilots funded by the EU Asylum Migration and Integration Fund (AMIF) and managed by the International Organization for Migration in Belgium, Ireland, Portugal and the United Kingdom are expected to facilitate refugees' access to such policies. Finland is also exploring such legal channels for refugees. Scalability, however, remains the key challenge to the effective development of active refugee admission policies (Vankova 2022a)—an aspect that brings refugee finance to the forefront as a highly desirable solution. As we explain in section two of this chapter, refugee finance presents itself as particularly suitable to the creation of 'protection-sensitive, accessible and scalable systems' for such admission policies (UNHCR 2019: 15).

---

4   See, for instance, EC (2018).
5   See the call from the Asylum, Migration and Integration Fund (AMIF 2020).
6   It must be noted, however, that at the time of finalising this chapter, Sweden had reduced the annual number of places offered for resettlement of refugees from 5,000 to 900 (UNHCR 2023).
7   The Global Refugee Forum is the global arrangement for international cooperation at the ministerial level established by the GCR (2023: para. 17). It is convened every four years and gives all UN member states and relevant stakeholders the opportunity to announce concrete pledges and contributions towards the objectives of the GCR, and to consider opportunities, challenges and ways in which burden and responsibility-sharing can be enhanced. According to the GCR (2023: para. 18), the pledges and contributions could include financial, material and technical assistance, resettlement places and complementary pathways for admission to third countries.

Even though some of these active refugee admission policies aim to provide international protection by targeting vulnerable refugees, states have leeway to impose additional criteria in line with their national strategic interests, following a migration-control rather than protection rationale (Welfens and Pisarevskaya 2020; see also van Selm 2004). One criterion often applied by receiving states is the 'integration potential' of refugees, which enables de facto cherry-picking of the most 'desirable and integratable' refugees on the basis of skills, education and cultural and religious beliefs (Westerby 2020).[8] At the same time, other stakeholders, such as NGOs, municipalities, educational institutions and employers, have started to play a greater implementation role in complementary pathways and have thus been able to influence outcomes and steer policy development. To sum up, a key issue with the implementation of all active refugee admission policies is their voluntary and discretionary nature,[9] reflected, for instance, in the application of selection criteria—a phenomenon that has been described as a 'legal abyss of discretion', resulting in a lack of procedural rights and legal remedies for refugees in the context of resettlement (Zieck and de Boer 2020).

Understanding refugee finance

To gain a clearer understanding of the link between active refugee admission policies and refugee finance, it is important to understand the emergence of this new financing mechanism. Refugee finance has developed over the past decade in response to the decline in aid from states, international organisations and/or donor agencies. We have thus witnessed a systemic shift in the way in which humanitarian responses to refugee movements are funded, with a major focus on mobilising private capital and social impact investors. The term 'refugee finance' broadly refers to social impact bonds (such as refugee bonds and humanitarian bonds), technical assistance funds and concessional loans (Cabot Venton et al. 2019). These financial instruments are promoted by international organisations, international financial institutions and states as innovative solutions to tackle the societal challenges related to international protection needs. The narrative

---

8   On 'cherry-picking' for refugee protection, see further de Boer and Zieck (2020). The Proposal for a Regulation Establishing a Union Resettlement Framework is silent on such criteria but poses other challenges. See further Ineli-Ciger (2022).

9   With the notable exception of family reunification, which is the only rights-based complementary pathway.

promoting refugee finance presents the need for a paradigmatic shift 'from funding to financing' (WEF 2019), based on the assumption that private capital will successfully complement public sector funds to resource refugee responses and support countries facing the fiscal stress of hosting refugees. Refugee finance thus promises to bridge the gap between humanitarian and development responses and to protect refugees in the region of origin, while at the same time supporting the economic development of the countries hosting them (Cabot Venton et al. 2019).

There are four main financial instruments of relevance in the refugee context. The first type is concessional loans to host states—that is, loans usually made to a borrower by an international financial institution or a philanthropic investor at a lower-than-market rate. These loans usually comprise one component at a market rate and one at a discounted rate.[10] The second type of instrument is technical assistance funds aimed at supporting refugees in starting a business and, more broadly, facilitating refugee entrepreneurship and integration in the host country, while also 'pump-priming' projects that can be scaled up to attract further investment (Davitti 2022). The third instrument is guarantees and risk insurance, provided below market rates by states, international financial institutions or philanthropic investors, with the idea that funds should then be immediately available at the onset of a refugee emergency (Davitti 2022). The fourth type are design-stage grants that are usually aimed at encouraging policy change, such as grants issued when legislation is passed to allow refugees to work. The Jordan and Lebanon compacts, for instance, established under the umbrella of the Comprehensive Refugee Response Framework and the GCR, include this type of grant (Howden et al. 2017).

As we will outline in section three, various refugee finance initiatives are already operational, yet very little is known about whether reliance on this financing modality by states and humanitarian organisations changes the way in which international protection is both understood and operationalised. In what follows, we provide some preliminary evidence to show that refugee finance plays a key role in the implementation, and indeed acceleration,

---

10   Examples of concessional loans for refugees are the World Bank's Global Concessional Financing Facility and loans by the European Bank for Reconstruction and Development used for the Regional Refugee & Resilience Plan (3RP) in response to the Syrian crisis, through which US$5.8 billion in loans were granted to Jordan, Lebanon, Iraq, Egypt and Türkiye in 2020 alone. See 3RP (2020).

of EU policies of containment, externalisation and 'cherry-picking' of refugees, because of its primary focus on solutions in the region of origin (Chimni 1998: 351) and on enhancing active refugee admission policies.

A new spectrum of refugeehood?

In our mapping of existing refugee finance instruments, we have observed a convergence between refugee finance and refugee 'solutions' that does not necessarily lead to long-lasting international protection (durable solutions) but instead appears to prioritise temporary measures for refugees and asylum seekers. Such convergence has so far occurred in two different operational spaces: in the region of origin, with more consolidated examples under the Jordan Compact (see the Refugee Impact Bond funded by partners in the Netherlands, Denmark, Norway, Belgium and the United States); and in some EU member states, which have carried out pilots of refugee bonds (both social impact bonds and development impact bonds).[11] Examples of initiatives in EU member states are the Finnish social impact bond KOTO SIB for labour market integration and the French Hémisphère Social Impact Fund financing accommodation for homeless people, refugees and asylum seekers. Finland and France, crucially, are also engaged in resettlement and the development of other complementary pathways. It is therefore not impossible to imagine the scaling up of these admission policies through the increased use of social or development impact bonds. This is in fact being proposed in various business case studies that promote the link between the two and, in practice, are being used to integrate Ukrainian refugees (OCHA 2022). Impact investing is also promoted as part of the AMIF framework, which has seen €9.9 billion in funding committed by the European Commission for the 2021–27 period. Within this context, the idea is to attract equity and quasi-equity investments in small and medium-sized enterprises providing 'social outcomes' such as services and facilities linked to AMIF policy objectives (that is, asylum, integration and return) (AMIF 2020).

As a result, we witness situations of precarity and non-durability in both these operational spaces. In non-European low and middle-income countries that host refugees in the region of origin, we see a continuous

---

11 Refugee bonds can be linked to any of the four types of instruments explained in the previous section, since their aim is to mobilise funds and their immediate availability though private markets. On the meaning of 'social' impact, see further Islam (2022: 709); and Maier et al. (2018: 1332).

inability to provide access to permanent solutions because of the high costs involved. The Jordan Compact is a good example of how refugee finance instruments (more specifically, design-stage grants) were provided by the EU in cooperation with the World Bank—in theory, to achieve both 'protection' and containment goals through financing (Gordon 2020). In practice, however, reviews of the Jordan Compact indicate that it was not successful in providing *durable* protection for those whom it assisted (Lenner and Turner 2019). The idea advanced under the Jordan Compact was to increase both work opportunities for 200,000 Syrian refugees and economic opportunities for local workers in Jordan, reflecting formal labour market participation as the 'new benchmark' for governments accountable to international donors.

The aim of the compact was also to use trade agreements to support refugee employment, as promoted by the two global compacts. This initiative saw the creation of special economic zones in Jordan dedicated to the garment manufacturing sector. Evaluations of the implementation of the Jordan Compact, however, point to its limited success. In the years after the adoption of the compact, only 500 Syrian refugees were working in the special economic zones, partly because of the low wages offered, the poor working conditions and the lack of opportunities for advancement in the garment sector (Gordon 2020). Some 45,000 Syrian work permit-holders were employed in the agricultural and construction sectors, which did not necessarily lead to improved working conditions for these refugees (Gordon 2020, referring to data from the World Bank and Norwegian Fafo Institute for Labour and Social Research). Because development and financial institutions were in the driver's seat when designing and negotiating the compact, the focus on expanding work opportunities for refugees at the bottom of global supply chains prevailed over ensuring decent work standards (Gordon 2020; see further Betts and Collier 2017).

The increased reliance on temporary solutions that prioritise *local* rather than *durable* protection is fuelled by current international policy trends that promote the idea of 'protection elsewhere' (Foster 2007: 223)— originally advanced by Australia and the United States but increasingly also favoured by the EU and its member states. Research provides ample evidence of increased efforts by states to prevent spontaneous arrivals and access to asylum claims on their territory or within their jurisdiction (Mountz 2020; see also Scott FitzGerald 2019; Ghezelbash 2018). Due to this general willingness to curtail access to territorial asylum, resettlement quotas in EU member states now serve the needs of a small fraction of the refugees in need of international protection and, as the initial welcoming of Ukrainian refugees has shown, states openly prefer refugees with racial and religious profiles akin to those of their own population (UNHCR 2022). Complementary pathways, therefore, are often portrayed as the only feasible alternative for people in need of protection who do not qualify for the limited resettlement quotas. This fundamentally changes the protection space and creates, we argue, a new spectrum of refugeehood.[12] At one end of the spectrum, we have the 'hyper-vulnerable' refugee, which is considered the only category eligible for resettlement, while at the other, we have the 'refugee entrepreneur'. The latter emerges from a longstanding emphasis on refugee 'self-reliance'[13] and embodies the characteristics of the 'ideal' refugee, capable of moulding themselves into businesspeople, migrant workers and/ or students to access the new complementary pathways made available to them, rather than requiring humanitarian support and demanding their rights be protected, respected and fulfilled (Turner 2020: 139). Spontaneous refugees inhabit the middle part of this new spectrum of refugeehood— a shrinking space for those who cannot meet the requirements of hyper-vulnerability or entrepreneurship, with little or no alternative for obtaining protection (Turner 2020: 155).

Conclusion: Of precarity and the changing meaning of 'protection'

Challenges related to precarity and non-durability of protection are common to refugees across the new refugeehood spectrum that is emerging. Achieving durable solutions for the refugee entrepreneur will depend on their qualifications, skills and opportunities to access permanent residence status in the host EU member state.[14] And the hyper-vulnerable refugees who once benefited from resettlement options or those who obtained refugee protection or other humanitarian status based on active refugee admission policies, such as humanitarian corridors or community sponsorship, are now increasingly at risk of being returned to their country of origin, due to a growing trend towards the adoption of cessation measures, especially in the Nordic countries (Tan 2021b; Schultz 2021: 170). EU member states

---

12   On the shift of the refugee regime towards more neoliberal notions, see further Ilcan and Rygiel (2015); Scott-Smith (2016).

13   On refugee entrepreneurship, see Betts et al. (2012); Turner (2020). On self-reliance, see Easton-Calabria and Omata (2018).

14   This usually happens after an average of five years. See further Vankova (2022b).

are increasingly stepping away from the concept of local integration towards the idea of 'enforced' cessation of refugee status, based on which refugees are sent back to their country of origin when the situation there is considered to have improved (Schultz 2021). How this 'improvement' is measured, however, remains unclear and often arbitrary, since legally a refugee can only go back to their country of origin on a voluntary basis and if their well-founded fear of persecution no longer persists (Fakhoury 2022; see also Ihlamur-Öner 2022).[15] Legally, a whole set of rights would also militate in favour of local integration when a refugee has established him or herself in the host country (Edwards 2005: 293; see also Hathaway and Foster 2014).

Against this backdrop of enforced cessation, involuntary returns and partiality for temporary protection, refugee finance delineates itself as the ideal set of financial instruments to scale up and mobilise private capital to accelerate short-term protection measures. Given the dearth of funding currently available for refugee responses, humanitarian organisations appear keen to embrace refugee finance, without critically questioning how this may be changing the nature of international protection at the macro level. In individual cases, undoubtedly complementary pathways can and do offer solutions for refugees in protracted situations who do not qualify for the limited resettlement places available (Vankova 2022a: 20). It is legitimate to ask ourselves what happens to durable solutions and international protection when the focus of refugee responses moves towards the creation of an enabling environment for sustainable investors and towards policies aimed at supporting refugees' self-reliance, including the facilitation of complementary pathways. Relatedly, who ultimately are the refugees that the international legal system *can* indeed 'protect' when protection measures are reoriented towards an increased dependence on private investors who become key enablers and co-providers of 'protection'? Despite the increasing calls to expand and strengthen refugee finance instruments, these questions remain unanswered and only time will tell how refugee finance will impact the trajectory of international protection measures currently deployed at the EU level and beyond.

---

15   On the geopolitics of the term 'return', see Cassarino (2020). On the inherent contradiction of 'voluntary' returns and cessation, see further Hathaway and Foster (2014).

References

Asylum, Migration and Integration Fund (AMIF). 2020. *AMIF Funding Call 2020: Complementary Pathways for Protection and Integration*. 15 October. Brussels: European Commission. ec.europa.eu/migrant-integration/news/amif-funding-call-2020-complementary-pathways-for-protection-and-integration.

Betts, A., L. Bloom, and N. Omata. 2012. *Humanitarian Innovation and Refugee Protection*. Working Paper Series. Oxford: Refugee Studies Centre.

Betts, A., and P. Collier. 2017. *Refuge: Transforming a Broken Refugee System*. London: Penguin.

Cabot Venton, C., J. Richardson, T. Clarey, and G. Jarmaine. 2019. *Innovative Financing for Responses to Refugee Crises*. March. London: Expert Advisory Call-Down Service Lot B: Strengthening Resilience and Response to Crises. www.rescue.org/sites/default/files/document/3888/innovativefinancingforresponsestorefugeecrises.pdf.

Cassarino, J.P. 2020. 'Généalogie d'un euphémisme: Quand retour rime avec expulsion [Genealogy of a Euphemism: When Return Rhymes with Expulsion].' *Les Cahiers de Tunisie* [*The Notebooks of Tunisia*] 72, nos 226–27: 75–99.

Chimni, B.S. 1998. 'The Geopolitics of Refugee Studies: A View from the South.' *Journal of Refugee Studies* 11, no. 4: 350. doi.org/10.1093/jrs/11.4.350-a.

Davitti, D. 2018. 'Biopolitical Borders and the State of Exception in the European Migration "Crisis".' *European Journal of International Law* 29, no. 4: 1173–96. doi.org/10.1093/ejil/chy065.

Davitti, D. 2022. 'Refugee Finance: External(ized) Protection and Investments for Refugees.' *Quaderni della Facoltà di Giurisprudenza/Series of the Faculty of Law, University of Trento* 65: 83–100. iris.unitn.it/handle/11572/364188.

de Boer, T., and M. Zieck. 2020. 'The Legal Abyss of Discretion in the Resettlement of Refugees: Cherry-Picking and the Lack of Due Process in the EU.' *International Journal of Refugee Law* 32, no. 1 (March): 54–85. doi.org/10.1093/ijrl/eeaa005.

Easton-Calabria, E., and N. Omata. 2018. 'Panacea for the Refugee Crisis? Rethinking the Promotion of "Self-Reliance" for Refugees.' *Third World Quarterly* 39: 1458–74. doi.org/10.1080/01436597.2018.1458301.

Edwards, A. 2005. 'Human Rights, Refugees, and the Right "To Enjoy" Asylum.' *International Journal of Refugee Law* 17, no. 2: 293–330. doi.org/10.1093/ijrl/eei011.

European Commission (EC). 2018. *Study on the Feasibility and Added Value of Sponsorship Schemes as a Possible Pathway to Safe Channels for Admission to the EU, Including Resettlement: Final Report.* Brussels: EC. op.europa.eu/en/publication-detail/-/publication/1dbb0873-d349-11e8-9424-01aa75ed71a1.

European Commission (EC). 2020. *Communication from the Commission to the European Parliament, the Council, the European Economic and Social Committee and the Committee of the Regions on a New Pact on Migration and Asylum.* 23 September, COM/2020/609 final. Brussels: EC. eur-lex.europa.eu/legal-content/EN/TXT/?uri=CELEX:52020DC0609.

Fakhoury, T. 2022. 'EU Engagement with Contested Refugee Returns in Lebanon: The Aftermath of Resilience.' *Geopolitics* 28, no. 3: 1007–32. doi.org/10.1080/14650045.2022.2025779.

Foster, M. 2007. 'Protection Elsewhere: The Legal Implications of Requiring Refugees to Seek Protection in Another State.' *Michigan Journal of International Law* 28, no. 2: 223–86. repository.law.umich.edu/cgi/viewcontent.cgi?referer=&httpsredir=1&article=1175&context=mjil.

Fratzke, S., M. Belén Zanzuchi, K. Hooper, H. Beirens, L. Kainz, N. Benson, E. Bateman, and J. Bolter. 2021. *Refugee Resettlement and Complementary Pathways: Opportunities for Growth.* Report, September. Washington, DC: Migration Policy Institute. www.migrationpolicy.org/research/refugee-resettlement-complementary-pathways.

Gammeltoft-Hansen, T., and J.C. Hathaway. 2015. 'Non-Refoulement in a World of Cooperative Deterrence.' *Columbia Journal of Transnational Law* 53, no. 2: 235–84. repository.law.umich.edu/cgi/viewcontent.cgi?article=2484&context=articles.

Ghezelbash, D. 2018. *Refuge Lost: Asylum Law in an Interdependent World.* Cambridge: Cambridge University Press. doi.org/10.1017/9781108349031.

Ghezelbash, D., and N.F. Tan. 2020. *The End of the Right to Seek Asylum? COVID-19 and the Future of Refugee Protection.* Working Paper, EUI RSCAS, 2020/55. Florence: Migration Policy Centre, European University Institute. hdl.handle.net/1814/68175. doi.org/10.2139/ssrn.3689093.

Global Compact on Refugees (GCR). 2023. *Global Compact on Refugees: Pledges & Contributions.* [Online database.] Geneva: UNHCR. globalcompactrefugees.org/pledges-contributions.

Goodwin-Gill, G.S., J. McAdam, and E. Dunlop. 2021. 'The Principle of Non-Refoulement: Part 1.' In *The Refugee in International Law*, edited by G.S. Goodwin-Gill and J. McAdam. Oxford: Oxford University Press.

Gordon, J. 2020. *Refugees and Decent Work: Lessons Learned from Recent Refugee Jobs Compacts*. Fordham Law Legal Studies Research Paper No. 3523247. New York: Fordham Law School.

Hashimoto, N. 2021. 'Are New Pathways of Admitting Refugees Truly Humanitarian and Complementary?' *Journal of Human Security Studies* 10: 15–31.

Hathaway, J.C., and M. Foster. 2014. 'Persons No Longer Needing Protection.' In *The Law of Refugee Status*, edited by J.C. Hathaway and M. Foster. 2nd edn. Cambridge: Cambridge University Press.

Howden, D., H. Patchett, and C. Alfred. 2017. 'The Compact Experiment: Push for Refugee Jobs Confronts Reality of Jordan and Lebanon.' *Refugees Deeply Quarterly*, December. s3.amazonaws.com/newsdeeply/public/quarterly3/RD+ Quarterly+-+The+Compact+Experiment.pdf.

Ihlamur-Öner, S.G. 2022. 'The Global Politics of Refugee Protection and Return: The Case of the Syrian Refugees.' In *The Informalisation of the EU's External Action in the Field of Migration and Asylum*, edited by E. Kassoti and N. Idriz. Cham, Switzerland: Springer. doi.org/10.1007/978-94-6265-487-7_13.

Ilcan, S., and K. Rygiel. 2015. '"Resiliency Humanitarianism": Responsibilizing Refugees through Humanitarian Emergency Governance in the Camp.' *International Political Sociology* 9: 333–51. doi.org/10.1111/ips.12101.

Ineli-Ciger, M. 2022. 'Is Resettlement Still a Durable Solution? An Analysis in Light of the Proposal for a Regulation Establishing a Union Resettlement Framework.' *European Journal of Migration and Law* 24, no. 1: 27–55. doi.org/ 10.1163/15718166-12340118.

Islam, S.M. 2022. 'Impact Investing in Social Sector Organisations: A Systematic Review and Research Agenda.' *Accounting & Finance* 62, no. 1: 709–37. doi.org/ 10.2139/ssrn.3850532.

Labman, S. 2016. 'Private Sponsorship: Complementary or Conflicting Interests?' *Refuge: Canada's Journal on Refugees* 32, no. 2: 67–80. doi.org/10.25071/1920- 7336.40266.

Lenner, K., and L. Turner. 2019. 'Making Refugees Work? The Politics of Integrating Syrian Refugees into the Labor Market in Jordan.' *Middle East Critique* 28: 65–95. doi.org/10.1080/19436149.2018.1462601.

Maier, F., G.P. Barbetta, and F. Godina. 2018. 'Paradoxes of Social Impact Bonds.' *Social Policy and Administration* 52, no. 7: 1332–53. doi.org/10.1111/spol. 12343.

Martin, S.F., R. Davis, G. Benton, and Z. Waliany. 2019. 'International Responsibility-Sharing for Refugees: Perspectives from the MENA Region.' *Geopolitics, History, and International Relations* 11: 59–91. doi.org/10.22381/GHIR11120193.

Moreno-Lax, V. 2017. *Accessing Asylum in Europe: Extraterritorial Border Controls and Refugee Rights under EU Law*. Oxford: Oxford University Press. doi.org/10.1093/oso/9780198701002.001.0001.

Moreno-Lax, V., and N. Vavoula. 2022. 'The (Many) Rules and Roles of Law in the Regulation of "Unwanted Migration".' *International Community Law Review* 24: 285–91. doi.org/10.1163/18719732-12341490.

Mountz, A. 2020. *The Death of Asylum: Hidden Geographies of the Enforcement Archipelago*. Minneapolis: University of Minnesota Press. doi.org/10.5749/j.ctv15d8153.

Regional Refugee & Resilience Plan (3RP). 2020. *Regional Refugee and Resilience Plan: Regional Strategic Overview 2021–2022*. December. reliefweb.int/sites/reliefweb.int/files/resources/RSO2021.pdf.

Ricci, C. 2020. 'The Necessity for Alternative Legal Pathways: The Best Practice of Humanitarian Corridors Opened by Private Sponsors in Italy.' *German Law Journal* 21: 265–83. doi.org/10.1017/glj.2020.7.

Schultz, J.L. 2021. 'An End to Asylum? Temporary Protection and the Erosion of Refugee Status.' In *Waiting and the Temporalities of Irregular Migration*, edited by C.M. Jacobsen, M.-A. Karlsen, and S. Khosravi. New York: Routledge.

Scott FitzGerald, D. 2019. *Refuge beyond Reach: How Rich Democracies Repel Asylum Seekers*. Oxford: Oxford University Press. doi.org/10.1093/oso/9780190874155.001.0001.

Scott-Smith, T. 2016. 'Humanitarian Neophilia: The "Innovation Turn" and Its Implications.' *Third World Quarterly* 37: 2229–51. doi.org/10.1080/01436597.2016.1176856.

Solf, B., and K. Rehberg. 2021. 'The Resettlement Gap: A Record Number of Global Refugees, But Few Are Resettled.' *Migration Information Source*, 22 October. Washington, DC: Migration Policy Institute. www.migrationpolicy.org/article/refugee-resettlement-gap.

Tan, N.F. 2021a. 'Community Sponsorship in Europe: Taking Stock, Policy Transfer and What the Future Might Hold.' *Frontiers in Human Dynamics* 3 (21 April). www.frontiersin.org/articles/10.3389/fhumd.2021.564084/full. doi.org/10.3389/fhumd.2021.564084.

Tan, N.F. 2021b. 'The End of Protection: The Danish Paradigm Shift and the Law of Cessation.' *Nordic Journal of International Law* 90: 60–85. doi.org/10.1163/15718107-bja10009.

Tan, N.F. 2022a. 'Externalisation of Asylum in Europe: Unpacking the UK–Rwanda Asylum Partnership Agreement.' *EU Immigration and Asylum Law and Policy*, Odysseus Academic Network blog, 17 May. eumigrationlawblog.eu/externalisation-of-asylum-in-europe-unpacking-the-uk-rwanda-asylum-partnership-agreement/.

Tan, N.F. 2022b. 'Visions of the Realistic? Denmark's Legal Basis for Extraterritorial Asylum.' *Nordic Journal of International Law* 91: 172–81. doi.org/10.1163/15718107-91010008.

Turner, L. 2020. '"#Refugees Can Be Entrepreneurs Too!" Humanitarianism, Race, and the Marketing of Syrian Refugees.' *Review of International Studies* 46, no. 1: 137–55. doi.org/10.1017/S0260210519000342.

United Nations General Assembly (UNGA). 2016. *New York Declaration for Refugees and Migrants*. Resolution 71/1, adopted by the General Assembly on 19 September 2016. Seventy-First Session, Agenda items 13 and 117. New York: UNGA. www.un.org/en/development/desa/population/migration/generalassembly/docs/globalcompact/A_RES_71_1.pdf.

United Nations High Commissioner for Refugees (UNHCR). 2019. *Complementary Pathways for Admission of Refugees to Third Countries*. Geneva: UNHCR.

United Nations High Commissioner for Refugees (UNHCR). 2020. *Make the SDGS a Reality: SDG Implementation*. Geneva: Department of Economic and Social Affairs, United Nations. sdgs.un.org/un-system-sdg-implementation/united-nations-high-commissioner-refugees-unhcr-24540.

United Nations High Commissioner for Refugees (UNHCR). 2022. 'UNHCR Chief Condemns "Discrimination, Violence and Racism" against Some Fleeing Ukraine.' Press release, 21 March. Geneva: UNHCR. news.un.org/en/story/2022/03/1114282.

United Nations High Commissioner for Refugees (UNHCR). 2023. 'Sweden Fact Sheet, February 2023.' News and press release, 6 March. Geneva: UNHCR. reliefweb.int/report/sweden/unhcr-sweden-fact-sheet-february-2023#:~:text=900%20resettlement%20places,refugees%20from%205%2C000%20to%20900.

United Nations Office for the Coordination of Humanitarian Affairs (OCHA). 2022. 'CEB's New USD 1 Billion Social Inclusion Bond to Benefit Ukraine Refugees.' News release, 9 June. New York: ReliefWeb. reliefweb.int/report/ukraine/cebs-new-usd-1-billion-social-inclusion-bond-benefit-ukraine-refugees.

Vankova, Z. 2022a. 'Refugees as Migrant Workers after the Global Compacts? Can Labour Migration Serve as a Complementary Pathway for People in Need of Protection into Sweden and Germany?' *Laws* 11, no. 6: 20. doi.org/10.3390/laws11060088.

Vankova, Z. 2022b. 'Work-Based Pathways to Refugee Protection under EU Law: Pie in the Sky?' *European Journal of Migration and Law* 24, no. 1: 86–111. doi.org/10.1163/15718166-12340120.

van Selm, J. 2004. 'The Strategic Use of Resettlement: Changing the Face of Protection?' *Refuge: Canada's Journal on Refugees* 22: 39–48. doi.org/10.25071/1920-7336.21316.

Welfens, N., M. Engler, A. Garnier, P. Endres de Oliveira, and J.O. Kleist. 2019. 'Active Refugee Admission Policies in Europe: Exploring an Emerging Research Field.' *Fluchtforschungsblog* [*German Network for Forced Migration Studies blog*], 13 May. blog.fluchtforschung.net/active-refugee-admission-policies-in-europe-exploring-an-emerging-research-field/.

Welfens, N., and A. Pisarevskaya. 2020. 'The "Others" amongst "Them": Selection Categories in European Resettlement and Humanitarian Admission Programmes.' In *European Societies, Migration and the Law: The 'Others' amongst 'Us'*, edited by J. Moritz, 81–104. Cambridge: Cambridge University Press. doi.org/10.1017/9781108767637.006.

Westerby, R. 2020. 'When Refugees Become Migrants: State "Cherry-Picking" for Refugee Protection.' *RLI Blog on Refugee Law and Forced Migration*, 20 October. London: Refugee Law Initiative, University of London. rli.blogs.sas.ac.uk/2020/10/20/when-refugees-become-migrants-state-cherry-picking-for-refugee-protection/.

World Economic Forum (WEF). 2019. *From Funding to Financing: Transforming SDG Finance for Country Success*. Geneva: WEF. www3.weforum.org/docs/WEF_From_Funding_to_Financing.pdf.

Yurdakul, G., R. Römhild, A. Schwanhäußer, and B. zur Nieden, eds. 2017. *Witnessing the Transition: Moments in the Long Summer of Migration*. Berlin: Berlin Institute for Empirical Integration and Migration Research. edoc.hu-berlin.de/bitstream/handle/18452/19415/witnessing-the-transition.pdf.

Zetter, R. 2021. 'Theorizing the Refugee Humanitarian–Development Nexus: A Political-Economy Analysis.' *Journal of Refugee Studies* 34: 1766–86. doi.org/10.1093/jrs/fez070.

5

The migration lottery: Luck, law and lotteries

Nicholas Simoes da Silva

Introduction

Lotteries, understandably, have a poor reputation. To speak of an unfair process might be to compare it to a lottery. There is something deeply discomforting about the notion that luck should determine a person's outcomes. Yet, randomised social decision-making—through deliberately designed social lotteries—is also understood as a just way of allocating some burdens or benefits. Lotteries have been used throughout history, such as for military conscription and jury duty. More recently, New Zealand used a social lottery to allocate scarce places in its Covid-19 quarantine program (MIQ 2022), enrolment in which was necessary to enter the country. Michael Sandel (2020: 184–88) has also proposed a 'lottery of the qualified' for entry to elite universities in the United States. This chapter argues that lotteries are a useful policy tool for allocating scarce goods to individuals with equal or indeterminate claims. Lotteries can help create the migration 'pathways' discussed in Chapter 1 of this volume that the European Union and its member states are increasingly exploring as they navigate the 'borders-to-pathways' moment.[1] As a policy tool, a migration lottery can help ensure pathways remain fairer and more accessible than if alternative tools, such as 'first-come, first-served', are used in building or maintaining pathways for migration to Europe.

---

1   The 'borders-to-pathways' image is critically examined in Chapter 1 of this volume.

Lotteries have been used in migration policy in the United States since 1989, in New Zealand since at least 2002 and in Canada since 2017 (Mares 2023: 27). In 2023, Australia announced the introduction of a lottery-based Pacific Engagement Visa.[2] Scholars and policymakers have studied the flawed origin of the United States' lottery program (Legomsky 1993: 319; Law 2002: 3; Wasem 2002: 239) and several have proposed or considered migration lottery designs (Woodward 1992: 59, 61; Bhattacharya 2012: 4; OECD 2014: 213; Farer 2020). This chapter builds on these contributions to argue that a migration lottery offers a useful tool for responding to a long-term challenge facing migration policy: allocating numerically limited (that is, capped) permanent and temporary migration visas to ever larger numbers of eligible migrants. I suggest migration lotteries offer a fairer means of allocating visas than the current policy alternatives of 'first-come, first-served', which is the dominant approach, or ranking migrants through points-based programs. Realising the European Union's goal of creating a 'fair, efficient and sustainable' migration system, as emphasised in the *New Pact on Migration and Asylum*, demands innovative policies and approaches (EC 2020: 28).

This chapter takes as given limits on migration and the current objectives of most states' immigration policies, including most European states. As explored empirically later in this chapter, these objectives include the promotion of family, labour and skilled migration, along with a relatively small humanitarian program. The concern of the chapter is not with the levels or distribution of migration among the various migration streams. Rather, I examine how, in a context of the number of eligible immigrants far exceeding limited migration places, policymakers can allocate visas more equitably within each migration stream. In this context, the discussion takes 'equality of opportunity' as its key fairness objective: ensuring that people with equal or indeterminate claims to migrate under visa criteria do in fact have a degree of meaningful equality of opportunity. Lotteries can be adapted to the existing economic and social objectives of most states' migration policies while increasing equality of opportunity among those who are eligible for family, labour or humanitarian visas. This research will be relevant to policymakers in countries with caps on migration or which are looking to implement points-based migration programs. These countries include Australia, the United Kingdom, Canada, the US and an

---

2   Under the proposed s. 46C(2) of the *Migration Act 1958*, inserted by the Migration Amendment (Australia's Engagement in the Pacific and Other Measures) Bill 2023 (Cth), 'participants' must be 'selected at random'.

increasing number of EU states.[3] Following the introduction of a points-based migration stream in the UK, both Germany and Czechia are looking to introduce similar programs (OECD 2022: 72). The consideration of lotteries will also be relevant to other European states that are increasingly looking to migration quotas as a way to address voter concerns. This chapter suggests that quotas will be quickly exceeded if EU and member state attempts to regularise migration patterns succeed, while excessive competition for points-based visas could eventually become arbitrary and exclude valued occupations such as nursing and teaching.

Section one argues that managing the policy challenge of limited visas fairly and justly is critical because the ability to migrate can offer enormous benefits to individuals. I then present the migration policy challenge facing decision-makers today and into the future: the ability to migrate remains intentionally restricted, yet the number of people who would be granted a visa but for limits on places is sizeable and increasing across most advanced economies. Concluding this section, I consider existing approaches to the policy challenge. Section two introduces social lotteries as a policy tool, identifying their features and requirements. I then examine the potential benefits of a migration lottery, discussing the US Diversity Visa lottery as a case study, before addressing how the allocation of scarce visas is strongly suited to the use of a lottery. I will then examine the most common alternative to a lottery, the approach of 'first-come, first-served', and explain how the benefits of this policy tool break down when demand is too high and waiting times are too long. Section three examines two suggestions for how a lottery could work within existing migration policies, before considering how a migration lottery could be introduced in the EU.

The policy challenge

The question of how to allocate visas and the right to migrate matters because the ability to migrate is critical to individuals and their opportunities in life. This is particularly because of the unequal distribution of basic goods such as security, health, education and human rights across countries (Hasell et al. 2023). National borders and inherited citizenship mean that an individual's position in this global distribution is largely fixed.[4]

---

3   As discussed later in this chapter, the following countries have introduced visas with caps or quotas: Austria, Czechia, Estonia, Italy, Greece, Hungary and Romania.
4   Except insofar as a person is able to be socially mobile within a state.

This results in 'the birthright lottery' (Shachar 2009: 3)—an arbitrary system of allocating the 'feudal privilege' of '[c]itizenship in Western liberal democracies' (Carens 1987: 251, 252). Milanović (2016) has identified the 'citizenship rent' from which citizens of developed economies benefit. His analysis, comparing incomes in countries globally, has concluded that 'we can "explain" … more than two-thirds of the variability in incomes across country-percentiles by only one variable: the country where people live'. Milanović suggests that '[j]ust by being born in the United States rather than in Congo, a person would multiply her income by 93 times' (2016: 133). Absent the abolition of political communities bounded by ostensibly impermeable borders, immigration is the only way to escape this birthright lottery and to gain access to the 'location bonus' or 'citizenship rent' of living in most Global North states (Bregman 2015: 217–21; Milanović 2016: 133).

Immigration also matters to individuals because of the social benefits it offers. This is obvious in the case of family migration, where parents, children or extended family can join a family member in another country. However, migration also matters to individuals in the context of 'transnational social networks', including in the diaspora (Van Hear et al. 2012: 11). Cultural differences or attractions across states may also make migration appealing, creating opportunities for human flourishing in different social contexts. These non-distributional motivations are obvious in the case of young people who migrate for study or work, even though the country from which they migrate may have a higher standard of living.[5] The EU's Erasmus+ mobility program, for example, has supported more than 12.5 million people to move for study, training or sport since 1987 (EC 2014; 2022: 17). The social motivations for migration are also found in the fact that many Bangladeshi women find in migration a way to escape marriages in a country that restricts divorce (Van Hear et al. 2012: 18). Apart from multiple economic gains, migration, therefore, brings significant social benefits that flow from shifting between different political communities that may be better suited or more attractive to particular individuals, regardless of whether these communities are better materially endowed.

The distributional inequalities persisting in the world today and the social opportunities afforded by migration require a migration policy that, to the maximum possible extent, ensures equality of opportunity among migrants

---

5   For discussion of the social benefits of migration for students, see EC (2014: 18).

with equal claims to a visa. I will return later to the 'equal claims' issue, but before doing so it is worth commenting on why formal equality of opportunity is a useful measure of fairness in migration policy. Formal equality of opportunity means 'that positions and posts that confer superior advantages should be open to all applicants. Applications are assessed on their merits, and the applicant deemed most qualified according to appropriate criteria is offered the position' (Arneson 2015).

In the context of migration policy, formal equality of opportunity means that all people eligible for a visa because they meet the criteria should have the meaningful opportunity to access that visa. For example, a person who meets the criteria for a parent visa in the UK should have the opportunity to receive that visa. I adopt a formal equality of opportunity approach because, while I consider equality of outcomes or substantive equality of opportunity are morally superior, they would require a revolutionary change in the principles and objectives of migration policy. This rethink has been proposed by many scholars (Carens 1987, 2013; Bregman 2015; Sager 2020) and rejected by others (Walzer 1983). Instead of joining this debate, I suggest that an immediately achievable fairer migration policy is one that distributes the opportunity to access the right to migrate as equally as possible among those with equal claims to a visa. The limits of 'formal equality' in this context are particularly acute. I make little comment in this chapter on the rules establishing who has a 'claim' to a visa—rules that may create a group of eligible persons that renders 'formal equality' entirely regressive and discriminatory. The aspirations of this chapter are relatively modest, seeking only to enhance the ability of the minority of people eligible for visas to access such visas.

The challenge of allocating visas

The policy challenge can be simply stated: the number of people wanting to permanently migrate far exceeds the number of available places. Gallup polling suggests about 750 million people would migrate if they could (Esipova et al. 2018). The US Diversity Visa Program, which simply requires a person to have a high school degree or two years of skilled experience, received 23,182,554 registrations in the 2020 financial year and 11,830,707 in the 2021 financial year (US State Department 2021b), with just 50,000 visas available under the program. Nuance can be added to this policy challenge: the number of people who would be granted a visa but for limits on visa places is significant. This second group is smaller than the total number of people who want to migrate because of states' restrictive visa requirements, such as for family and skill visas, but it remains large.

The available data support the proposition that the number of persons eligible for family, labour and humanitarian visas exceeds the number of visas available. The waiting list for family visas is particularly startling. A person making a new application for an Australian Contributory Parent visa will wait 12 years before they have their application processed (Department of Home Affairs 2022a). New successful applicants for Parent and Aged Parent visas can expect to wait 29 years, with the wait for eligible Remaining Relative and Aged Dependent Relative visa applications about 24 years (Department of Home Affairs 2022a, 2022b). In the US, family and employment visas are also substantially oversubscribed. The waiting list for the 226,000 family-preference visas (which exclude 'immediate relatives', an uncapped category) was 3,969,573—a 5.5 per cent increase on the previous year (US State Department 2021a: 2). This belies the true waiting times for people from oversubscribed countries, because the US imposes a cap per country for most visa classes. The 2022 financial year country cap was 15,820 (US State Department 2021a: 5), which means people on the list of 1,209,633 Mexican applicants will wait decades and someone making a new application faces a wait of more than 70 years.[6] This reality is acknowledged by the US consular service, which frequently culls 'visa cases to remove from the count those unlikely to see further action' (US State Department 2021a: 4). For humanitarian visas, the number of eligible refugees far exceeds the number of humanitarian visa places in advanced economies, with more than 20 million people registering as refugees between 2010 and 2019 (UNHCR 2020: 4). The number of UNHCR resettlement refugees a country accepts is capped at whatever discretionary figure that country applies in a given year (OECD 2006: 111).

The allocation of scarce visas to ever larger numbers of applicants will become increasingly important among member states of the European Union. Several countries, including Austria, Czechia, Estonia, Italy, Greece, Hungary and Romania, have numerical limits on their temporary and permanent migration programs (Chaloff and Lemaitre 2009: 43; OECD 2017: 200, 236, 238, 268; 2018: 222; 2019: 224, 228). Many EU countries also have small humanitarian programs (see Table 5.1), which have become

---

6   Assuming the country cap is not substantially increased.

largely meaningless in the context of large-scale irregular migration, as observed in Greece and Italy. However, this is changing as the EU and its member states seek to strengthen common borders and regularise migration—both central objectives of the European Commission's *New Pact on Migration and Asylum* (2020: 2–3). If these attempts succeed, regular migration pathways will face greater demand, perhaps comparable to that seen in Australia and the United States. For example, Romania reached its annual permanent migration quota for the first time in November 2017 and, but for rises in the quota over both years, it would have exceeded it in 2018 and 2019 (OECD 2018: 276; 2019: 268). Estonia reached its cap on residence permits in 2018 (OECD 2019: 228). The increase in regular migration comes as many countries are promising stronger controls on migration more generally. The French Government, promising to 'take back control of our migration policy' (BBC News 2019), is looking to introduce migration quotas for the first time (Chrisafis 2019), while Austria did so in 2017 for humanitarian visas (ECRE 2017; Rettman 2016).

It is in this context—of a move to both regularise migration and introduce quotas on immigration that are being exceeded or likely to be exceeded—that the fundamental question of *how* to allocate the ability to migrate becomes crucial to policymakers. In other words, how can the 'borders-to-pathways' aspiration be meaningfully realised in Europe and how should new or increasingly busy pathways to migration be (re)designed?

Current approaches to the policy challenge

Three core long-term migration streams have developed that focus on different migrant characteristics: labour, family and humanitarian. Table 5.1 shows the prevalence of these streams in permanent or long-term migration programs across selected Organisation for Economic Co-operation and Development (OECD) states. European states have introduced a suite of new policies to encourage temporary and permanent skilled labour migration, often seeking to move away from migration programs dominated by family or low-skilled migrants. In Germany, for example, the *Skilled Workers Immigration Act* has simplified the processes for skilled migrants to obtain visas (OECD 2022: 236). Countries such as Lithuania, Slovakia and Poland have taken similar steps (OECD 2022: 254, 255, 272).

Table 5.1 Permanent or long-term migration streams in selected countries (per cent)

Country	Labour	Family	Humanitarian	Total migration in three streams
Slovenia	57.00	42.00	n.a.	**98.30**
Canada	32.50	51.80	13.80	**98.10**
United States	11.00	72.00	11.00	**93.90**
New Zealand	22.00	65.00	6.00	**93.20**
Australia	26.60	58.20	8.00	**92.80**
Lithuania	88.00	4.00	n.a.	**92.00**
Estonia	41.50	43.50	n.a.	**85.00**
Czechia	57.10	24.70	n.a.	**81.80**
Portugal	41.00	35.00	0.00	**75.90**
Poland	60.00	15.00	n.a.	**75.20**
United Kingdom	18.00	41.00	14.00	**73.50**
Finland	23.60	35.90	12.20	**71.70**
France	18.00	35.00	12.00	**65.00**
Italy	6.00	47.00	9.00	**62.30**
Spain	10.00	33.00	15.00	**57.70**
Greece	8.00	42.00	n.a.	**50.20**
Belgium	3.70	28.10	6.40	**38.20**
Netherlands	12.00	21.00	4.00	**38.00**
Denmark	18.40	17.90	1.50	**37.80**
Germany	10.00	14.00	12.00	**35.80**
Austria	7.40	11.40	10.90	**29.70**

n.a. = not applicable

Source: Data from OECD country reports published in the *International Migration Outlook* (2022).

Policymakers can rely on a mix of policy tools to limit migration within the framework of either formal or informal numerical limits (OECD 2006: 111). The two key policy tools are restrictions on eligibility criteria (for example, the types of relatives able to apply for a family visa or requirements for certain educational standards for skilled migrants) and ranking potential migrants based on their characteristics, with only applicants of a certain rank or score able to apply to migrate (Elster 1992: 58–59). For example, Australia's migration scheme for skilled migrants assigns points based on age, language, skilled work in Australia and overseas, educational qualifications and several other criteria (Sumption 2019: 3). In 2019, applicants who did not have a job offer needed at least 65 out of 100 points to be eligible under the criteria. However, due to Australia's capping of visa numbers and reliance on ranking migrants, successful applicants really needed at least 85 points to succeed in June 2019—up from 70 in December 2018 (Sumption 2019: 3). The scope for this kind of ranking or for restricting applicant criteria is limited in relation to humanitarian migrants applying for resettlement. Instead, humanitarian visas are allocated on a waiting list basis administered by the UNHCR or through a natural lottery of who is physically able to get to a country that may accept them (asylum seekers) (UNHCR 2020: 4). Many advanced economies, even when using policy tools to limit the pool of eligible migrants, will still see more eligible applicants than available places, as the beginning of this section demonstrated.

Wherever the number of eligible applicants exceeds the supply of available migration places, policymakers have several options. First, as the Australian example demonstrates, eligible migrants can simply be ranked and excluded if they do not meet the shifting cut-off score, which is the point at which the number of ranked applicants meets the maximum number of places. However, this does not apply to family and humanitarian streams. As Table 5.1 shows, family migrants make up a significant proportion of migrants to most EU countries, as well as to the US, Australia and Canada (Ferrie and Hatton 2015: 53, 78). Despite their use in Australia, points-based systems that comparatively rank applicants, whether for labour or family visas, are used by few other countries. Instead, minimum standards are generally used, such as minimum educational qualifications, skills or a job offer. In this case, the primary policy tool for allocating visas is 'first-come, first-served'—an approach that is often used in conjunction with a *waiting list* or *queue* (Elster 1989: 70). Where there is no formal waiting list, an informal but unordered one effectively operates for people who are eligible but were unable to access a visa due to a cap on places and the operation of 'first-come, first-served'. It is also worth noting that the challenge of allocating scarce permanent or long-term labour visas can be avoided by relying on short-term migrant schemes. These are often uncapped, but they leave individuals in precarious situations, needing to frequently reapply for their visas and having limited economic and social rights. In 2016, OECD countries received 4.2 million temporary labour migrants—an increase of 11 per cent on 2015 and dwarfing the 500,000 permanent labour migrants moving to an OECD country (OECD 2018: 26).

In summary, policymakers who do not use points-based systems generally attempt, at least in relation to labour and family migration, to restrict the number of persons eligible for visas, such as through minimum skills, educational qualifications or familial connections. Where this fails to reduce the number of eligible persons below a numerical limit, the policymaker can simply declare that the country will not accept migrants above the cap and implement a 'first-come, first-served' policy. In this circumstance, which also applies to humanitarian migrants, all eligible persons have equal claims to a visa. Policymakers then use time and the order in which people applied as the tiebreaker between equal claims to the visa (through a waiting list).

Proposals for a migration lottery

This section first considers what randomised social decision-making in the form of a lottery looks like, how lotteries have been used historically, how they can be flexibly designed and their ethics and efficacy. It then examines the US Diversity Visa lottery, before considering why European and other policymakers may want to use a migration lottery, particularly in place of 'first-come, first-served' approaches, to allocate scarce visas.

What is a lottery?

Kornhauser and Sager (1988: 483, 485) define a social lottery as a scheme that

> allocates a benefit (sometimes called a 'prize') among a designated group of potential beneficiaries ('candidates' who comprise a 'pool') according to a stipulated procedure (the 'pay-off condition'). The payoff condition is stipulated by some person or persons with the authority to effectuate the allocation (the 'allocating agency').

A social lottery can be contrasted with a natural lottery, such as a person's genetic inheritance or birthplace, both of which have no human 'allocating agency' (Goodwin 1992: 62–64; Shachar 2009: 3–4, 11). A social lottery is therefore manufactured by an authority able to impose it as a decision-making process for allocating a particular benefit or burden. Social lotteries are most famously used in the allocation of jury duty and military service through draft lotteries (Elster 1989: 95; Fienberg 1971: 255). They have also been used 'to settle sporting matters, to determine which citizens should be subject to tax inspections, to recruit employees, to determine which immigration applications should be successful [referring to the US Diversity Visa Program], [and] to assign judges' (Duxbury 1999: 43–44). The use of social lotteries has therefore been significant.

For a process to be a lottery, the 'stipulated procedure (the "payoff condition")' must be random (Kornhauser and Sager 1988: 485). What this means in practice is much debated and is dependent on the design of the 'stipulated procedure'. For the purposes of this chapter, I take this randomness requirement to be satisfied so long as the entries in a pool are selected in an 'equiprobable' way (Kornhauser and Sager 1988: 485). This means that if there are 100 slips of paper in a hat, each has the same chance of being selected. This does not mean that each person has an equal chance of being selected, because a person may have been entered multiple times under a 'weighted lottery' approach. However, each entry to the lottery is as likely to be picked.

The members of the pool for the lottery can be selected on almost any basis. This makes social lotteries amoral: the morality of any lottery depends on how the pool is selected and what the lottery is being used to allocate. For example, the candidates for a military conscription lottery may be persons aged 18–40, while the pool for a kidney transplant may be those likely to die within one year absent a transplant. An immoral lottery may be one that allocates a burden, such as military service, among a pool solely comprising a minority ethnic community. An immoral lottery may only permit white people to access a benefit such as a dialysis machine. Structural factors may also—deliberately or not—affect access to lotteries and therefore their fairness. Such structural factors can include language, location, knowledge and other social capital. For example, and as discussed further below, the Irish diaspora significantly helped Irish migrants 'win' the US Diversity Visa lottery during its early years. Social lotteries are deliberate human creations generated to address allocative challenges and they are inherently neither moral nor immoral. Ultimately, lotteries offer almost endless flexibility in selecting entrants to the pool of potential 'winners' and in weighing each applicant within the pool (whether equally or through some formula).

The US Diversity Visa lottery

The history of the US Diversity Visa begins with the US Congress's concern that family migrants in the 1980s were coming from a limited number of countries, largely in Asia and South and Central America (Legomsky 1993: 328). This was the result of the *Immigration and Nationality Act of 1965* and its removal of many explicitly discriminatory features of US immigration policy, such as a ban on Asian immigration (Law 2002: 4). After a transition period that ended on 30 June 1968, discriminatory national quotas were eliminated and s. 202(a) of the *Immigration and Nationality Act* introduced a limit of 20,000 migrants per country, covering all visa streams.[7] Section 203 of the Act provided for a new system of preferences, which assigned visas to people based on labour and family connection requirements (Law 2002: 6–12). The legislation immediately reduced migration from European states, which had benefited from the discriminatory rules in the earlier legislation. In 1965, the total quota for migrants from European states was 149,697, or 94 per cent of the total quota in that year. Migrants from Asia and Africa had a total quota of less than 8,000, and only 4,624 people were actually allowed to migrate from those regions in 1965 (US Immigration and Naturalization Service 1965: 34). By 1970, European migrants accounted for 57 per cent of Eastern Hemisphere migrants admitted through the new system—a figure that dropped to 37 per cent in 1975 (US Immigration and Naturalization Service 1970: 47; 1975: 42).

Beginning in 1986, Congress began experimenting with policy tools to allocate permanent residency visas to migrants from countries that had been 'adversely affected' by the 1965 *Immigration and Nationality Act* (Legomsky 1993: 328). As Law (2002) demonstrates, the Diversity Visa lottery was classic 'pork-barrel politics' aimed at benefiting Americans of European, particularly Irish, heritage.[8] European migrants had been impacted by the new preferences system, under which it appears many were ineligible or uncompetitive relative to migrants from other regions. This meant that, by the 1980s, many European states had relatively low migration flows to the United States and used little of their quota of 20,000 visas. The 1986 NP-5 program created a total of 10,000 visas that were granted 'first-come, first-served' to nationals of 'adversely affected countries'. This meant any 'country that did not use more than 25 percent of its 20,000 annual allotment of visas'—a definition that generally captured European states (Law 2002: 15). This program ran for four years and, though not strictly a lottery, functioned with a significant degree of luck. A total of 1.4 million applications were received in the seven-day registration period for 1986,

---

7   There were exceptions to this rule, so that some migrants could enter without counting towards the numerical limits. Most importantly, ss. 201(a)–(b) of the *Immigration and Nationality Act* provided that exempt migrants included 'immediate relatives'—defined to mean children, spouses and parents of a citizen of the United States.

8   This view was echoed by Miller (2017); and Alvarez (2017).

with applications approved as they arrived in the mail (Dunn 1991; Law 2002: 15). Applicants easily manipulated the program. Irish applicants arranged charter flights for their applications and held parties where attendees filled in visa applications, which were unlimited, for potential Irish migrants (Gaiba 2016; Law 2002: 15). Applications received in 1986 were used to award a further 10,000 visas annually in 1987, 1988 and 1989, resulting in Irish migrants receiving more than 40 per cent of visas. The scheme had a strong racial aspect to it, as European migrants tended to be white (Gaiba 2016; Law 2002: 15).

Following this first period, the NP-5 program was replaced with an actual randomised lottery with one entry per person. In 1990, an initial program (OP-1) offered 10,000 visas to nationals of 'underrepresented countries'. OP-1 used the same criteria as the 1986 NP-5 program but genuinely randomised the process. This resulted in a vastly different cohort from the NP-5's Irish-dominated stream, with the top 10 countries in 1990 being Bangladesh, Pakistan, Egypt, Peru, Trinidad and Tobago, Fiji, Poland, Iran, Malaysia and Indonesia (Dunn 1991). The lottery was made permanent as part of the *Immigration Act 1990*. From 1992 to 1994, a transitional lottery was operated (visa program AA-1), with 40,000 visas granted annually, subject to national limits and an Irish preference that guaranteed at least 40 per cent of visas to Irish nationals (Wasem 2002: 241). Since 1995, the modern Diversity Visa has provided 50,000 visas (down from 55,000 in its first two years of operation) to nationals from countries 'from which immigrant admissions were lower than a total of 50,000 over the preceding five years' (Wilson 2019: 4). Numerical limits are applied to applicants from certain regions, each country is capped at 7 per cent of the total number of available visas and there is no cost to enter the lottery (US State Department 2020: 1). Along with being from an eligible country, an applicant must have a 'high school education or its equivalent' or 'two years of work experience within the past five years in an occupation that requires at least two years of training or experience to perform' (US State Department 2020: 2).

The US Diversity Visa illustrates the potential flexibility of lotteries in increasing equality of opportunity while still achieving the longstanding objectives of migration policy. As Figures 5.1 and 5.2 show, the Diversity Visa produces a notably different cohort of migrants than other migration streams. The figures show the visa provides far more visas to African migrants (43 per cent) than other streams (11 per cent). It also results in a substantially younger migrant cohort, with 85 per cent of visa recipients under the age of 30 (compared with 46 per cent in other migration streams).

The Diversity Visa delivers on the 'diversity' objective while using skill requirements to achieve a migrant cohort that reflects the labour objectives of US migration policy. The evolution of the program over its first decade from 1986 demonstrates how the criteria used to select the 'pool' of potential 'winners' can be flexibly altered as the objectives of migration policy shift. It is notable that the shift from a 'first-come, first-served' approach in the 1986 NP-5 program, which rewarded informed and mobilised migrants such as the Irish, to a lottery approach significantly improved the equality of opportunity, as reflected in the far more diverse cohort since the 1995 lottery. It should be noted that if a 'first-come, first-served' approach had been retained, the waiting time for migrants at the end of the waiting list for the Diversity Visa would be measured in hundreds of years.

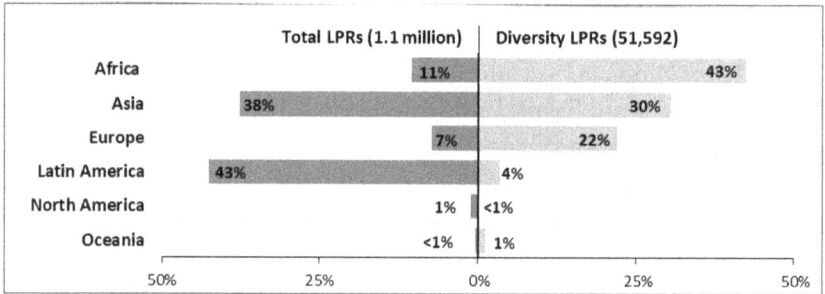

Figure 5.1 Regional composition of US Diversity Visas and general immigration stream
Note: LPR refers to legal permanent resident.
Source: Wilson (2019: 7).

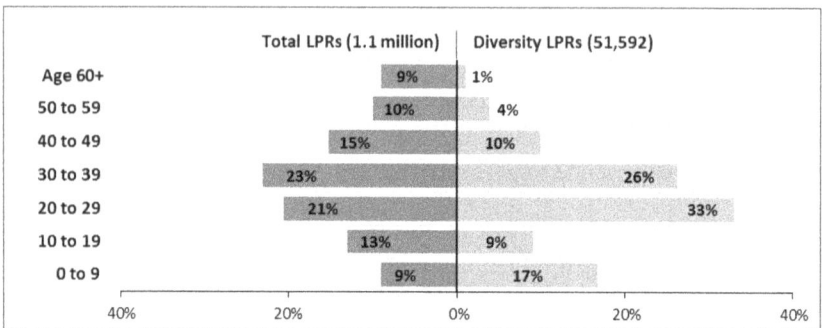

Figure 5.2 Age composition of US Diversity Visas and general immigration stream
Source: Wilson (2019: 8).

Why use a migration lottery for allocating visas?

Scholars who have previously considered the use of a migration lottery have assumed that it would need to draw from the entire population of people wishing to migrate (Bhattacharya 2012; Woodward 1992: 61). This may be true from a purely moral standpoint of ensuring complete equality of opportunity. However, it is not consistent with the objectives of modern migration policies. Migration policies, including those from European states identified in Table 5.1, tend to focus on family and labour migration, with a component of humanitarian migration. So, how can a lottery be used to serve the objectives of migration policies?

As a tool for allocating benefits, a social lottery is useful for situations in which people are: 1) equally or indeterminately entitled to a benefit, and 2) the benefit is not sufficiently available to satisfy people's demand for it. Indeterminate claims are those where there is no fair or practical way to distinguish between multiple people. Policymakers instead rely on other mechanisms to distinguish indeterminate claims, such as 'first-come, first-served' or a lottery. Indeterminacy arises 'when claims are determined by considerations that are matters of degree' or where 'sources of claims may be intrinsically vague, so that it may be impossible even in principle to say that claims are exactly equal' (Broome 1984: 38, 49). Duxbury (1999: 44–45) identifies the use of lotteries in the allocation of benefits among indeterminate or equal claims to 'plots of land, public housing, church pews, proceeds of charity, oil-drilling leases, broadcasting licenses, prospecting rights, tickets for public events, vaccines and other drugs, haemodialysis machines, and places at medical and other schools'. Sandel (2020: 184–88) has proposed a lottery for the allocation of places at top universities, given the indeterminacy of many applicants' claims to such places. Lotteries are useful in these situations because the decision-maker has determined that all the people in the 'pool' of eligible applicants have an equal or indistinguishable claim to the good. Allocation of visas for family and humanitarian migration obviously satisfies both criteria: as discussed in section one, the number of people satisfying the eligibility criteria far outweighs the number of visas. New Zealand's migration lottery is a classic case of indeterminacy: it awards a very small number of permanent residency visas through its Samoan Quota and Pacific Access programs among large numbers of applicants who are all equally eligible (New Zealand Immigration 2023; RNZ 2019).

Where a decision-maker is faced with a pool of equally or indeterminately entitled applicants, a lottery brings in two key benefits that ensure the decision-making process remains fair: a sanitising effect and equality of opportunity. Both are shared, in theory, with a 'first-come, first-served' approach, though the second of these breaks down when the pool of eligible applicants is too large. A lottery has 'sanitising effects' because it suppresses 'all reasons for making an allocative choice' among a group of people with equal or indeterminate entitlements to a good (Kornhauser and Sager 1988: 488). This means that the risk of 'falling into error and delusion' as a result of our 'rational capacities' trying to discern reasons for distinguishing claims 'that simply aren't there' is reduced (Stone 2009: 375, 383; see also Goodwin 1992: 97). In the context of migration, this can reduce the need for decision-makers to try to artificially distinguish between applicants, though the decision-maker can still apply criteria to determine who is in the eligible 'pool' for the lottery.

Second, a lottery provides equality of opportunity by giving everyone within the pool a chance to access the good (Duxbury 1999: 61). This led Greely (1977: 113, 122) to regard 'random selection' as 'the only allocative method which can claim the objective equality of opportunity from which the satisfaction of equality of expectation springs. It is the allocative method which maximises the goal of equality.' It should be noted that this pure conception of 'equality of opportunity' as giving everyone within the pool an equal opportunity to access the good is modified in the case of weighted lotteries. Under a weighted lottery, some people within the pool are more likely to 'win' because they have been entered multiple times. However, I suggest that even a weighted lottery delivers a degree of equality of opportunity to access a good, at least when compared with adjudicatory or market mechanisms. Such mechanisms would otherwise simply exclude people from the opportunity to access a good because a person did not rank sufficiently high or have enough funds. Formal equality of opportunity is preserved in weighted lotteries because any entrant still has the possibility of 'winning' and has the (theoretical) opportunity to satisfy whatever criteria lead to greater weighting, thereby increasing the number of entries.[9]

Last, lotteries can be useful and flexible for decision-making because policymakers can use them in conjunction with other allocative mechanisms—notably, adjudicatory and market mechanisms (Kornhauser

---

9   As long as the factors increasing a person's weighting are not the product of a natural lottery, such as height, race or sex.

and Sager 1988: 483). For example, access to a lottery for haemodialysis machines may be conducted through adjudication, with access to the pool limited to patients with a reasonable postoperative life expectancy, good prospects of a successful operation and a significant need for the treatment. In contrast, access to a lottery for broadcasting licences may be determined by a market mechanism that requires payment of a fee to enter the lottery. Lotteries only become necessary if the number of people in the pool exceeds the number of haemodialysis machines or broadcasting licences, which themselves are indivisible. In both cases, a small pool could be achieved by relying solely on the adjudicatory or market mechanism. For example, the criteria for access to haemodialysis machines could be set in such a way to limit the pool to the number of machines, and broadcasting licences could be auctioned (Broome 1984: 41). However, reliance on market mechanisms is often inappropriate or regarded as immoral for scarce goods that bring significant benefits because such mechanisms reward privilege and wealth (Sandel 2012). A market mechanism would be inappropriate for allocating humanitarian or family visas and reliance on market mechanisms, such as reference to a person's income, often leaves a pool of eligible labour migrants that is greater than the number of available visas. Reliance on adjudicatory mechanisms to reduce the size of the pool to less than the number of places is often impossible or so resource-intensive as to be impractical. The impracticality stems from the challenges of indeterminate claims. The impossibility of adjudication due to indeterminate claims is obvious for humanitarian and family visas, where policymakers are limited in the criteria that can be used to restrict applications. The current approach to managing this migration policy challenge is to rely on the principle of 'first-come, first-served'.

The problem with 'first-come, first-served'

Several scholars have analysed the normative basis of 'first-come, first-served' and the system of queuing (that is, standing in line) or waiting lists (Perry and Zarsky 2014: 1595; Larson 1987: 895; Sandel 2012: 18–36). The concern in migration policy is largely with waiting lists, given these predominate over physically or virtually standing in a line waiting for a visa, as a way of allocating the visas (rather than as a final step in collecting a visa, for instance). Waiting lists do not require standing in line and therefore lack many of the justifications that relate to physical queues, such as the fact that physically waiting in line is 'seen as generating desert' (Elster 1992: 74). Instead, the applicant submits their application and then joins a waiting list. While they are on the waiting list, they can continue to live their life with no other sacrifice stemming from having joined the list. In some contexts, time on the waiting list is a proxy for need (Saunders 2008: 359, 370). For example, Elster (1992: 74) notes that time spent waiting for a kidney transplant can be used as 'a proxy for medical need, since a patient's condition often deteriorates over time'. Irrespective of whether queuing is a meaningful proxy for need in the context of migration, the metaphorical power of the 'queue' is significant and 'the queue is seen to represent a system in which legitimate claims are ordered and rendered orderly by a recognizable system of allocation' (Young 2016: 65, 137). Perry and Zarsky's (2014: 1602–14) extensive review of the literature on the issue suggests that it is widely agreed that 'first-come, first-served' is fair, both normatively and in people's perceptions. For others, though, 'first-come, first-served' and waiting lists are justified largely because they are 'assumed to be natural lotteries' where a person's entry into the line and the amount of time they have to wait are dependent on need and/or luck rather than privilege or wealth (Saunders 2008: 370). Indeed, Perry and Zarsky (2014: 1609) acknowledge that several of the normative justifications for 'first-come, first-served' are shared with social lotteries, including their apparent commitment to egalitarianism. Stone also notes that '[a]llocation on a "first-come, first-served" basis is frequently mentioned as an equivalent alternative to allocation by lottery, especially in the biomedical literature', though he suggests they are 'not equivalent' (2009: 2011; Childress 1970: 339, 347–48; Scanlon 1969: 620, 621).

Regardless, my key reservation about 'first-come, first-served' and waiting lists is that they become unfair for a group of people with equal claims to a resource where the waiting time becomes excessive. If a group of people with equal claims to a resource waits for an hour, a day or even a month to access the resource, this arguably does not significantly impair the equality of opportunity among them. Each has a reasonable prospect of accessing the resource within a fair time. However, equality of opportunity and a sense of egalitarian fairness disappear when waiting times become unreasonable or so long as to effectively deny later applicants the chance to access the resource. This is particularly true where the scarce resource is as important as a visa. Under the policy challenge discussed in section one, many people who apply for a visa under 'first-come, first-served' models will never have the opportunity to get a visa: the waiting list is simply too long. This makes waiting time arbitrary—a product of birthdate and the luck of joining the line before it became too long (OECD 2014: 213). This offers no meaningful sense of equality of opportunity despite applicants' equal claims to the visa.

Implementing a migration lottery

Lotteries can be a powerful alternative or complement to 'first-come, first-served', offering enhanced equality of opportunity in situations where demand among people with equal claims is significant, while also preserving many of the normative benefits of 'first-come, first-served'. This section considers two potential designs for a migration lottery. First, it discusses a 'non-weighted migration lottery' in which each person who meets the entry criteria has an equal chance of 'winning'. Second, it explores a 'weighted migration lottery', which offers an alternative to the 'first-come, first-served' arrangement that still considers the time spent waiting in a lottery system. The section concludes by discussing the implementation of a migration lottery in the EU.

Non-weighted migration lotteries

A non-weighted migration lottery offers a useful policy tool where a policymaker does not want to prioritise among equal or indeterminate claimants to visas, which includes every situation where a policymaker currently uses 'first-come, first-served' as the decision-making tool. A non-weighted migration lottery would see policymakers use a simple set of minimum criteria, such as a type of familial connection, skill level or status such as recognised resettlement refugee. People who meet these criteria would form the pool of eligible persons for the lottery. Key to this type of lottery is that people within the pool are not assessed comparatively so everyone has an equal or indeterminate claim to the visa. This means there is no need to weight the lottery. For example, every person eligible for a parent visa is equally entitled, as is everyone who satisfies a minimum high school qualification or job offer requirement for a labour visa. Within the pool, there is complete equality of opportunity, even if the criteria for getting into the pool have comparatively ranked people. For example, to get in the pool for a 'high-risk' humanitarian visa a person may need to meet certain criteria of need and risk. The lottery will only be used if the 'pool' of people meeting those criteria is larger than the number of eligible places and the waiting time becomes so long as to be an obstacle to equality of opportunity.

Weighted migration lotteries

A weighted migration lottery can be used where a policymaker wants to favour certain characteristics of a migrant or if disregarding waiting time entirely is seen as unfair. For example, time spent on the waiting list could be used to accrue additional entries in the lottery. This would mean that a person who has been waiting five years for a visa might be entered into the lottery five times, while a person who has been waiting for less than one year would have just one entry. Increasing the number of entries can be used to achieve equality of opportunity when compared with a 'first-come, first-served' approach while still reflecting the values of a society that considers waiting time as 'generating desert'. Another way a weighted lottery can be used to increase equality of opportunity while still reflecting migration policy objectives is in skilled migration. It is possible to build a weighted lottery that favours skills, attributes or occupations but still gives an opportunity to workers who would otherwise be excluded by an exclusively points-based system that ranks and excludes lower-scoring people. For example, we might turn here to Australia's points-based migration system, which requires eligible migrants to achieve a score of at least sixty-five. However, due to the caps on visas and the approach to comparatively ranking applicants, people need far higher scores to be successful. Using a lottery could complement this ranking, with everyone above 65 points placed in the lottery pool but people given more entries in the pool depending on their score. This preserves a greater degree of equality of opportunity while still favouring highly skilled migrants. This reasoning—preserving the opportunity for qualified persons to access valuable benefits—also underlies Sandel's (2020: 184–88) proposal for a lottery for admission to elite US universities.

At least two additional benefits flow from a lottery used in conjunction with a points-based approach, the first of which deserves more attention to verify. First, randomisation reduces the need for state prioritisation of economic sectors. For example, in the UK, prioritisation based solely on points for non-EU migrants has resulted in doctors, nurses and other critical health workers largely being excluded from the skilled migration stream. The *Financial Times* noted in 2018 that, due to high demand for capped places, '[t]he minimum salary needed to qualify [for a skilled visa], which used to be £30,000, hit £55,000 in December and £50,000 in January' (Wright 2018). When demand is high, many health professionals fall down the rankings relative to other better-paying professions, such as finance and legal. The UK is taking steps to address this for National Health

Service staff, but the example demonstrates that this requires a highly interventionist approach to managing migration. A carefully designed and executed lottery can reduce this need for extensive government management of migration streams by producing distributions of migrants that are more likely to reflect the skill needs of the economy more broadly, rather than delivering only for industries in need of very highly skilled, qualified or paid migrants. Second, a migration policy that favours high-skilled migrants but does not exclude lower-ranked applicants is arguably one that better sees migrants as humans rather than simply economic units, while still working to achieve economic objectives in a migration policy.

A migration lottery in the European Union

As the member states of the EU move from 'borders to pathways', they will increasingly face the challenge of 'indeterminate claims' to limited visa places, as discussed in section one. In the context of the growing demand for limited visas, section two has demonstrated how a migration lottery could produce a fairer policy than a 'first-come, first-served' approach. However, introducing a migration lottery to the EU or any of its member states raises unique issues.

The failure of 'first-come, first-served' is already acute in countries that have traditionally experienced high levels of migration, such as Australia, the US and Canada. In those states, the federal government has sole competence over migration and naturalisation.[10] Federal governments can implement a visa lottery for one or more migration streams, as Canada has done (Marcs 2023: 27) and Australia is presently legislating.[11] However, the European Union has a substantially more complex legal structure in which visa arrangements are subject to shared competence with member states.[12] The European Union has the authority to legislate with respect to both short-term and long-term visas,[13] and these powers are extensive (Thym 2016: 277–78). It appears possible that an EU member state could nonetheless

---

10   *The Australian Constitution*, s. 51(xix); *Constitution of the United States*, art. I, s. 8; *Canada Act 1982 (UK)* c. 11, Sch B s. 91(25).

11   Under the proposed s. 46C(2) of the *Migration Act 1958* (Cth), inserted by the Migration Amendment (Australia's Engagement in the Pacific and Other Measures) Bill 2023 (Cth), 'participants' must be 'selected at random'.

12   The EU can make legislation with respect to migration under its competence for the 'area of freedom, security and justice'. *Treaty on the Functioning of the European Union*, Opened for Signature 7 February 1992, [2016] OJ C 202/1 (Entered into Force 1 November 1993), title V [hereinafter *TFEU*]. This is a shared competence under Article 4 of the treaty.

13   *TFEU*, arts. 77(2)(a), 79(2)(a).

create a visa allocated by lottery, so long as the state complied with existing EU directives and other legislation. For example, EU law restricts long-term visas to five years.[14] Alternatively, the EU could consider legislating the use of a migration lottery in circumstances where 'first-come, first-served' is proving unsuitable due to excessive demand, such as for economic and family migration. In particular, Article 79(2)(a) of the *Treaty on the Functioning of the European Union* (*TFEU*) provides that the EU may create 'standards on the issue by Member States of long-term visas and residence permits, including those for the purpose of family reunification'. Legislation under Article 79 of the *TFEU* must be made through the ordinary legislative procedure, but achieving this level of support across the EU for a migration lottery could prove difficult.[15] The EU's unique decision-making processes perhaps make it more likely that a member state could experiment with a migration lottery, before it is adopted by other states or the EU. Ultimately, the exact legal method through which a migration lottery is adopted is outside the scope of this chapter, though any migration lottery should be designed to be appropriate for the circumstances of the member state in which it is being introduced. For example, the criteria for entry may vary between states and some states may wish to adopt weighted lotteries. The EU principle of subsidiarity could help guide the matters for which EU legislative action with respect to a migration lottery would be desirable.[16]

Conclusion

As critically reviewed in Chapter 7 of this volume, the EU has enthusiastically adopted the rhetoric of 'safe, legal pathways' into the EU and its member states. The promise of such pathways may be exaggerated, but the EU's increasingly sophisticated attempts to strengthen its borders[17] are likely to force more people onto the narrow pathways that exist today or may be created in the future. Moreover, the European states are increasingly seeking to attract 'legal' migrants in the face of growing demographic challenges and

---

14   *Regulation (EC) No. 810/2009 of the European Parliament and of the Council of 13 July 2009 Establishing a Community Code on Visas (Visa Code)* [2009] OJ L 243/1 art. 24(1).

15   The ordinary legislative procedure requires a qualified majority, which is defined to mean '55% of the members of the Council representing the participating Member States, comprising at least 65% of the population of these States'. See *TFEU*, art. 238(3)(a).

16   *Treaty on European Union*, Opened for Signature 7 February 1992, [2009] OJ C 115/13 (Entered into Force 1 November 1993) art. 5(3)–(4).

17   See the discussion of Frontex in Chapter 1 of this volume.

to do so while maintaining 'fair' migration policies.[18] As demonstrated in section one, European policymakers face the possibility of enormous demand for visas from people with equal or indeterminate claims to such visas, as some member states are already experiencing. The existing approaches to allocating visas, particularly 'first-come, first-served', will prove inadequate to this challenge, as they have in Australia, the US and Canada. The failure of 'first-come, first-served' or sole reliance on points-based migration has a very real impact on people's opportunities to escape the distributional inequalities present in the world today. Innovative solutions are therefore required, particularly to ensure equality of opportunity among those eligible for a visa.

The review of randomised social decision-making in this chapter has sought to provide a basis for debate about the role that lotteries can play in increasing equality of opportunity among eligible migrants. Migration lotteries are flexible policy tools that offer a fairer method for allocating scarce visas when compared with existing approaches. Migration lotteries can also be adapted to the existing economic and social objectives of most states' migration policies while increasing equality of opportunity among those who are eligible for family, labour or humanitarian visas. Explicitly introducing randomness into migration policy may appear unsettling, arbitrary or unfair. However, for those who wish to defend the existing system of allocating visas, one must grapple with how 'first-come, first-served' or points-based migration is not itself a natural lottery that rewards, respectively, people making applications earlier and those who are highly skilled, highly qualified and highly paid. A migration lottery offers a means to manage and minimise the impact of natural lotteries already present in migration policy, while still supporting the labour, family and humanitarian objectives of modern migration policies.

References

Alvarez, P. 2017. 'The Diversity Visa Program Was Created to Help Irish Immigrants.' *The Atlantic*, 1 November. www.theatlantic.com/politics/archive/2017/11/diversity-visa-program/544646/.

Arneson, R. 2015. 'Equality of Opportunity.' In *Stanford Encyclopedia of Philosophy*. Stanford: Stanford University.

---

18   *TFEU*, s. 67(2).

BBC News. 2019. 'France "Takes Back Control" with Non-EU Migrant Quotas.' *BBC News*, 6 November. www.bbc.com/news/world-europe-50317442.

Bhattacharya, A. 2012. 'Does Justice Require a Migration Lottery?' *Global Justice: Theory Practice Rhetoric* 5: 4–15. doi.org/10.21248/gjn.5.0.27.

Bregman, R. 2015. *Utopia for Realists: How We Can Build the Ideal World*. Boston: Little, Brown and Company.

Broome, J. 1984. 'Selecting People Randomly.' *Ethics* 95, no. 1: 38–55. doi.org/10.1086/292596.

Carens, J.H. 1987. 'Aliens and Citizens: The Case for Open Borders.' *Review of Politics* 49, no. 2: 251–73. doi.org/10.1017/S0034670500033817.

Carens, J.H. 2013. *The Ethics of Immigration*. Oxford: Oxford University Press.

Chaloff, J., and G. Lemaitre. 2009. *Managing Highly-Skilled Labour Migration: A Comparative Analysis of Migration Policies and Challenges in OECD Countries*. OECD Social, Employment and Migration Working Papers No. 79. Paris: OECD Publishing.

Childress, J. 1970. 'Who Shall Live When Not All Can Live?' *Soundings* 53, no. 4: 339–55.

Chrisafis, A. 2019. 'France to Set Migrant Worker Quotas in Bid to Appeal to Rightwing Voters.' *The Guardian*, 6 November. www.theguardian.com/world/2019/nov/05/france-migrant-workers-quotas-rightwing-voters-marine-le-pen-emmanuel-macron.

Department of Home Affairs. 2022a. 'Capping and Queuing of Parent Visa Applications.' *Visa Processing Times*. [Online.] Canberra: Australian Government. immi.homeaffairs.gov.au/visas/getting-a-visa/visa-processing-times/family-visa-processing-priorities/parent-visas-queue-release-dates.

Department of Home Affairs. 2022b. 'Other Family Visas: Queue Release Dates and Processing Times.' *Visa Processing Times*. [Online.] Canberra: Australian Government. immi.homeaffairs.gov.au/visas/getting-a-visa/visa-processing-times/family-visa-processing-priorities/other-family-visas-queue-release-dates.

Dunn, A. 1991. 'U.S. Plans Lottery with Jackpot of Legal Residency: Immigration Officials Brace for Deluge of Applicants for 40,000 Visas. Critics Say the Process Favors Europeans.' *Los Angeles Times*, 6 September. www.latimes.com/archives/la-xpm-1991-09-06-mn-1739-story.html.

Duxbury, N. 1999. *Random Justice: On Lotteries and Legal Decision-Making*. Oxford: Oxford University Press. doi.org/10.1093/acprof:oso/9780198268253. 001.0001.

Elster, J. 1989. *Solomonic Judgments: Studies in the Limitations of Rationality*. Cambridge: Cambridge University Press.

Elster, J. 1992. *Local Justice: How Institutions Allocate Scarce Goods and Necessary Burdens*. Cambridge: Cambridge University Press.

Esipova, N., A. Pugliese, and J. Ray. 2018. 'More Than 750 Million Worldwide Would Migrate If They Could.' *Gallup*, 10 December. news.gallup.com/poll/245255/750-million-worldwide-migrate.aspx.

European Commission (EC). 2014. *The Erasmus Impact Study*. Report. Brussels: EC.

European Commission (EC). 2020. *Communication from the Commission to the European Parliament, the Council, the European Economic and Social Committee and the Committee of the Regions on a New Pact on Migration and Asylum*. 23 September, COM/2020/609 final. Brussels: EC. eur-lex.europa.eu/legal-content/EN/TXT/?uri=CELEX:52020DC0609.

European Commission (EC). 2022. *Annual Report 2021*. Brussels: EC.

European Council of Refugees and Exiles (ECRE). 2017. 'Austria: Proposals to Restrict Humanitarian Visas and Family Reunification.' News, 20 January. Brussels: ECRE. ecre.org/austria-proposals-to-restrict-humanitarian-visas-and-family-reunification/.

Farer, T. 2020. *Migration and Integration: The Case for Liberalism with Borders*. Cambridge: Cambridge University Press. doi.org/10.1017/9781108757997.

Ferrie, J.P., and T.J. Hatton. 2015. 'Two Centuries of International Migration.' In *Handbook of the Economics of International Migration*, edited by B.R. Chiswick and P.W. Miller, 53–88. Amsterdam: North-Holland. doi.org/10.1016/B978-0-444-53764-5.00002-5.

Fienberg, S.E. 1971. 'Randomization and Social Affairs: The 1970 Draft Lottery.' *Science* 171, no. 3968: 255–61. doi.org/10.1126/science.171.3968.255.

Gaiba, F. 2016. 'I'm a White Immigrant and I Benefited from a Racist Visa Lottery.' *TIME*, 8 December. time.com/4593985/immigration-visa-lotter-racism/.

Goodwin, B. 1992. *Justice by Lottery*. London: Harvester Wheatsheaf.

Greely, H. 1977. 'The Equality of Allocation by Lot.' *Harvard Civil Rights–Civil Liberties Review* 12, no. 1: 113–41.

Hasell, J., P. Arriagada, E. Ortiz-Ospina, and M. Roser. 2023. 'Economic Inequality.' *Our World in Data*. [Online.] ourworldindata.org/global-economic-inequality.

Kornhauser, L.A., and L.G. Sager. 1988. 'Just Lotteries.' *Rationality and Society* 27, no. 4: 483–516. doi.org/10.1177/053901888027004001.

Larson, R.C. 1987. 'Perspectives on Queues: Social Justice and the Psychology of Queuing.' *Operations Research* 35, no. 6: 799–933. doi.org/10.1287/opre.35.6.895.

Law, A.O. 2002. 'The Diversity Visa Lottery: A Cycle of Unintended Consequences in United States Immigration Policy.' *Journal of American Ethnic History* 21, no. 4: 3–29. doi.org/10.2307/27501196.

Legomsky, S.H. 1993. 'Immigration, Equality and Diversity.' *Columbia Journal of Transnational Law* 31, no. 2: 319–35.

Managed Isolation and Quarantine (MIQ). 2022. *The Managed Isolation Booking System: Virtual Lobby*. [Online.] Wellington: Ministry of Business, Innovation and Employment, New Zealand Government. web.archive.org/web/20220305173031/https://www.miq.govt.nz/travel-to-new-zealand/secure-your-place-in-managed-isolation/the-managed-isolation-booking-system/virtual-lobby/.

Mares, P. 2023. *The Parent Conundrum: Considering Australia's Troubled Approach to Parent Migration*. Narrative No. 11, July. Melbourne: Scanlon Foundation Research Institute. scanloninstitute.org.au/sites/default/files/2023-07/FINAL%20Scanlon%20Foundation%20Research%20Institute%20Report%20%20NARRATIVE%2011%20%28002%29-compressed.pdf.

Milanović, B. 2016. *Global Inequality: A New Approach for the Age of Globalization*. Cambridge: The Belknap Press of Harvard University Press. doi.org/10.4159/9780674969797.

Miller, M.E. 2017. 'Diversity Visa Lottery, Criticized after New York Terrorist Attack, Was Invented to Help the Irish.' *Washington Post*, 1 November. www.washingtonpost.com/news/retropolis/wp/2017/05/02/straight-up-pork-barrel-politics-how-the-green-card-lottery-was-invented-to-help-the-irish/.

New Zealand Immigration. 2023. *Pacific Access Category Resident Visa*. [Online.] Wellington: New Zealand Government. www.immigration.govt.nz/new-zealand-visas/apply-for-a-visa/visa-factsheet/pacific-access-category-resident-visa.

Organisation for Economic Co-operation and Development (OECD). 2006. *International Migration Outlook*. Paris: OECD Publishing.

Organisation for Economic Co-operation and Development (OECD). 2014. *International Migration Outlook*. Paris: OECD Publishing.

Organisation for Economic Co-operation and Development (OECD). 2017. *International Migration Outlook*. Paris: OECD Publishing.

Organisation for Economic Co-operation and Development (OECD). 2018. *International Migration Outlook*. Paris: OECD Publishing.

Organisation for Economic Co-operation and Development (OECD). 2019. *International Migration Outlook*. Paris: OECD Publishing.

Organisation for Economic Co-operation and Development (OECD). 2022. *International Migration Outlook*. Paris: OECD Publishing.

Perry, R., and T.Z. Zarsky. 2014. 'Queues in Law.' *Iowa Law Review* 99, no. 4: 1595–658.

Rettman, A. 2016. 'Austria Imposes Asylum Cap to "Shake Up" Europe.' *EU Observer*, [Brussels], 20 January. euobserver.com/rule-of-law/131928.

RNZ. 2019. 'Pacific Immigration Quotas to NZ Drawn Today.' *Radio New Zealand*, 7 June. www.rnz.co.nz/international/pacific-news/391448/pacific-immigration-quotas-to-nz-drawn-today.

Sager, A. 2020. *Against Borders*. Lanham: Rowman & Littlefield.

Sandel, M.J. 2012. *What Money Can't Buy: The Moral Limits of Markets*. London: Allen Lane.

Sandel, M.J. 2020. *The Tyranny of Merit: What's Become of the Common Good?* London: Allen Lane.

Saunders, B. 2008. 'The Equality of Lotteries.' *Philosophy* 83, no. 3: 359–72. doi.org/10.1017/S0031819108000727.

Scanlon, T.M. 1969. 'Scarce Medical Resources.' *Columbia Law Review* 69, no. 4 (April): 620–92. doi.org/10.2307/1121120.

Shachar, A. 2009. *The Birthright Lottery: Citizenship and Global Inequality*. Cambridge: Harvard University Press. doi.org/10.4159/9780674054592.

Stone, P. 2009. 'The Logic of Random Selection.' *Political Theory* 37, no. 3: 375–97. doi.org/10.1177/0090591709332329.

Sumption, M. 2019. *The Australian Points-Based System: What Is It and What Would Its Impact Be in the UK?* Report, 22 July. Oxford: The Migration Observatory, University of Oxford.

Thym, D. 2016. 'Legal Framework for EU Immigration Policy.' In *EU Immigration and Asylum Law: A Commentary*, edited by K. Hailbronner and D. Thym, 272–300. 2nd edn. Oxford: Hart. doi.org/10.5771/9783845259208-272.

United Nations High Commissioner for Refugees (UNHCR). 2020. *Global Trends: Forced Displacement in 2019*. Copenhagen: Statistics and Demographics Section, UNHCR. www.unhcr.org/5ee200e37.pdf.

United States Immigration and Naturalization Service. 1965. *Annual Report of the Immigration and Naturalization Service*. Washington, DC: US GPO. searchworks. stanford.edu/view/488273.

United States Immigration and Naturalization Service. 1970. *Annual Report of the Immigration and Naturalization Service*. Washington, DC: US GPO. searchworks. stanford.edu/view/488273.

United States Immigration and Naturalization Service. 1975. *Annual Report of the Immigration and Naturalization Service*. Washington, DC: US GPO. searchworks. stanford.edu/view/488273.

United States State Department. 2020. *Instructions for the 2021 Diversity Immigrant Visa Program (DV-2021)*. Washington, DC: Department of State. travel.state. gov/content/dam/visas/Diversity-Visa/DV-Instructions-Translations/DV-2021-Instructions-Translations/DV-2021-%20Instructions-English.pdf.

United States State Department. 2021a. *Annual Report of Immigrant Visa Applicants in the Family-Sponsored and Employment-Based Preferences Registered at the National Visa Center as of November 1, 2021*. Washington, DC: Department of State. cis.org/sites/default/files/2022-10/WaitingListItem_2021vF.pdf.

United States State Department. 2021b. *Diversity Visa Program, DV 2019–2021: Number of Entries During Each Online Registration Period by Region and Country of Chargeability*. Washington, DC: Department of State. travel.state.gov/content/dam/visas/Diversity-Visa/DVStatistics/DV-applicant-entrants-by-country-2019-2021.pdf.

Van Hear, N., O. Bakewell, and K. Long. 2012. *Drivers of Migration*. Migrating Out of Poverty Research Programme Consortium Working Paper 1, March. Brighton: University of Sussex.

Walzer, M. 1983. *Spheres of Justice: A Defense of Pluralism and Equality*. New York: Basic Books.

Wasem, R.E. 2002. 'Diversity Immigrant Visa Lottery Issues.' *Current Politics and Economics of the United States, Canada and Mexico* 14, nos 2–3: 239–53.

Wilson, J.H. 2019. *The Diversity Immigrant Visa Program.* CRS Report R45973. [Updated 15 October.] Washington, DC: Congressional Research Service. crsreports.congress.gov/product/pdf/R/R45973.

Woodward, J. 1992. 'Commentary: Liberalism and Migration.' In *Free Movement*, edited by B. Barry and R.E. Goodin. London: Routledge.

Wright, R. 2018. 'UK Hits Cap on Letting in Skilled Non-EU Migrants.' *Financial Times*, [London], 31 January.

Young, K.G. 2016. 'Rights and Queues: On Distributive Contests in the Modern State.' *Columbia Journal of Transnational Law* 55, no. 1: 65–137.

Part 3.
Recolonisation, siege mentalities and the myth of difference

6

The activation of the Temporary Protection Directive: The protection of non-Ukrainian displaced persons within a dichotomous EU asylum *acquis*

Clare McBride-Kelly

Introduction

On 4 March 2022, the Council of the European Union made the landmark decision to activate the Temporary Protection Directive (TPD) in response to the mass influx of persons into the European Union from Ukraine.[1] This decision has been widely celebrated in the international public discourse as the TPD provides displaced persons in mass influx situations with immediate group-based protection in the EU.[2]

---

1   *Council Implementing Decision (EU) 2022/382 of 4 March 2022 Establishing the Existence of a Mass Influx of Displaced Persons from Ukraine within the Meaning of Article 5 of Directive 2001/55/EC, and Having the Effect of Introducing Temporary Protection* [2022] OJ L 71/1, art. 2(1) [hereinafter *Implementing Decision*].
2   *Council Directive 2001/55/EC of 20 July 2001 on Minimum Standards for Giving Temporary Protection in the Event of a Mass Influx of Displaced Persons and on Measures Promoting a Balance of Efforts between Member States in Receiving Such Persons and Bearing the Consequences Thereof* [2001] OJ L 212/12 [hereinafter *TPD*].

However, the Implementing Decision narrowed the class of persons to whom the TPD applies from what was contemplated in the European Commission's proposal.[3] Crucially, the proposal extended temporary protection to all non-Ukrainian nationals 'residing legally in Ukraine … who are unable to return in safe and durable conditions to their country or region of origin'.[4] However, the Implementing Decision removed this class of non-Ukrainian nationals from the mandatory scope of beneficiaries, instead inserting an ambiguous provision, Article 2(2), which provides that EU member states

> shall apply either this Decision or *adequate protection under their national law* [to non-Ukrainian nationals] who can prove that they were legally residing in Ukraine … on the basis of a valid permanent residence permit … and who are unable to return in safe and durable conditions to their country or region of origin.[5]

More than 85 per cent of non-Ukrainian nationals who have entered the EU after fleeing Ukraine have African, Syrian or Afghan nationalities (see, for example, IOM 2022: 1).

The Visegrád Group—Hungary, Poland, Czechia and Slovakia—voiced their opposition to the commission's proposal (Reuters 2022). While the council must adopt a decision by qualified majority voting to activate the TPD,[6] the council chose to adopt the decision through unanimity voting. Commentators have thus inferred that the insertion of art. 2(2) into the Implementing Decision arose from concessions made to the Visegrád Group (Carrera et al. 2022: 11). Visegrád states have an enduring history of politicised racism (Tyler 2018: 1783, 1787) and have shown an aversion to providing protection to populations deemed culturally and linguistically different from their own.[7]

A critical concern is that the legally ambiguous language of 'adequate protection' could enable states to confer a lower standard of rights on non-Ukrainian nationals compared with Ukrainian nationals. Indeed, both Hungary and Poland have sought to justify the conferral of a lower standard

---

3   *Implementing Decision*, art. 2(1); *Proposal for a Council Implementing Decision* [2022] COMM(2022) 91 final, art. 2(1) [hereinafter *Commission Proposal*].

4   *Commission Proposal*, art. 2(1)(b).

5   *Implementing Decision*, art. 2(2).

6   *TPD*, art. 4(2).

7   *Slovak Republic and Hungary v. Council of the EU* (CJEU, C-643/15 and C-647/15, ECLI:EU: C:2017:618, 6 September 2017) [302] [hereinafter *Slovak Republic and Hungary v. Council*].

of rights on non-Ukrainian displaced persons by claiming they are conferring 'adequate protection' on them. This differentiation is particularly pertinent given the widescale reports of violence and discrimination directed towards non-Ukrainian nationals fleeing Ukraine (UN 2022).

Hungary and Poland's practice of conferring a lower standard of rights on non-Ukrainian displaced persons has occurred within the broader picture of the EU adopting contrasting responses to the influx of persons from Syria in 2015 and Ukraine in 2022 (Costello and Foster 2022: 244, 245). Policies of containment, externalisation and criminalisation underpinned the EU's response to the influx of persons from Syria in 2015, standing in stark contrast to the swift activation of the TPD in 2022 (de Boer and Zieck 2020: 54, 55).

This chapter considers two central questions raised by the activation of the TPD. First, what is required for 'adequate national protection' under EU law and does Hungary and Poland's purported implementation of adequate protection meet that standard? Second, how are we to understand the EU's contrasting responses to Ukrainian and non-Ukrainian displaced persons, evidenced both in the singling out of non-Ukrainians in art. 2(2) of the Implementing Decision and in the EU's failure to activate the TPD in 2015?

This chapter argues that while art. 2(2) was inserted into the Implementing Decision to attain the 'buy-in' of the Visegrád states, the correct interpretation of 'adequate protection', employing the teleological method of construction of the Court of Justice of the European Union (CJEU), requires member states to confer on non-Ukrainians the minimum standards in the TPD. Further, if a member state confers higher than the minimum standard of rights on Ukrainians, 'adequate protection' demands this higher standard be conferred on non-Ukrainian displaced persons. Thus, despite the apparent intentions of the Visegrád states to allow for superior rights to be afforded to Ukrainian nationals, this chapter argues that the correct interpretation of 'adequate protection' requires commensurate rights to be conferred on Ukrainian nationals and non-Ukrainian nationals captured by art. 2(2) of the Implementing Decision. This interpretative process reveals that Hungary and Poland's purported implementation of adequate protection is not adequate and hence not compatible with EU law.

Commentators have noted the ambiguity in the phrase 'adequate protection', however, no scholarship or jurisprudence to date construes this provision (Carrera et al. 2022: 13). This chapter fills a critical lacuna in the literature and provides a basis for strategic litigation advocating for the protection of non-Ukrainian displaced persons in compliance with EU law.

While the correct legal interpretation of 'adequate protection' requires commensurate rights to be conferred on Ukrainian and non-Ukrainian nationals, the insertion of art. 2(2) into the Implementing Decision, singling out non-Ukrainians, reflects the politics inherent in the EU asylum *acquis*. Member states have consolidated the 'myth of difference'— a concept expounded by B.S. Chimni (1998: 350, 351)—to justify the EU's contrasting responses to the mass influx of persons from Syria and Ukraine. This myth has been further constructed by the singling out of non-Ukrainians in the Implementing Decision. Echoing the title of this book, while the activation of the TPD was internationally celebrated as an innovative and progressive step forward for refugee protection in the EU, an in-depth analysis of the terms of the directive, its implementation— in particular, in the Visegrád states—and its inactivation in 2015 reflects persistent regression and discrimination within the EU asylum *acquis*.

While the TPD is shrouded in the politically neutral language of humanitarianism, it acts as a tool either of protection when it is activated or of containment when the European Council justifies its inactivation, dictated by the political interests of the EU. This results in a dichotomous EU border, prioritising persons deemed to have ideological value while dehumanising others, based not on their need for protection but solely on their 'fate of birth' and purported geopolitical value.

This chapter analyses the consequences of the activation of the TPD using the following structure. The first section situates the TPD within the European asylum *acquis* and examines the purported implementation of adequate protection in Hungary and Poland. Further, the abandonment of solidarity in 2015 is examined, elucidating why the council chose to employ unanimity voting to activate the TPD, making concessions to the Visegrád Group. The second section adopts doctrinal methodology, employing the CJEU's method of interpretation to construe the phrase 'adequate protection under their national law'[8] contained in Article 2(2) of the Implementing Decision. In accordance with the hierarchy of norms

8   *TPD*, art. 2(2).

in EU law, art. 2(2) is construed in the spirit of the TPD, the inviolable right to human dignity and principles of non-discrimination law. Three sources of non-discrimination law are drawn on: Article 21 of the Charter of Fundamental Rights, the general principle of equal treatment in EU law and the non-discrimination provision contained in Article 3 of the *Convention Relating to the Status of Refugees*. The final section turns to a theoretical analysis, employing Third-World approaches to international law methodology to analyse the EU's construction of a dichotomous border. This section examines both the EU's failure to activate the TPD in response to the mass influx of Syrian persons in 2015 and the singling out of non-Ukrainians in the Implementing Decision in 2022.

Situating the activation of the TPD: The legal and political context

This section situates the TPD within the EU asylum *acquis* and examines its activation in 2022. Before interpreting art. 2(2) of the Implementing Decision, it is necessary to consider why the EU used unanimity voting to activate the TPD, making concessions to the Visegrád Group. Against the backdrop of the dual crisis of asylum and constitutional governance in 2015, I argue that the European Council chose to employ unanimity voting to restore the EU's integrationist project, re-engaging states' commitment to the Common European Asylum System (CEAS).

The TPD and the EU asylum *acquis*

The EU must act within the limits of competencies conferred on it by member states through treaties to achieve treaty objectives, and competencies not given to the EU remain with the member states.[9] A core objective of the EU is to offer citizens 'an area of freedom, security and justice without internal borders', allowing for the free movement of persons alongside 'measures with respect to external border controls, asylum and immigration'.[10] Both the EU and national governments may legislate in this area as it is of shared competence,[11] however, member states can only

---

9   *Treaty on European Union*, Opened for Signature 7 February 1992, [2009] OJ C 115/13 (Entered into Force 1 November 1993) art. 5(1)–5(2) [hereinafter *TEU*].
10   Ibid., art. 3(2).
11   *Treaty on the Functioning of the European Union*, Opened for Signature 7 February 1992, [2009] OJ C 155/199 (Entered into Force 1 November 1993) art. 4(2)(j) [hereinafter *TFEU*].

exercise their competence to the extent that the EU has not exercised its competence.[12] The development of the CEAS is one means through which the EU has exercised its competence in this field, with Article 78 of the *Treaty on the Functioning of the European Union* (*TFEU*) requiring the EU to develop 'a common policy on asylum, subsidiary protection and temporary protection' in accordance with the Refugee Convention.[13] The TPD falls within the CEAS, providing for an EU-wide model of temporary protection in circumstances of a mass influx of displaced persons.[14]

The TPD is activated when the council, on a proposal by the European Commission, adopts a decision by qualified majority voting (QMV) establishing the existence of a mass influx.[15] QMV requires 55 per cent of member states to vote in favour of a decision supported by states accounting for at least 65 per cent of the population of the EU (Rosas and Armati 2010: 82). A mass influx situation is defined as the arrival in the EU of 'a large number of displaced persons, who came from a specific country or geographical area'.[16]

Once the TPD is activated, member states must provide the directive's beneficiaries with residence permits and authorise them to engage in employed or self-employed activities.[17] Member states are further obliged to ensure beneficiaries have access to suitable accommodation, necessary assistance in terms of social welfare and means of subsistence, and access to medical care, which at a minimum includes emergency care and essential treatment of illness.[18] Beneficiaries under the age of 18 must be granted access to education on the same basis as nationals of the host state.[19] The duration of temporary protection is one year, which can be extended for a maximum of three years.[20] On 10 October 2022, the European Commission extended the TPD until March 2024 (Genovese 2022).

12 Ibid., art. 2(2).
13 Ibid., art. 78(1); Rosas and Armati (2010: 166).
14 *TPD*.
15 Ibid., art. 5(2).
16 Ibid., art. 2(d).
17 Ibid., arts. 8(1), 12.
18 Ibid., art. 13(1)–(3).
19 Ibid., art. 14 (1).
20 Ibid., art. 4(1)–(2).

Implementation of 'adequate protection'

In this chapter, I use the term 'non-Ukrainian nationals' to describe the class of persons captured by art. 2(2) of the Implementing Decision—namely, non-Ukrainian nationals who were living on a permanent residence permit in Ukraine and were unable to return to their country or region of origin in safe and durable conditions.[21] At the time of writing, Hungary and Poland are the only member states purporting to confer adequate protection on non-Ukrainian nationals (UNHCR 2022b: 2).

On 7 March 2022, the Hungarian Government introduced *Government Decree No. 86/2022*, applying the temporary protection scheme to Ukrainian nationals, persons benefiting from international protection in Ukraine and their family members.[22] Under this scheme, these classes of persons are conferred residence permits for one year and are entitled to all the rights expounded in the TPD.[23]

The decree is silent on the position of non-Ukrainian nationals who had not formally applied for international protection in Ukraine but nonetheless cannot return 'in safe and durable conditions'[24] to their country of origin. However, the UNHCR and Hungarian Helsinki Committee report that border guards are providing non-Ukrainian nationals with certificates for temporary stays (Hungarian Helsinki Committee 2022; UNHCR 2022a). These certificates entitle holders to legally reside in Hungary for 30 days, which can be extended for 'a maximum of 3 months at each occasion' (Hungarian Helsinki Committee 2022; European Council 2013). Persons holding such a certificate are conferred minimal rights, entitling them to remain in Hungary and access emergency health care and schooling for minors. According to the Hungarian Helsinki Committee (2022), this document does not give holders a right to 'any other type of assistance from the Hungarian state', including social welfare, family reunification or permission to engage in employed or self-employed activities. Further, there is no obligation on the Hungarian Government to ensure certificate holders have access to accommodation or means to obtain housing.

---

21 *Implementing Decision*, art. 2(2).
22 Hungarian Helsinki Committee, *Government Decree No. 86/2022*, [Hungary], Gazette No. 44 of 2022, 7 March 2022, Section 1, Unofficial translation, 8 March 2022, helsinki.hu/en/wp-content/uploads/sites/2/2022/03/HUgovdecree_implementing_councildecision_tempprotEN.pdf, art. 2(2) [hereinafter *Government Decree No. 86/2022*].
23 Ibid., ss. 6–7.
24 *Implementing Decision*, art. 2(2).

Poland adopted the *Special Act on Assistance to Ukrainian Nationals* on 12 March 2022, providing Ukrainian nationals full access to the labour market, healthcare system, social benefits and education for minors on the same basis as Polish nationals.[25] All non-Ukrainians are excluded from the scope of the Act, instead receiving a certificate of temporary protection.[26]

While the rights conferred on non-Ukrainian nationals in Poland are higher than the rights granted under Hungarian law, differentiation remains between Ukrainians and non-Ukrainians (Morales 2022). Holders of a certificate of temporary protection are permitted to remain in Poland for one year and have a right to work and to access accommodation, family reunification, education for minors and medical care.[27] However, while Ukrainian nationals are granted full access to the social welfare system (Office for Foreigners 2022), non-Ukrainian nationals may merely apply for a 'one-off cash payment' if they decide to live outside the Centre for Foreigners (Republic of Poland 2022b; EUAA 2022: 14). Further, while Ukrainians are entitled to access free state medical care under 'the same conditions as Polish citizens' (Office for Foreigners 2022), non-Ukrainians may only access basic medical care via the Office for Foreigners (Republic of Poland 2022a). The Special Rapporteur on the human rights of migrants Felipe González Morales has called on the Polish Government to cease 'the double standards' in legal entitlements conferred on Ukrainians and non-Ukrainians fleeing the same war (Morales 2022: 2).

Consensus-based voting: The shadow of the 2015 constitutional crisis

The European Council's decision to employ consensus-based voting to activate the TPD, making concessions to the Visegrád Group, must be understood against the backdrop of the dual crises of asylum and constitutional governance in 2015, marked by states' abandonment of solidarity (Byrne et al. 2020: 871).

---

25 At the time of writing there is no English translation of this Act. I have relied on the Polish Government's English-language summary of the Act in Office for Foreigners (2022).
26 *Act of 13th of June 2003 on Granting Protection to Aliens within the Territory of the Republic of Poland* (Poland) Journal of Laws of 2003 No. 128 item 1176, 13 June 2003 [hereinafter *Act on Granting Protection to Aliens*]; Republic of Poland (2022c).
27 *Act on Granting Protection to Aliens*, art. 112–17.

In *Slovak Republic and Hungary v. Council of the EU*, Advocate-General Bott highlights that 'solidarity is a founding and existential value of the Union, at the heart of the process of integration'.[28] Article 2 of the *Treaty on European Union* enshrines solidarity as a fundamental value of the EU, and art. 3(2) holds that the EU shall promote solidarity 'among generations … and between Member States'.[29] While the concept of solidarity lacks a single definitive meaning, in the context of migration policies, art. 80 of the *TFEU* indicates that the principle of solidarity requires 'the fair sharing of responsibility' between member states.[30]

In 2015, in response to the arrival in the EU of 1.3 million people from Syria, Afghanistan and Iraq, states adopted siloed self-help measures to insulate themselves from flows of protection seekers (Byrne et al. 2020: 873; Clayton and Holland 2015). As Morano-Foadi (2017: 223, 225) argues, the adoption of unilateral measures challenged the 'integrity of the whole EU project' as states abandoned EU-wide solidarity in pursuit of individual self-interest.

Frontier states undermined their commitment under the Dublin Regulation—which generally dictates that the country in which an asylum seeker first enters the EU is responsible for processing their asylum claim[31]—instead 'waving them through' at border posts (Armstrong 2020: 332, 337). Responsibility-sharing was further undermined by states reasserting internal borders to inhibit entry of asylum flows, constructing legal and physical barriers across the EU (Armstrong 2020: 335).

As highlighted by Byrne et al. (2020: 873), the events of 2015 started as a crisis of asylum and transpired into a constitutional crisis. The proliferation of internal borders not only struck at the heart of solidarity but also undermined EU citizens' fundamental rights to free movement (Byrne et al. 2020: 873). This revealed the fragility of the 1985 Schengen Agreement, which guarantees EU citizens' enjoyment of the fundamental rights to the

---

28   *Slovak Republic and Hungary v. Council of the EU* (Opinion of Advocate-General Bott in the CJEU, C-643/15 and C-647/15, ECLI:EU:C:2017:618, 6 September 2017) [18]–[20] [hereinafter *AG: Slovak Republic v. Council*].

29   *TEU*, arts. 2, 3(2).

30   *TFEU*, art. 80.

31   *Regulation (EC) 604/2013 of 29 June 2013 Establishing the Criteria and Mechanisms for Determining the Member State Responsible for Examining an Application for International Protection Lodged in One of the Member States by a Third-Country National or a Stateless Person (Recast)* [2013] OJ L180/31, art. 13(1).

free movement of goods, persons, services and capital.[32] Lengthy queues at border crossings undermined free movement, with the cost to businesses estimated to have reached €18 billion (Dennison and Pardijis 2016: 3–4).

Member states' abandonment of solidary was further reflected in the failure of the emergency relocation decisions (Marin et al. 2020: 1, 5) that, passed through QMV, established a quota system for the mandatory relocation of 160,000 asylum seekers from Greece and Italy across the EU.[33] Only two EU member states, Ireland and Malta, met their relocation targets, with a mere 20,000 asylum seekers relocated by the end of 2017 (EC 2017: 2). Strikingly, the Visegrád states voted against the relocation decisions, with Czechia relocating just 12 asylum seekers, while Hungary and Poland offered no relocation positions.[34] As argued by Advocate-General Bott in *Slovak Republic and Hungary v. Council*, the failure of states to uphold their quota obligations demonstrates 'the crisis of the European integration project', which is underpinned by solidarity between member states.[35]

This notion is supported by Goldner Lang (2020: 39, 49), who contends that the violation by member states of asylum law in 2015 symbolised a process of 'EU disintegration'. Goldner Lang draws on the concepts of 'exit' and 'voice' as conceived by Hershman and developed in the European context by Weiler (Weiler 1990: 2403, 2411; Hershman 1970). 'Voice' refers to 'the mechanism of interorganisational correction' (Weiler 1990: 2411), which, in the EU context, is member states' capacity to protect their interests during decision-making processes (Goldner Lang 2020: 49). 'Exit' refers to 'the mechanism of organisational abandonment in the face of unsatisfactory performance', with the United Kingdom's exit from the EU in 2020 reflecting a 'complete exit' (Weiler 1990: 2411; Goldner Lang 2020: 49). Where states have a stronger outlet for 'voice' this reduces pressure on 'exit', while 'the closure of exit leads to demands for enhanced voice' (Weiler 1990: 2411). Goldner Lang (2020: 49) posits that in 2015

---

32   *Convention Implementing the Schengen Agreement of 14 June 1985* [22 September 2000] OJ L239.
33   *Council Decision (EU) 2015/1523 of 14 September 2015 Establishing Provisional Measures in the Area of International Protection for the Benefit of Italy and of Greece* [2015] OJ L 239/136 [hereinafter *Council Decision 2015/1523*]; *Council Decision (EU) 2015/1601 of 22 September 2015 Establishing Provisional Measures in the Area of International Protection for the Benefit of Italy and Greece* [2015] OJ L 248/80 [hereinafter *Council Decision 2015/1601*].
34   *European Commission v. Republic of Poland and Others* (CJEU, C-715/17, C718/17 and C-719-17, ECLI:EU:C:2020:257, 2 April 2020) [24]–[25].
35   *AG: Slovak Republic v. Council*, 3.

Visegrád states experienced reduced 'voice' as the relocation decisions were adopted through QMV, hence they sought to 'selectively exit' the EU, retaining membership while avoiding EU obligations.

The events of 2015 highlighted that states must collectively engage with the CEAS to protect the fundamental values of solidarity and free movement on which the EU project relies. Against this backdrop, the council's decision to use consensus-based voting to activate the TPD was likely made to restore the EU's integrationist project by re-engaging member states' commitment to the CEAS. This decision could reflect a broader move within EU governance towards unanimity voting on matters concerning the CEAS.

Buy-in from the Visegrád Group was crucial as they border Ukraine. Visegrád states have shown an aversion to protecting non-European refugees.[36] In *Slovak Republic and Hungary v. Council*, Hungary, Poland and Slovakia sought to nullify the 2015 emergency relocation decisions, arguing that receiving Syrian refugees would 'disproportionally burden' their 'ethnically homogeneous societies'.[37] The CJEU dismissed this argument, holding that the ethnic origin of protection seekers cannot be considered in relocation decisions, as this would be contrary to the non-discrimination provision contained in Article 21 of the Charter of Fundamental Rights.[38] The Visegrád states' opposition to non-European refugees occurred alongside a rise in populist nationalist parties which asserted a connection between migration and the destabilisation of public order, terrorism and loss of national culture (Byrne et al. 2020: 880).

It can hence be inferred that the Visegrád states may have advocated for the insertion of art. 2(2) into the Implementing Decision to enable a lower standard of rights to be conferred on non-Ukrainian nationals who have fled Ukraine. However, as the next section will explore, the CJEU's interpretation of 'adequate protection' would require non-Ukrainians to be conferred rights commensurate to Ukrainians.

---

36 *Slovak Republic and Hungary v. Council,* [302].
37 Ibid., [302].
38 Ibid., [305].

Interpreting the directive: A doctrinal analysis

In accordance with the spirit of the TPD, the inviolable right to human dignity and principles of non-discrimination, the CJEU would construe 'adequate protection'[39] to require Ukrainian and non-Ukrainian nationals to be afforded commensurate rights. Article 2(2) may come before the CJEU for construction if the European Commission or a member state brings direct proceedings alleging Hungary and Poland are failing to fulfil an obligation under the Implementing Decision.[40] Alternatively, a national court may refer the interpretation of the phrase 'adequation protection' to the CJEU, with the national court subsequently determining whether national law complies with EU law.[41]

The scope of this analysis is limited to art. 2(2), as this provision includes the legally ambiguous terminology of 'adequate protection',[42] thus this chapter applies to non-Ukrainian nationals who had a permanent residence visa in Ukraine and cannot return in safe and durable conditions to their country of origin. Article 2(3) of the Implementing Decisions stipulates that states 'may apply' temporary protection to non-Ukrainian nationals legally residing in Ukraine who did *not* hold a permanent residence permit and cannot return to their country of origin.[43] While the non-discrimination analysis is likely equally applicable to this class of non-Ukrainians, a complete analysis of art. 2(3) lies outside the scope of this chapter.

The CJEU's method of construction

1. The teleological approach

As outlined by the CJEU in *Merck v. Hauptzollamt Hamburg-Jonas*, when interpreting a provision of EU law, the court considers 'not only its wording but also the context in which it occurs and the objects of the rules of which it is part'.[44] Linguistic arguments are inherently limited in the CJEU due to the multilingual nature of EU law (Ceruti 2019: 253, 265).

---

39 *Implementing Decision*, art. 2(2).
40 *TFEU*, arts. 258–59.
41 Ibid., art. 267.
42 Ibid., art. 2(2).
43 Ibid., art. 2(3).
44 *Merck v. Hauptzollamt Hamburg-Jonas* (CJEU, C-292/82, ECLI:EU:C:1983:335, 17 November 1983) [12] [hereinafter *Merck*].

Writing extrajudicially, Koen Lenaerts (2007: 1011, 1016), President of the Court of Justice, posits that the teleological method of interpretation commands a prominent place in the CJEU, with the court seeking to adopt the interpretation of a provision that 'best serves the purpose' for which the overall instrument was made. It is not only the *telos* of the rules that the court considers but also the 'telos of the legal context in which those rules exist' (Poiares Pessoa Maduro 2007: 137, 140), with the court seeking to resolve legal ambiguity in a manner that furthers the European integrationist project (Lenaerts 2007: 1030).

2. The hierarchy of norms

There is a hierarchy of norms within the EU legal order, with the Implementing Decision, as a form of secondary EU law, sitting at the bottom of the hierarchy (Rosas and Armati 2010: 41). It thus must be interpreted in accordance with the values of the EU, the general principles of EU law, the EU's constituent treaties, the Charter of Fundamental Rights, international agreements binding on the EU and general international law (Rosas and Armati 2010: 41). Within the purview of secondary EU law, implementing acts fall below legislative and delegated acts (Craig and de Búrca 2015: 117; Rosas and Armati 2010: 50), hence the Implementing Decision must also be interpreted in light of the TPD, which is a legislative act.[45]

The spirit of the TPD

The CJEU determines the overall 'spirit' of instruments by considering the 'design and purpose of the instrument and the effect which it sought to achieve', construing an ambiguous provision to produce this desired effect.[46] As demonstrated in *Van Gend & Loose v. Netherlands Inland Revenue*, to elucidate an instrument's spirit, the CJEU draws on the instrument's preamble, objectives and general scheme in a non-hierarchical manner.[47]

Article 1 of the TPD stipulates that the 'purpose of this Directive is to establish minimum standards for giving temporary protection in the event of a mass influx of displaced persons from third countries who are unable to return to their country of origin'.[48] Emphasis is placed on the fact that

---

45 *TPD*.
46 *NV Algemene Transport- en Expeditie Onderneming van Gend & Loos v. Netherlands Inland Revenue Administration* (CJEU, C-26/62, ECLI:EU:C:1963:1, 5 February 1963) [12].
47 *Merck*, [12].
48 *TPD*, art. 1.

displaced persons are 'unable to return to their country of origin',[49] making no distinctions based on their nationality. Likewise, the definition of a 'mass influx' refers to the arrival of 'a large number of displaced persons … from a specific country or geographical area'[50] and hence does not distinguish between displaced persons' nationalities. This indicates that the spirit of the TPD is to confer a minimum standard of protection on displaced persons in mass influx situations who have come from a specific country, regardless of their nationality.

The TPD's second objective is to 'promote a balance of efforts between Member States' in receiving displaced persons.[51] This objective is linked to the preambular statement that the TPD introduces minimum standards to 'avert the risk of secondary movements' across the EU.[52] If adequate protection consisted of a lower standard of rights than the minimum standard contained in the TPD, non-Ukrainian nationals would be incentivised to move across the EU into states which have chosen under Article 2(2) to extend temporary protection to them. This would therefore undermine the purpose of the TPD to mitigate secondary movements.

Imbued throughout the TPD is a further objective of militating against 'overwhelming national asylum systems' in mass influx situations. The preamble states that the directive benefits member states by limiting 'the need for displaced persons to seek international protection'.[53] To meet this objective, there is a high degree of consistency between the rights conferred on refugees under the Qualifications Directive, and beneficiaries of the TPD, such that there is no immediate need for displaced persons to seek international protection.[54] If adequate protection allowed a lower threshold of rights to be conferred on non-Ukrainians, this would encourage them to apply for international protection, undermining the spirit of the TPD.

The spirit of the TPD thus indicates that 'adequate protection' must be construed to require the member states to extend the minimum standards contained in the TPD to non-Ukrainian nationals. This conclusion is

---

49   Ibid.
50   Ibid., art. 2(d).
51   Ibid., art. 1.
52   Ibid., Preamble, para. 9.
53   *Implementing Decision*, Preamble, para. 16.
54   *Directive 2011/95/EU on Standards for the Qualification of Third-Country Nationals or Stateless Persons as Beneficiaries of International Protection, for a Uniform Status for Refugees or for Persons Eligible for Subsidiary Protection and for the Content of the Protection Granted (Recast)* [2011] OJ L 337/9 [hereinafter *Qualifications Directive*]; *TPD*, art. 1.

consistent with a statement made in the commission's proposal, stipulating that 'to respect the spirit' of the TPD, member states should extend temporary protection to all non-Ukrainian nationals who cannot return to their country of origin.[55]

Human dignity and the Charter of Fundamental Rights

The CJEU interprets EU law in accordance with the Charter of Fundamental Rights, which is a legally binding instrument elevated to the same status as EU treaties after the entry into force of the *Treaty of Lisbon* on 1 December 2009.[56] Article 1 of the charter provides that 'human dignity is inviolable'.[57] *Cimade, Gisti v. Ministre de l'Intérieur* (hereinafter *Cimade*) reflects the instructive role that human dignity plays in the CJEU's interpretation of directives within the CEAS.[58]

In *Cimade*, the French Council of State referred the interpretation of the Reception Conditions Directive to the CJEU.[59] In this directive, the minimum reception conditions afforded to asylum seekers in the EU are the rights to housing, food, clothing, health care, education for minors and access to employment within nine months.[60] The critical question was whether member states were required to grant these minimum standards to an asylum seeker for whom the member state decided, pursuant to the Dublin Regulation, to call on another member state to examine the asylum application.[61] The CJEU held that to respect the fundamental right to human dignity, the Reception Conditions Directive must be construed to oblige member states to confer the minimum standards on all asylum seekers on its territory, including those for whom a member state decides that another

---

55 *Commission Proposal*, 7.

56 *Treaty of Lisbon Amending the Treaty on European Union and the Treaty Establishing the European Community*, Opened for Signature 13 December 2007, [2007] OJ C 306/1 (Entered into Force 1 December 2009) art. 6(1).

57 *Charter of Fundamental Rights of the European Union*, [2000] OJ C 326/392, art. 1 [hereinafter *Charter of Fundamental Rights*].

58 *Cimade, Group d'information et de soutien des immigrés (GISTI) v. Ministre de l'Intérieur, de l'Outre-mer, des Collectivités territoriales et de l'Immigration* (CJEU, C-179/11, ECLI:EU:C:2012:594, 27 September 2012) [hereinafter *Cimade*].

59 *Council Directive 2003/9/EC of 27 January 2003 Laying Down Minimum Standards for the Reception of Asylum Seekers* [2003] OJ L 31/18.

60 Ibid., Ch. II, arts. 7–15.

61 *Cimade*, [36].

state is responsible for processing their application.[62] This obligation only ceases when the transfer of the asylum seeker to the responsible member state occurs.[63]

The present matter is highly analogous to *Cimade*, as both the TPD and the Reception Conditions Directive contain minimum standards of protection for displaced persons. Further, both directives stipulate that they 'respect the fundamental rights recognised by the Charter'.[64] The reasoning in *Cimade* demonstrates the importance the CJEU places on ensuring human dignity is upheld for all third-country nationals whom CEAS directives capture. Following this approach, the CJEU would hold that to respect the right to human dignity, the minimum standards expounded in the TPD must be extended to all persons whom the Implementing Decision captures, including non-Ukrainians unable to return to their country of origin. Indeed, the rights in the Reception Conditions Directive mirror the minimum standards within the TPD, indicating that the latter are necessary to constitute a 'dignified standard of living'.[65]

Non-discrimination

Thus far, the interpretative process has revealed that adequate protection requires member states to confer on non-Ukrainians *at least* the minimum standards within the TPD. The critical question raised is what 'adequate protection' requires when a member state, pursuant to art. 3(5) of the TPD,[66] opts to confer higher than the minimum standards on Ukrainian nationals. The following non-discrimination analysis is instructive in demonstrating that adequate protection requires commensurate rights to be conferred on Ukrainian and non-Ukrainian nationals.

Multiple sources require the CJEU to construe secondary EU law consistent with the principle of non-discrimination. First, all EU acts must be interpreted in accordance with the general principle of equal treatment, drawn from the constitutional traditions of member states.[67] Second, the

---

62   Ibid., [50].
63   Ibid., [55].
64   *TPD*, art. 3(2).
65   *Cimade*, [61].
66   *TPD*, art. 3(5).
67   *Christopher Sturgeon, Gabriel Sturgeon and Alana Sturgeon v. Condor Flugdienst GmbH* (C-402/07) and *Stefan Böck and Cornelia Lepuschitz v Air France SA* (C-432/07) (ECLI:EU:C:2009:716, 19 November 2009) [48] [hereinafter *Sturgeon*].

charter prohibits discrimination including on the basis of nationality.[68] While the orthodox view was that this provision prohibited discrimination between EU citizens,[69] recent jurisprudence affirms the court's openness to invoking considerations of non-discrimination between two classes of non-EU nationals.[70] Indeed, Lenaerts (2014: 1) argues that equal treatment has 'grown out of its internal market origins' and now pervades the entire body of EU law, 'standing at the apex of the hierarchy of norms'. Third, art. 78 of the *TFEU* provides that the TPD must be developed in accordance with the Refugee Convention.[71] In compliance with the hierarchy of norms, the TPD must be interpreted in accordance with the *TFEU*, necessitating consideration of Article 3 of the Refugee Convention, which prohibits discrimination among refugees.[72]

As outlined by the CJEU, the principle of equal treatment stipulates that 'comparable situations must not be treated differently ... unless such treatment is objectively justifiable' and is proportionate to the aim pursued.[73] This test mirrors the non-discrimination test applicable within art. 3 of the Refugee Convention (Hathaway 2021: 26).

Are Ukrainian and non-Ukrainian nationals in comparable positions?

Ukrainian nationals and the class of non-Ukrainians in question are in comparable positions. Both have suffered comparable harm in needing to flee Ukraine due to the Russian invasion and cannot return in safe and durable conditions to Ukraine. Further, both Ukrainian nationals and the class of non-Ukrainian nationals in question cannot return in 'safe and durable conditions' to their country of nationality.[74] It is inferred that the reference in art. 2(2) to 'country of origin' is to non-Ukrainian nationals'

---

68   *Charter of Fundamental Rights*, art. 21(1)–(2).
69   *Athanasios Vatsouras and Josif Koupatantze v.* Arbeitsgemeinschaft (CJEU, C-22/08 and C-23/08, ECLI:EU:C:2009:344, 4 June 2009) [52] [hereinafter *Vatsouras*].
70   See, for example, *Kreis Warendorf v. Ibrahim Alo and Amira Osso v. Region Hannover* (CJEU, C-443/14 and C-444/14, ECLI:EU:C:2016:127, 1 March 2016) 54.
71   *TFEU*, art. 78.
72   *Convention Relating to the Status of Refugees*, Opened for Signature 28 July 1951, 189 UNTS 150 (Entered into Force 22 April 1954) art. 1A, as amended by the *Protocol Relating to the Status of Refugees*, Opened for Signature 31 January 1967, 606 UNTS 267 (Entered into Force 4 October 1967) art. 3 [hereinafter *Refugee Convention*].
73   *Wolfgang v. Freistaat* (CJEU, C-356/12, ECLI:EU:C:2014:350, 22 May 2014) [43] [hereinafter *Wolfgang*].
74   *Implementing Decision*, art. 2(2).

country of nationality, as it is a necessary assumption of the Implementing Decision that persons cannot return to Ukraine. This is consistent with the definition of 'country of origin' in the Qualifications Directive.[75]

The TPD explicitly acknowledges that persons falling within the scope of the directive may fall within the scope of the Refugee Convention.[76] The reference to non-Ukrainians unable to return in 'safe and durable conditions' echoes terminology used in the voluntary repatriation of refugees 'in safety and in dignity' (UNGA 2018: 3.1), indicating that the class of non-Ukrainians captured by art. 2(2) may meet the art. 1A(2) definition of a refugee in the Refugee Convention.[77] Indeed, 69 per cent of non-Ukrainians who entered Germany from Ukraine had Ghanaian or Nigerian nationality, with the remainder having Syrian, Sudanese or Afghan nationalities—countries widely recognised as refugee-producing (IOM 2022: 1).

Is differentiation objectively justifiable?

There is no objective ground capable of justifying the conclusion that 'adequate protection' allows for a lower standard of protection to be conferred on non-Ukrainian nationals unable to return to their country of origin.

CJEU case law indicates that member states may legitimately differentiate between EU and non-EU citizens,[78] however, the matter at hand concerns two categories of non-EU citizens. While Ukraine has applied to join the EU, this process will take years to finalise (BBC News 2022), and hence does not provide a justifiable basis on which to differentiate between the protection provided to Ukrainian and non-Ukrainian nationals fleeing Ukraine.

It could be argued that Ukrainian citizens enjoy a special legal status in the EU, as they are entitled to travel in the EU for 90 days in a 180-day period.[79] However, in the context of displaced persons fleeing the Russian invasion, Ukrainian nationals having access to this generous holiday visa is not an objectively justifiable reason to confer less protection on persons

---

75 *Qualifications Directive*, art. 2(n).
76 *TPD*, art. 2(c).
77 *Refugee Convention*, art. 1A(2).
78 *Vatsouras*, [52].
79 *Regulation EU 2018/1806 of the European Parliament and the Council Listing the Third-Country Nationals Who Must Be In Possession of Visas When Crossing the External Borders and Those Whose Nationals Are Exempt* [2018] OJ L303/39, art. 4(1).

who do not have access to this visa. Indeed, this visa is issued on the basis that Ukrainian nationals will leave the EU and return to Ukraine after 90 days and hence is not relevant to considerations of the protection of displaced persons.

Consistent with the argument raised in *Slovak Republic and Hungary v. Council*, member states may posit that 'adequate protection' entails a lower standard of protection to disincentivise non-Ukrainians from remaining in these states, as protecting non-Ukrainians 'disproportionally burdens' their 'ethnically homogeneous' societies.[80] Should such a spurious argument be again made, this would be given short shrift by the CJEU as manifestly discriminatory and not a legitimate justification for less protection to be provided to non-Ukrainians.[81]

Proportionality

If differentiation is found to be based on an objective justification, the principle of equal treatment demands that the differentiation must be proportionate to the aim pursued.[82] In *Saidoun v. Greece*, the European Court of Human Rights held that Greek authorities denying a family allowance to an Iraqi refugee contravened the principle of equal treatment, stipulating that 'only very strong reasons' could lead the court to conclude that a difference in treatment exclusively based on nationality is proportionate.[83] The CJEU draws on the jurisprudence of the European Court of Human Rights, particularly in the field of non-discrimination law (Craig and de Búrca 2015: 935). There appears to be no objective ground justifying a lower standard of rights being conferred on non-Ukrainian nationals unable to return to their country of origin and, even if a justification was accepted by the CJEU, it is unlikely to meet the high standard of a 'very strong reason'[84] for differentiation.

---

80   *Slovak Republic and Hungary v. Council*, [302].
81   Ibid., [305].
82   *Wolfgang*, [43].
83   *Saidoun v. Greece* (European Court of Human Rights, Application No. 40083/07, 28 October 2010) [30].
84   Ibid., [30].

Applying Article 3 of the 1951 Refugee Convention

As the class of non-Ukrainian nationals in question may meet the art. 1A(2) definition of a refugee, this necessitates consideration of art. 3 of the 1951 Refugee Convention.[85] Refugee status determination is declarative, not constitutive, hence a person meeting the definition of a refugee is a refugee even before formal recognition (Hathaway 2021: 80). The need to consider art. 3 is reinforced by the *TFEU* holding that the TPD must be developed in accordance with the Refugee Convention.[86] The critical strength of art. 3 as an interpretative tool is that it explicitly prohibits discrimination among classes of refugees on the basis of 'race, religion or country of origin'.[87]

While nationality is not an enumerated ground for non-discrimination, eminent jurists argue that art. 3 is non-exhaustive and its parameters must be understood in light of the non-discrimination provisions in the *International Covenant on Civil and Political Rights* (*ICCPR*).[88] Crucially, Article 26 of the *ICCPR* prohibits any discrimination including on the basis of 'race, colour … national or social origin',[89] with General Comment 18 of the UN Human Rights Committee holding that this article prohibits discrimination in 'any field regulated and protected by public authorities'.[90] Thus, the non-discrimination provision is not textually limited and, when read in light of the *ICCPR*, it encompasses a prohibition of discrimination between refugees based on nationality (Hathaway 2021: 286; Marx and Staff 2011: 648).

While there is limited jurisprudence on art. 3, Hathaway (2021: 113) posits that it is necessary to consider whether there is 'a real difference in need' between the two classes of persons. Here, there is no justifiable basis to hold that Ukrainians need a higher standard of rights than non-Ukrainians, as both groups had to flee Ukraine and cannot return to their country of nationality. This reinforces the conclusion that 'adequate protection' cannot be construed to allow differential treatment between Ukrainian and non-Ukrainian refugees.

---

85 *Refugee Convention*, art. 3.
86 *TFEU*, art. 78.
87 *Refugee Convention*, art. 3.
88 *International Covenant on Civil and Political Rights*, Opened for Signature 16 December 1966, 999 UNTS 171 (Entered into Force 23 March 1976) [hereinafter *ICCPR*]; Hathaway (2021: 286); Marx and Staff (2011: 654).
89 *ICCPR*, art. 26.
90 Human Rights Committee, *General Comment No. 18: Non-Discrimination*, 37th session (10 November 1989) 3 [12].

Non-discrimination conclusion

This analysis reveals that any differentiation in rights conferred on Ukrainian and non-Ukrainian nationals unable to return to their country of origin would constitute unlawful discrimination. Thus, in accordance with the general principle of equal treatment, Article 21 of the Charter of Fundamental Rights and Article 3 of the Refugee Convention, the CJEU must construe adequate protection to require member states to confer commensurate rights on Ukrainian and non-Ukrainian nationals.

This conclusion is consistent with the Advocate-General's view in *LW v. Bundesrepublik Deutschland*, which concerned an interpretation of the Qualifications Directive.[91] This critical CEAS instrument sets out the rights afforded to refugees and beneficiaries of subsidiary protection.[92] Crucially, this directive contains a provision mirroring art. 3(5) of the TPD, enabling states to confer on protection seekers 'more favourable conditions' than the minimum standards within the directive.[93] The advocate-general in this matter noted that member states' discretion to provide 'more favourable treatment' to protection seekers allows states to raise the minimum standards for all protection seekers on their territory, as exercise of this discretion 'cannot result in a breach of equal treatment'.[94] This indicates that the 'more favourable' standards provision in art. 3(5) of the TPD similarly permits states to raise protection standards for all displaced persons captured by the Implementing Decision, and does not allow for differentiation between classes of persons in comparable positions.

Interpretative outcome

Conferring a lower standard of protection on non-Ukrainian nationals would be inconsistent with the spirit of the TPD, the inviolable right to human dignity and fundamental principles of non-discrimination. As outlined in *Zoi Chatzi v. Ypourgos Oikonomikon*, the CJEU will interpret a community measure 'as far as possible in such a way as to not affect its validity and in compliance with primary EU law'.[95] Thus, while 'adequate

---

91   *LW v. Bundesrepublik Deutschland* (Opinion of Advocate-General, C-91/20, ECLI:EU:C:2021:384, 12 May 2021) [85] [hereinafter *LW*].
92   *Qualifications Directive.*
93   Ibid., art. 3; *TPD*, art. 3(5).
94   *LW*, [85].
95   *Zoi Chatzi v. Ypourgos Oikonomikon* (CJEU, C-149/10, ECLI:EU:C:2010:534, 16 September 2010) [43].

protection' in ordinary language appears to connote a lower standard of protection, when read in the context of the EU hierarchy of norms, the CJEU would construe 'adequate protection' to require commensurate rights to be conferred on Ukrainian and non-Ukrainian nationals.

Hungary and Poland are likely to argue, first, that this outcome is inconsistent with their drafting intention, and second, that it disregards the textual distinction between 'adequate' and 'temporary' protection drawn in art. 2(2).[96]

However, the CJEU gives limited, if any, consideration to drafting history when interpreting secondary law, due to difficulties in determining the collective intention of all member states (Lenaerts and Gutiérrez-Fons 2013: 20–22). Indeed, the CJEU has consistently held that preparatory work 'cannot be used for the purpose of interpreting secondary acts' where no reference is made to the content of the drafting history in the provision, as it therefore 'has no legal significance'.[97] Instead, the court presumes the drafters intended to comply with EU law.[98]

In regard to the textual distinction, the CJEU's teleological method gives limited weight to strict textualism, reading textual distinctions out of provisions where this is necessary to guarantee compliance with primary law (Ceruti 2019: 267).[99] In this matter, reading the textual distinction out of art. 2(2) is necessary to comply with the spirit of the TPD, EU non-discrimination law and the right to human dignity.

Hungary's purported implementation of 'adequate protection' is manifestly contrary to EU law, as it does not confer on non-Ukrainian nationals the minimum standards expounded in the TPD. The conferral of residency for a 30-day period falls far below the strict temporal requirement in the TPD to provide protection for a minimum initial period of 12 months.[100] Further, Hungary is failing to provide non-Ukrainian nationals with a right to engage in employed or self-employed activities or to access social assistance (Hungarian Helsinki Committee 2022).

---

96 *TPD*, art. 2(2).
97 See, for example, *The Queen v. Immigration Appeal Tribunal, ex parte Gustaff Desiderius Antonissen* (CJEU, C-292/89, ECLI:EU:C:1991:80, 26 February 1991) [18].
98 *Sturgeon*, 37.
99 *Merck*, [12].
100 *TPD*, art. 4(1).

While Polish law confers the minimum standards expounded in the TPD on non-Ukrainians unable to return to their country of origin, it nevertheless fails to meet the standard of 'adequacy', as it confers a higher standard of rights on Ukrainian nationals compared with non-Ukrainians. In particular, Polish law provides superior social assistance and medical care to Ukrainians, thus failing to meet the standard of 'adequate protection' (Republic of Poland 2022a, 2022b).

While this interpretative outcome provides a powerful tool for non-Ukrainians to demand commensurate rights to Ukrainian nationals, it must be acknowledged that due to the significant lag between the commencement of litigation and the handing down of a judgement in the CJEU, non-Ukrainians will continue to be subject to conditions falling below the standard of 'adequacy'. This outcome continues Poland's and Hungary's policies of 'quiet neglect' under which refugees of colour are produced as outsiders to the social and economic order (Cantat 2020: 183, 186).

Discriminatory (in)activation of the TPD: A critical analysis

While the correct interpretation of 'adequate protection' requires commensurate rights to be conferred on Ukrainian and non-Ukrainian nationals, the fact that art. 2(2) was inserted into the Implementing Decision to single out non-Ukrainians reflects the politics inherent in the EU asylum *acquis*. Hungary's and Poland's practices of conferring a lower standard of rights on non-Ukrainians must be understood within the broader picture of the EU adopting contrasting responses to the influx of persons from Syria in 2015 and Ukraine in 2022. Policies of containment, externalisation and criminalisation underpinned the EU's response to the Syrian crisis, standing in stark contrast to the European Council's swift activation of the TPD in 2022 (de Boer and Zieck 2020).

This section first examines the reasons outlined by commentators writing before 2022 for the council's failure to activate the TPD in 2015. Examination of the events of 2022 demonstrates that the theorised barriers to activating the TPD in 2015 proved inconsequential in 2022. Further, the threshold of a 'mass influx' likely was met in 2015. This necessitates consideration of the 'myth of difference', providing insight into why the EU adopted contrasting responses to the mass influx of Ukrainian and Syrian displaced persons.

Factors given for the inactivation of the TPD in 2015

'Mass influx': An ambiguous standard

Scholars argued that the inherent vagueness of the term 'mass influx' was a critical barrier to the TPD's activation in 2015, as a 'large number' of displaced persons is an undetermined legal concept (see, for example, Gluns and Wessels 2017: 57, 62; Arenas 2006: 435, 438). Article 2(a) of the TPD holds that the directive is particularly applicable where 'there is a risk that the asylum system will be unable to process this influx without adverse effects for its efficient operation'.[101]

Despite scholarly contentions that the TPD was 'obsolete' (Ineli-Ciger 2015: 226), it was efficiently activated in 2022, indicating that the ambiguous standard of a 'mass influx' is not a barrier to the TPD's activation. Arguably, the concept of a 'mass influx' is strategically vague enough to leave the activation of the TPD to the political will of the council.

More than 1.3 million displaced persons entered the EU in 2015, 75 per cent of whom were from Syria, Iraq and Afghanistan (Clayton and Holland 2015). At the time of the TPD's activation on 4 March 2022, 650,000 displaced persons had entered the EU from Ukraine[102]—significantly fewer than the number of displaced persons who entered the EU in 2015 (USA for UNHCR 2021). Further, the Implementing Decision notes that 4 million people were expected to flee Ukraine in 'the worst case scenario'.[103] It is likely the 'worst case scenario' in 2015 was comparable: 7.6 million Syrian people were internally displaced and 12.2 million required humanitarian assistance (UNHCR 2015: 1).

The TPD was developed in reaction to the influx of 672,000 persons into the EU in 1992 due to the Balkan crisis. The number of persons who entered the EU in 2015 significantly exceeded the 1992 influx, further indicating that the former likely met the threshold of a 'mass influx' (European Council 2022; Gluns and Wessels 2017: 61).

---

101 Ibid., art. 2(a); Gluns and Wessels (2017: 63).
102 *Implementing Decision*, Preamble, para. 5.
103 Ibid., Preamble, para. 6.

Further, asylum systems in Greece and Germany were under significant pressure in 2015 and 'unable to process the influx without adverse effects on their efficient operation'.[104] In 2011, the European Court of Human Rights held in *M.S.S. v. Belgium and Greece* that there were serious 'deficiencies in the asylum procedure in Greece', with no guarantee that Greek authorities would 'seriously examine' asylum applications.[105] This decision was closely mirrored in the CJEU's decision of *N.S. v. Secretary of State for the Home Department and ME*,[106] which highlights that the Greek asylum system was unprepared for the arrival of 1.3 million displaced persons in 2015—the majority entering the EU via Greece. Reflecting the failed asylum system in Greece, only 1.5 per cent of asylum seekers who entered were registered by the end of 2015 (EC 2016: 1).

The German asylum system was also unable to process the influx of persons in 2015, with more than 600,000 asylum seekers unable to lodge their claims with local authorities (Gluns and Wessels 2017: 60). The European Council's adoption of two emergency relocation decisions, in which it acknowledged that member states were experiencing an 'emergency situation characterised by a sudden inflow of third-country nationals',[107] further indicates that the EU experienced a mass influx in 2015.

Difficulty in securing QMV

Scholars also argued that difficulties in securing QMV contributed to the non-activation of the TPD in 2015. Ineli-Ciger (2015: 230) posits that QMV is particularly difficult to reach as influx situations tend to seriously affect a small number of member states along the EU's borders. Member states may thus prefer to rely 'on the structural imbalances reinforced by existing rules' in the Dublin Regulation, which disproportionately burden frontline states with the processing of asylum claims (Marin et al. 2020: 5). Scholars also argued that member states were unlikely to activate the TPD due to concerns it would create 'pull factors for migrants seeking to access the EU' (see, for example, Klug 2011: 133).

---

104 *TPD*, art. 2(a).
105 *M.S.S. v Belgium and Greece* (2011) 1 European Court of Human Rights 1, 55.
106 *N.S. v. Secretary of State for the Home Department and ME* (CJEU, C 411/10 and C494/10, ECLI:EU:C:2011:865, 21 December 2011).
107 *Council Decision 2015/1601*, art. 1(1); *Council Decision 2015/1523*, art. 1; Ineli-Ciger (2016: 1, 17).

However, the council used unanimity voting to activate the TPD in 2022, despite displaced persons from Ukraine being concentrated in Hungary and Poland.[108] Member states did not indicate a concern with creating 'pull factors' for migrants. Instead, EU political figures openly voiced their desire to welcome displaced populations from Ukraine (Faiola et al. 2022).

Activation procedures

Commentators also theorised that the TPD was not implemented in 2015 because of its lengthy and complex activation mechanism (Gluns and Wessels 2017: 80). Gluns and Wessels (2017: 82) argued that the 'lengthy debates' that would occur within the council to activate the TPD were a critical 'transaction cost' deterring Germany from advocating for the TPD's activation in 2015. They thus contended that Germany, as a rational actor, chose to focus its resources on 'important issues of relocation' rather than seeking to trigger the TPD. Lengthy activation procedures were, however, not an issue in 2022, with the council adopting the Implementing Decision a mere two days after the European Commission's proposal.[109]

The 'myth of difference'

Thus far this analysis has shown that theorised barriers to activating the TPD in 2015 proved inconsequential in 2022. Further, the standard of a 'mass influx' likely was met by the influx of persons in 2015. There was no obstacle to the TPD being activated in 2015, as 75 per cent of the displaced persons came from the 'same geographical area'[110]—namely, the Middle East. Yet, no member state sought to trigger the TPD in 2015.

Founding the myth of difference

Chimni's (1998: 351) 'myth of difference' explains how states of the Global North systematically use refugee law to pursue ideological and political agendas. This narrative is consolidated by the arbitrary distinctions made between Syrian and Ukrainian refugees to justify the activation of the TPD in 2022. Chimni (1998: 351) posits that the arrival of Third-World asylum seekers in the Global North in the 1990s caused a paradigm shift in refugee law. The 'myth of difference' was born, with refugee flows from the Third World characterised as 'radically different' to flows of European

---

108 *Implementing Decision*, Preamble, para. 4.
109 Ibid.; *Commission Proposal*.
110 *TPD*, art. 2(d).

refugees. During the Cold War, an image was constructed of the 'normal' refugee as 'white, male and anti-communist' (Chimni 1998: 351), causing what Johnson (2014: 48) terms a 'crisis of authenticity' for asylum seeker flows from the Global South whose claims were depicted as spurious. A 'repatriation turn' in refugee governance occurred, with the Global North advocating for voluntary repatriation and the provision of assistance in refugees' countries of origin as the key solutions to refugee flows (Chimni 1998: 351).

Chimni highlights that at the end of the Cold War refugees ceased possessing ideological value, as they were no longer persons fleeing communism. Thus, the myth of difference was constructed to justify the imposition of containment policies. The new post–Cold War approach to refugee governance, while shrouded in the politically neutral language of humanitarianism, was dictated by the political agenda of the Global North (Chimni 1998: 351).

Proponents of this myth argued that the number of refugees from the Global South was of an 'unprecedented' magnitude and could not satisfy the requirement of individualised persecution (Chimni 1998: 356). However, mass refugee movements were not new. The First Balkan War in 1912 forced more than 400,000 people to flee their homes and World War II displaced 30 million people (Skran 1995: 4; Chimni 1998: 357). Further, no serious exercise had been undertaken to ensure that Cold War refugees were not leaving for mixed motives (Chimni 1998: 360). Indeed, Melander (1990: 137, 146) notes that in the case of persons fleeing Hungary in 1956, not every asylum seeker would have been recognised as a refugee if they had been assessed individually.

The notion that the Refugee Convention acts as a containment mechanism for refugees from the Global South can be traced back to Article 1B(1) of the convention, which limited its applicability to 'events occurring in Europe' (Tuitt 1997: 96, 100).[111] Although this provision was removed by the 1967 protocol,[112] it indicates the assumed European racial category of a refugee (Tuitt 1997: 100). As highlighted by Hathaway (1990: 129, 156), the common view among the European drafters of the convention was that

---

111 *Refugee Convention*, art. 1B(1)(a)–(b).
112 *Protocol Relating to the Status of Refugees*, Opened for Signature 31 January 1967, 606 UNTS 267 (Entered into Force 4 October 1967) art. 1(2) [hereinafter *1967 Protocol*].

European refugees were 'the proper object of a universal convention, while the needs of non-European refugees ought to be dealt with by adjacent states'.

Tuitt (1997: 100–1) posits that the definition of a refugee remains 'peculiarly geared to the European refugee' as it is guided by European understandings of fault, with the emphasis on 'deliberate, culpable' actions by states, aligning with conduct attracting legal responsibility in Western jurisdictions. Despite developments in the jurisprudence in which courts have rejected this 'state accountability' theory, the discipline retains echoes of this period. Indeed, Hathaway and Foster note that common law jurisdictions tend to require protection seekers to prove their home state failed to exercise 'due diligence', which acts as 'a significant barrier to successful claims where the state is not the actor of persecution' (Hathaway and Foster 2014: 305, 307).

Further, as highlighted by Matthew Zagor (2015: 373, 378), public discourse continues to promote a dichotomy between 'good' refugees, who remain in refugee camps passively awaiting 'our redemption touch', and 'bad' refugees, who are unauthentic as they 'jump the queue' by seeking to 'illegally' enter host states (see also McAdam 2013: 435, 437). Jane McAdam (2013: 438) notes that the modes of arrival that are deemed illegal by the Global North tend to be used by refugee populations of the geopolitical South due to both a lack of resources and the absence of legal protection in neighbouring states, perpetuating the tendency of refugee law discourse to privilege refugees from the Global North.

Consolidating the myth: Ukrainian and non-Ukrainian refugees

EU member states have consolidated the myth of difference to justify the activation of the TPD, relying on arbitrary distinctions between Syrian and Ukrainian refugees (Brito 2022). The TPD can therefore act as a tool of protection when it is activated or of containment when the council justifies its inactivation, which is dictated by the political interests of the EU.

Arbitrary distinctions in the political discourse

Recent political discourse reflects the ways in which seemingly arbitrary distinctions are made. For instance, during the forty-ninth session of the UN Human Rights Council, the Hungarian Minister of Foreign Affairs and Trade stated that Hungary distinguishes between two kinds of refugees

(Brito 2022). The first were 'illegal immigrants … from far away', who were 'aggressive, uncooperative and did not show respect towards Hungarian regulations or culture'. The second were Ukrainian refugees, who 'waited patiently in line for hours, entered legally, cooperated with the authorities and were grateful for the help they are receiving' (Brito 2022). Comments by politicians in France, Bulgaria, Denmark, Austria and Sweden echo this xenophobic distinction between Ukrainian and non-Ukrainian refugees. These politicians were elected on anti-immigration agendas but argue that Ukrainian refugees are different to other refugees as they are 'women and children', 'Christian', 'civilised', 'white' and 'just like us' (Linderberg et al. 2022).

Strikingly, the Bulgarian Prime Minister stated that Ukrainian refugees were 'not the refugees we are used to' as they were 'Europeans, intelligent, educated people', unlike other refugees flows, who were 'people with unclear pasts, who could have been even terrorists' (Faiola et al. 2022). Further, the leader of the Polish Law and Justice Party warned in 2015 that Syrian refugees were 'bringing parasites' (Cienski 2015). This same political party, which is now in power in Poland, has welcomed more than 2 million Ukrainian refugees to Poland, stipulating that Ukrainians are 'our guests and our brothers' (The White House 2022).

The language of the Implementing Decision is also revealing, placing stress on the purportedly 'extraordinary'[113] and 'exceptional'[114] nature of the influx of persons from Ukraine, perpetuating the notion that this is radically different from the 2015 influx. However, as explored in section one, this is not the case.

While the protection needs of Ukrainians and non-Ukrainians unable to return to their country of origin are analogous, the singling out of non-Ukrainian persons in Article 2(2) of the Implementing Decision further constructs an image that there is a 'radical difference' between Ukrainian and non-Ukrainian refugees (Chimni 1998: 356).

Consistent with Chimni's (1998: 352) contention, the Implementing Decision places great emphasis on considerations of repatriation for non-Ukrainian displaced persons fleeing Ukraine, as they are required to prove that they are 'unable to return in safe and durable conditions to their country

---

113 *Implementing Decision*, Preamble, para. 16.
114 Ibid.

or region of origin'.[115] The 'repatriation turn' in refugee policy resulted in states engaging in practices of 'involuntary' reparation in which states assessed the safety of a country of origin based on 'abstract theorisation rather than evidence on the ground' (Chimni 1998: 364).

This concern remains alive in the EU's response to Ukraine, as there is a distinct absence of information provided within the implementing decision for how national authorities are to assess whether non-Ukrainians can return in safe and durable conditions. This raises concern that states may abuse this provision to return non-Ukrainians to their country of origin despite them needing equal protection. Further, the inclusion of the language of 'region of origin'[116] highlights the desire of EU states, as members of the Global North, to contain refugees in the Global South, even if they cannot safely return to their country of origin.

A safe third country?

The EU–Turkey Statement, introduced in 2016, provided for the return of Syrian refugees to Türkiye from Greece on the basis that Türkiye is a 'safe third country' (European Council 2016). A similar argument could hold that a genuine basis for differentiating between Syrian and Ukrainian refugees is the fact that displaced persons from Ukraine directly entered the EU, while Syrian refugees traversed a 'safe third country' (European Council 2016).

However, the EU–Türkiye deal is based on a dubious idea of safety (Costello 2016: 601, 621). There are widescale reports of Türkiye systematically detaining and deporting Syrian refugees, coercing them to sign voluntary repatriation forms—contrary to the principle of non-refoulement (see, for example, HRW 2019, 2022b). Further, non-European refugees in Türkiye are often denied legal protection as Türkiye made a reservation to the 1967 protocol, limiting the scope of its application to persons 'who have become refugees as a result of events occurring in Europe'.[117]

While the EU–Türkiye deal has been challenged before the CJEU, the court, in *NF v. European Council*, held that the deal is a measure adopted by national authorities and cannot be subject to judicial review by the

---

115 Ibid., art. 2(2).
116 Ibid., art. 2(2).
117 *1967 Protocol.*

CJEU.[118] This decision has been criticised by commentators, who argue that the statement is a binding agreement concluded by the EU with member states (see, for example, Hilary 2021: 127, 128). In the absence of a judicial decision on the safety of Türkiye for Syrian refugees, the reports of practices contrary to the principle of non-refoulement and the exclusion of non-European refugees from protection in Türkiye are sufficient to counter any proposition that it is a 'safe third country' for Syrian refugees (Costello 2016: 621).

Ideological value attached to Ukrainian refugees

Consistent with Chimni's observations on the role of refugee law in Cold War politics, EU member states have reconstructed the myth of difference to serve their ideological interest in receiving Ukrainian refugees.

Soviet invasion

Visegrád Group states hold shared memories of the Soviet invasion and occupation during World War II. After the Soviet Union invaded Poland, there were mass arrests and executions, with 20,000 Polish soldiers killed and 1 million people forced to resettle in the Far East of the USSR. As Roszkowksi (2015: 237, 262) powerfully writes, Poland emerged from World War II 'devastated and depopulated … subordinated to the Soviet Union, one of its wartime oppressors'. Hungary also suffered a great loss after the Soviet invasion in early 1945, with the country 'practically defenceless in the face of Soviet troops who plundered, murdered and raped' (Roberts 2007: 263). However, Hungary's relations with Russia remain complex, dichotomously characterised by its deep-seated suspicion of Russian influence fuelled by the history of invasion and President Orbán's affinity for Russia (Kim 2022).

The threat of Russian aggression is not distant history, with much scholarship and broader political discourse speculating that Russia's national strategy is to move 'its frontiers as far west as possible'. This raises serious questions about Moscow's intentions towards Eastern Europe (Tiryaki 2022). Protecting Ukrainian refugees thus has deep ideological value for EU member states and, in particular, the Visegrád Group, as Ukrainians are fleeing a shared historical and emerging enemy.

---

118 *NF v. European Council* (CJEU, T-192/16, ECLI:EU:T:2017:128, 28 February 2017) [71].

Ukrainian–Polish relations

While public discourse has identified common 'cultural' ties as a fundamental basis for Poland's welcoming approach to Ukrainian refugees (see, for example, Wamsley 2022), it risks simplifying the complex narrative of Polish–Ukrainian relations, which is characterised by deep political tensions. As highlighted by Rapaway (2016: 19), Ukrainian–Polish relations are marked by 'deeply ingrained cultural and religious divisions combined with incompatible claims to mutually settled territories'. From 1943 until the end of 1944, the Ukrainian insurgent army killed an estimated 100,000 Polish people in Volhynia in an effort to control territories that both Ukraine and Poland viewed as their 'cultural inheritance' (Roszkowski 2015: 264; Rapaway 2016: 19). In retaliation, a group of Polish partisans forming the anti-Nazi and anti-Soviet Home Army killed an estimate 20,000 Ukrainians (Roszkowski 2015: 264).

These events remain in the Polish and Ukrainian national consciousnesses, with a survey conducted in Poland in 2018 finding that just one in four respondents felt positively towards Ukrainians, while 40 per cent reported 'a strong feeling of dislike' (UNIAN 2018). The history of conflict and deep political tensions between Poland and Ukraine indicates that there is a much greater driving force for Poland's welcoming approach to Ukrainian refugees than mere 'cultural ties', which can be understood through the ideological lens of the shared Russian enemy.

Conclusion

The analysis in this section demonstrates that EU member states have consolidated the myth of difference to justify the EU's failure to activate the TPD in 2015. This myth has been further constructed by the singling out of non-Ukrainians within the Implementing Decision. The TPD is hence not a politically neutral instrument of humanitarianism, but rather acts as a tool either of protection, when it is activated, or of containment, when the European Council justifies its inactivation, which is dictated by the political interests of the EU.

Conclusion

While the move towards consensus-based decision-making in the European Council re-engages member states' commitment to the CEAS, protecting the fundamental value of solidarity and thereby indirectly protecting the right to free movement, it raises the risk of concessions being made that deplete the rights of displaced persons. This risk is particularly pertinent given the rise of populist nationalist parties across the EU and the Visegrád Group's pattern of resisting obligations within the EU asylum *acquis*.

However, the teleological method of interpretation, in which the spirit of instruments and the fundamental rights framework sit at the heart of the interpretative process, provides the CJEU with a powerful tool to protect the rights of displaced persons. If the CJEU follows its jurisprudence in good faith, it will command a prominent role in ensuring instruments developed through unanimity voting comply with EU law, including the fundamental right to human dignity and equal treatment. Time will tell whether the CJEU steps up to this challenge.

This chapter has argued that, despite the apparent intentions of the Visegrád Group to allow for superior rights to be afforded to Ukrainian nationals, the correct interpretation of 'adequate protection' under Article 2(2) of the Implementing Decision requires commensurate rights to be conferred on Ukrainian and non-Ukrainian nationals. Hungary and Poland's purported implementation of 'adequate protection' is hence inadequate and incompatible with EU law. Filling a critical lacuna in the literature, this chapter provides a basis for strategic litigation advocating for the protection of non-Ukrainian displaced persons in compliance with EU law.

Further, this chapter has argued that member states have consolidated the 'myth of difference'—a concept expounded by B.S. Chimni to justify the EU's contrasting responses to the mass influxes of persons from Syria and Ukraine. While the correct legal interpretation of 'adequate protection' requires the same rights to be conferred on Ukrainian and non-Ukrainian nationals, the singling out of non-Ukrainians in the Implementing Decision further perpetuates the myth of difference. While the TPD is shrouded in the politically neutral language of humanitarianism, it is either used or neglected by the EU, depending on the ideological value of a 'mass influx' of protection seekers. This results in a dichotomous EU border, prioritising persons with ideological value while dehumanising others, based not on their need for protection but solely on their 'fate of birth' and purported geopolitical value.

References

Abdelaaty, L.E. 2021. *Discrimination and Delegation: Explaining State Responses to Refugees*. Oxford: Oxford University Press. doi.org/10.1093/oso/97801975300 61.001.0001.

Amnesty International. 2017. *Greece: A Blueprint for Despair: Human Rights Impact of the EU–Turkey Deal*. Report, 14 February. London: Amnesty International.

Arenas, N. 2006. 'The Concept of "Mass Influx of Displaced Persons" in the European Directive Establishing the Temporary Protection System.' *European Journal of Migration and Law* 7, no. 4: 435–50. doi.org/10.1163/15718160577 6293246.

Armstrong, A. 2020. 'You Shall Not Pass! How the Dublin System Fuelled Fortress Europe.' *Chicago Journal of International Law* 20, no. 2: 332–83. chicago unbound.uchicago.edu/cgi/viewcontent.cgi?article=1772&context=cjil.

Arnardóttir, O.M. 2002. *Equality and Non-Discrimination under the European Convention on Human Rights*. Leiden, Netherlands: Martinus Nijhoff Publishers. doi.org/10.1163/9789004481534.

BBC News. 2022. 'How Could Ukraine Become An EU Member and What Does Russia Say?' *BBC News*, 24 June. www.bbc.com/news/world-61844552.

Brito, R. 2022. 'Europe Welcomes Ukrainian Refugees—Others, Less So.' *Associated Press*, 1 March. apnews.com/article/russia-ukraine-war-refugees-diversity-230b0 cc790820b9bf8883f918fc8e313.

Brittain, S. 2015. 'The Relationship Between the EU Charter of Fundamental Rights and the European Convention on Human Rights: An Originalist Analysis.' *European Constitutional Law Review* 11, no. 3: 482–511. doi.org/10.1017/ S1574019615000255.

Byrne, R., G. Noll, and J. Vedsted-Hansen. 2020. 'Understanding the Crisis of Refugee Law: Legal Scholarship and the EU Asylum System.' *Leiden Journal of International Law* 33, no. 4: 871–92. doi.org/10.1017/S0922156520000382.

Cannizzaro, E. 2017. 'Denialism as the Supreme Expression of Realism: A Quick Comment on NF v. European Council.' *European Papers* 2, no. 1.

Cantat, C. 2020. 'Governing Migrants and Refugees in Hungary: Politics of Spectacle, Negligence, and Solidarity in a Securitising State.' In *Politics of (Dis) integration*, edited by S. Hinger and R. Schweitzer, 183–99. Cham, Switzerland: Springer. doi.org/10.1007/978-3-030-25089-8_10.

Carrera, S., M. Ineli Ciger, L. Vosyliute, and L. Brumat. 2022. *The EU Grants Temporary Protection for People Fleeing the War in Ukraine: Time to Rethink Unequal Solidarity in EU Asylum Policy*. Report No. 2022-09, 14 March. Brussels: Centre for European Policy Studies. www.ceps.eu/ceps-publications/eu-grants-temporary-protection-for-people-fleeing-war-in-ukraine.

Ceruti, A.P. 2019. 'The European Court of Justice: Legal Interpretation and the Dynamics of European Integration.' *Columbia Journal of European Law* 25, no. 2.

Chimni, B.S. 1998. 'The Geopolitics of Refugee Studies: A View from the South.' *Journal of Refugee Studies* 11, no. 4: 350–37.

Cienski, J. 2015. 'Migrants Carry "Parasites and Protzoa" Warns Polish Opposition Leader.' *Politico*, [Washington, DC], 14 October. www.politico.eu/article/migrants-asylum-poland-kaczynski-election/.

Clayton, J., and H. Holland. 2015. 'Over One Million Sea Arrivals Reach Europe in 2015.' *Stories*, 30 December. Geneva: UNHCR. www.unhcr.org/news/latest/2015/12/5683d0b56/million-sea-arrivals-reach-europe-2015.html#:~:text=UNHCR%20figures%20show%20over%20one,with%20almost%204%2C000%20feared%20drowned.

Costello, C. 2016. 'Safe Country? Says Who?' *International Journal of Refugee Law* 28, no. 4: 601–22. doi.org/10.1093/ijrl/eew042.

Costello, C., and M. Foster. 2022. '(Some) Refugees Welcome: When Is Differentiating Between Refugees Unlawful Discrimination?' *International Journal of Discrimination and the Law* 22, no. 3: 244–80. doi.org/10.1177/13582291221116476.

Craig, P., and G. de Búrca. 2015. *EU Law: Text, Cases and Materials*. 6th edn. Oxford: Oxford University Press.

de Boer, T., and M. Zieck. 2020. 'The Legal Abyss of Discretion in the Resettlement of Refugees: Cherry Picking and the Lack of Due Process in the EU.' *International Journal of Refugee Law* 32, no. 1: 54–85. doi.org/10.1093/ijrl/eeaa005.

den Heijer, M. 2018. 'Visas and Non-Discrimination.' *European Journal of Migration and Law* 20, no. 4: 470–89. doi.org/10.1163/15718166-12340039.

Dennison, S., and D. Pardijis. 2016. *The Future of Schengen*. Report, 14 April. Berlin: European Council on Foreign Relations.

European Commission (EC). 2016. *The Refugee Crisis in Greece in the Aftermath of the 20 March 2016 EU–Turkey Agreement*. Report, 5 August. Brussels: EC.

European Commission (EC). 2017. *Relocation: EU Solidarity Between Member States*. Report, 3 November. Brussels: EC.

European Council. 1999. *Presidency Conclusions, Tampere European Council, 15–16 October 1999*. 16 October. Brussels: Council of the European Union. www.refworld.org/docid/3ef2d2264.html.

European Council. 2013. *Ideiglenes Tartózkodásra Jogosító Igazolás* [*Temporary Residence Certificate*]. Document: HUN-HO-07005, 1 January. Brussels: Council of the European Union. www.consilium.europa.eu/prado/en/HUN-HO-07005/index.html.

European Council. 2016. 'EU–Turkey Statement.' Press release, 18 March. Brussels: Council of the European Union. www.consilium.europa.eu/en/press/press-releases/2016/03/18/eu-turkey-statement/.

European Council. 2022. 'What Is Temporary Protection?' *Refugee Inflow from Ukraine*. Brussels: Council of the European Union. www.consilium.europa.eu/en/infographics/temporary-protection-displaced-persons/#:~:text=On%204%20March%202022%2C%20the,Bosnia%20and%20Herzegovina%20and%20Kosovo.

European Union Agency for Asylum (EUAA). 2022. *Poland*. Report, 4 June. Valletta: EUAA.

Faiola, A., R. Noack, and K. Adam. 2022. 'Suddenly Welcoming, Europe Opens the Doors to Refugees Fleeing Ukraine.' *Washington Post*, 28 February [updated 1 March]. www.washingtonpost.com/world/2022/02/28/ukraine-refugees-europe/.

Fennely, N. 2010. 'Legal Interpretation at the European Court of Justice.' *Fordham International Law Journal* 20, no. 1.

Genovese, V. 2022. 'Brussels Extends Ukrainian Refugee Rights to Live and Work in the EU Until 2024.' *Euronews*, [Brussels], 10 October. www.euronews.com/my-europe/2022/10/10/brussels-extends-ukrainian-refugee-rights-to-live-and-work-in-eu-until-2024.

Gluns, D., and J. Wessels. 2017. 'Waste of Paper or Useful Tool? The Potential of the Temporary Protection Directive in the Current "Refugee Crisis".' *Refugee Survey Quarterly* 36, no. 2: 57–83. doi.org/10.1093/rsq/hdx001.

Goldner Lang, I. 2020. 'No Solidarity without Loyalty: Why Do Member States Violate EU Migration and Asylum Law and What Can Be Done.' *European Journal of Migration and Law* 22, no. 1: 39–59. doi.org/10.1163/15718166-12340068.

Grimmel, A. 2018. *The Crisis of the European Union: Challenges, Analyses, Solutions.* London: Routledge. doi.org/10.4324/9781315443683.

Hathaway, J.C. 1990. 'A Reconsideration of the Underlying Premise of Refugee Law.' *Harvard International Law Journal* 31, no. 1: 129–83.

Hathaway, J.C. 2021. *The Rights of Refugees Under International Law.* 2nd edn. Cambridge: Cambridge University Press. doi.org/10.1017/9781108863537.

Hathaway, J.C., and M. Foster. 2014. *The Law of Refugee Status.* 2nd edn. Cambridge: Cambridge University Press. doi.org/10.1017/CBO9780511998300.

Hilary, L. 2021. 'Down the Drain with General Principles of EU Law? The EU–Turkey Deal and "Pseudo-Authorship".' *European Journal of Migration and Law* 23, no. 2: 127–51. doi.org/10.1163/15718166-12340097.

Hirshman, A. 1970. *Exit, Voice, and Loyalty.* Cambridge: Harvard University Press.

Human Rights Watch (HRW). 2019. *Turkey: Syrians Being Deported to Danger.* Report, 24 October. New York: Human Rights Watch. www.hrw.org/news/2019/10/24/turkey-syrians-being-deported-danger.

Human Rights Watch (HRW). 2022a. *Ukraine: Unequal Treatment for Foreigners Attempting to Flee.* Report, 4 March. New York: Human Rights Watch. www.hrw.org/news/2022/03/04/ukraine-unequal-treatment-foreigners-attempting-flee.

Human Rights Watch (HRW). 2022b. *Turkey's Threatened Incursion into Northern Syria.* Report, 17 August. New York: Human Rights Watch. www.hrw.org/news/2022/08/17/questions-and-answers-turkeys-threatened-incursion-northern-syria.

Hungarian Helsinki Committee. 2022. *Information for Non-Ukrainian Citizens Fleeing from Ukraine.* 7 June [last updated 15 April 2023]. Budapest: Hungarian Helsinki Committee. helsinki.hu/en/information-for-nonukrainian-citizens-fleeing-from-ukraine/.

Ibrahim, A. 2022. '"There's Poland, Now Walk": Arab Students' Ordeal Out of Ukraine.' *Al Jazeera*, 5 March. www.aljazeera.com/news/2022/3/5/thats-poland-now-walk-arab-students-plight-out-of-ukraine.

Ineli-Ciger, M. 2015. 'Has the Temporary Protection Directive Become Obsolete? An Examination of the Directive and Its Lack of Implementation in View of the Recent Asylum Crisis in the Mediterranean.' In *Seeking Asylum in the European Union*, edited by C. Bauloz, M. Ineli-Ciger, S. Singer, and V. Stoyanova, 223–46. Leiden, Netherlands: Brill Nijhoff. doi.org/10.1163/9789004290167_008.

Ineli-Ciger, M. 2016. 'Time to Activate the Temporary Protection Directive: Why the Directive Can Play a Key Role in Solving the Migration Crisis in Europe.' *European Journal of Migration and Law* 18, no. 1: 1–33. doi.org/10.1163/15718166-12342088.

International Organization for Migration (IOM). 2022. *Germany: Third Country Nationals Arriving from Ukraine in Germany (June 2022)*. Report, 18 July. Geneva: IOM. dtm.iom.int/reports/germany-third-country-nationals-arriving-ukraine-germany-june-2022.

Ippolito, F. 2014. 'Establishing the Common European Asylum System: "It's a Long Way to Tipperary".' In *Regional Approaches to the Protection of Asylum Seekers: An International Legal Perspective*, edited by A. Abass and F. Ippolito. London: Routledge.

Johnson, H.L. 2014. *Borders, Asylum and Global Non-Citizenship: The Other Side of the Fence*. Cambridge: Cambridge University Press. doi.org/10.1017/CBO9781107449404.

Kayacik, L. 2022. *Report of the Fact Finding Mission to Poland by Ms Leyla Kayacik, Special Representative of the Secretary General on Migration and Refugees 30 May— 3 June 2022*. Information Documents SG/Inf(2022)30, 18 October. Brussels: Council of the European Union. rm.coe.int/CoERMPublicCommonSearchServices/DisplayDCTMContent?documentId=0900001680a7acc9.

Kim, V. 2022. 'Hungary's Oil Embargo Exemption is the Latest Sign of its Leader's Affinity for Russia.' *New York Times*, 31 May. www.nytimes.com/2022/05/31/world/europe/hungary-oil-embargo-russia.html.

Klug, A. 2011. 'Regional Developments: Europe.' In *The 1951 Convention Relating to the Status of Refugees and its 1967 Protocol: A Commentary*, edited by A. Zimmermann, F. Machts, and J. Dörschner. Oxford: Oxford University Press.

Lemmens, P. 2001. 'The Relationship Between the Charter of Fundamental Rights of the European Union and the European Convention on Human Rights— Substantive Aspects.' *Maastricht Journal of European and Comparative Law* 8, no. 1: 49–67. doi.org/10.1177/1023263X0100800104.

Lenaerts, K. 2007. 'Interpretation and the Court of Justice: A Basis for Comparative Reflection.' *The International Lawyer* 41, no. 4: 1011–32.

Lenaerts, K. 2014. 'The Principle of Equal Treatment and the European Court of Justice.' *European Law Review* 8, no. 1.

Lenaerts, K., and J. Gutiérrez-Fons. 2013. 'To Say What the Law of the EU Is: Methods of Interpretation and the European Court of Justice.' *Columbia Journal of European Law* 20, no. 2: 3–61. api.semanticscholar.org/CorpusID:153519355.

Linderberg, A., A. Franck, A. Azis, A. Jung, A. Bousiou, J. Jern, and J. Anderson. 2022. 'Who Deserves to Be a Refugee? Ukraine, Racialization and "Grievable" Lives.' *School of Global Studies Blog*, 30 March. Gothenburg, Sweden: University of Gothenburg. www.blogalstudies.com/post/who-deserves-to-be-a-refugee-ukraine-racialization-and-grievable-lives.

Marin, L., S. Penasa, and G. Romeo. 2020. 'Migration Crises and the Principle of Solidarity in Times of Sovereignism: Challenges for EU Law and Polity.' *European Journal of Migration and Law* 22, no. 1: 1–10. doi.org/10.1163/15718166-12340066.

Marx, R., and W. Staff. 2011. 'Article 3.' In *The 1951 Convention Relating to the Status of Refugees and its 1967 Protocol: A Commentary*, edited by A. Zimmerman, F. Machts, and J. Dörschner. Oxford: Oxford University Press.

McAdam, J. 2013. 'Australia and Asylum Seekers.' *International Journal of Refugee Law* 25, no. 3: 435–48. doi.org/10.1093/ijrl/eet044.

Melander, G. 1990. 'Refugee Policy Options: Protection or Assistance.' In *The Uprooted: Forced Migration as an International Problem in the Post-War Era*, edited by G. Rystad, 137–57. Lund, Sweden: Lund University Press.

Morales, F.G. 2022. 'End of Visit Statement of the Special Rapporteur on the Human Rights of Migrants, Felipe González Morales, on His Visit to Poland and Belarus (12–25 July 2022).' Press release, 28 July. Geneva: Office of the High Commissioner for Human Rights. www.ohchr.org/en/press-releases/2022/07/un-expert-praises-generosity-towards-ukrainian-refugees-poland-and-urges.

Morano-Foadi, S. 2017. 'Solidarity and Responsibility: Advancing Humanitarian Responses to EU Migratory Pressures.' *European Journal of Migration and Law* 19, no. 3: 223–54. doi.org/10.1163/15718166-12340011.

Nowak, T., and M. Glavina. 2020. 'National Courts as Regulatory Agencies and the Application of EU Law.' *Journal of European Integration* 43, no. 6: 739–53. doi.org/10.1080/07036337.2020.1813734.

Office for Foreigners. 2022. *Amendment to the Law on Assistance to Ukrainian Citizens in Connection with the Armed Conflict on the Territory of the Country.* 28 March. Warsaw: Republic of Poland. www.gov.pl/web/udsc-en/the-law-on-assistance-to-ukrainian-citizens-in-connection-with-the-armed-conflict-on-the-territory-of-the-country-has-entered-into-force.

Pobjoy, J. 2010. 'Treating Like Alike: The Principle of Non-Discrimination as a Tool to Mandate the Equal Treatment of Refugees and Beneficiaries of Complementary Protection.' *Melbourne University Law Review* 34, no. 1.

Poiares Pessoa Maduro, L.M. 2007. 'Interpreting European Law: Judicial Adjudication in a Context of Constitutional Pluralism.' *European Journal of Legal Studies* 1, no. 2. doi.org/10.2139/ssrn.1134503.

Rapaway, S. 2016. *The Culmination of Conflict: The Ukrainian–Polish War and the Expulsion of Ukrainians after the Second World War*. Stuttgart, Germany: Ibidem Press.

Republic of Poland. 2022a. 'Health and Social Security.' *Services for the Citizen*. 24 March. Warsaw: Republic of Poland. www.gov.pl/web/ochrona-en/medical-care.

Republic of Poland. 2022b. 'Social Assistance and Medical Care.' *Temporary Protection for Foreigners*. 24 March. Warsaw: Republic of Poland. www.gov.pl/web/ochrona-en/social-assistance.

Republic of Poland. 2022c. 'Temporary Protection for Foreigners Who Are Not Citizens of Ukraine.' 24 March. Warsaw: Republic of Poland. www.gov.pl/web/ochrona-en/temporary-protection-for-foreigners-who-are-not-citizens-of-ukraine.

Reuters. 2022. 'Hungary Does Not Back EU Proposal on Temporary Protection for Ukrainian Refugees.' *Euronews*, [Brussels], 4 March. www.euronews.com/2022/03/04/uk-ukraine-crisis-hungary-refugees?.

Roberts, G. 2007. *Stalin's Wars: From World War to Cold War, 1939–1953*. New Haven: Yale University Press.

Rosas, A., and L. Armati. 2010. *EU Constitutional Law: An Introduction*. Oxford: Hart Publishing.

Roszkowski, W. 2015. *East Central Europe: A Concise History*. Warsaw: The Institute of Political Studies of the Polish Academy of Sciences.

Skran, C.M. 1995. *Refugees in Inter-War Europe: The Emergence of a Regime*. Oxford: Oxford University Press. doi.org/10.1093/acprof:oso/9780198273929.001.0001.

Takle, M. 2018. 'Is the Migration Crisis a Solidarity Crisis?' In *The Crisis of the European Union*, edited by A. Grimmel. New York: Taylor & Francis. doi.org/10.4324/9781315443683-9.

The White House. 2022. 'Remarks by President Biden and President Andrzej Duda of Poland in Briefing on the Humanitarian Efforts for Ukraine.' Rzeszów-Jasionka Airport, Rzeszów, Poland, 25 March. www.whitehouse.gov/briefing-room/speeches-remarks/2022/03/25/remarks-by-president-biden-and-president-andrzej-duda-of-poland-in-briefing-on-the-humanitarian-efforts-for-ukraine/.

Tiryaki, S. 2022. *Putin's Invasion Strengthens Resolve in Central and Eastern Europe*. Report, 11 March. London: Royal United Services Institute for Defence and Security Studies. rusi.org/explore-our-research/publications/commentary/putins-invasion-strengthens-resolve-central-and-eastern-europe.

Tsourdi, E. 2017. 'Solidarity at Work? The Prevalence of Emergency-Driven Solidarity in the Administrative Governance of the Common European Asylum System.' *Maastricht Journal of European and Comparative Law* 24, no. 5: 667–86. doi.org/10.1177/1023263X17742801.

Tuitt, P. 1997. 'Defining the Refugee by Race: The European Response to "New" Asylum Seekers.' In *The Critical Lawyers' Handbook 2*, edited by P. Ireland and P. Laleng. London: Pluto Press.

Tyler, I. 2018. 'The Hieroglyphics of the Border: Racial Stigma in Neoliberal Europe.' *Ethnic and Racial Studies* 41, no. 10: 1783–801. doi.org/10.1080/01419870.2017.1361542.

UNIAN. 2018. 'Poles' Attitude to Ukrainians Worst in the Last Decade.' *UNIAN*, [Kyiv], 13 March. www.unian.info/society/10040087-poles-attitude-to-ukrainians-worst-in-last-decade-poll.html.

United Nations (UN). 2022. 'UNHCR Chief Condemns "Discrimination, Violence and Racism" Against Some Fleeing Ukraine.' *UN News*, 21 March. New York: United Nations. news.un.org/en/story/2022/03/1114282.

United Nations General Assembly (UNGA). 2018. *Global Compact on Refugees*. GA Res. 12107, UN GAOR, 53 Comm, 73rd Session, 55th & 56th Meetings, Agenda Item 1, UN DOC A/73/12 (Part II), 2 August. New York: UNGA.

United Nations High Commissioner for Refugees (UNHCR). 2015. *Update on UNHCR's Operations in the Middle East and North Africa*. Report, 24 September. Geneva: UNHCR.

United Nations High Commissioner for Refugees (UNHCR). 2022a. 'Temporary Protection.' *Help Hungary*. Geneva: UNHCR. help.unhcr.org/hungary/temporary-protection/.

United Nations High Commissioner for Refugees (UNHCR). 2022b. *The EU Temporary Protection Directive in Practise 2022*. Report, 16 June. Geneva: UNHCR.

USA for UNHCR. 2021. *Refugee Crisis in Europe*. Washington, DC: USA for UNHCR. www.unrefugees.org/emergencies/refugee-crisis-in-europe/.

Wamsley, L. 2022. 'Race, Culture and Politics Underpin How—Or If—Refugees Are Welcomed in Europe.' *NPR*, [Washington, DC], 3 March. www.npr.org/2022/03/03/1084201542/ukraine-refugees-racism.

Weiler, J.H.H. 1990. 'The Transformation of Europe.' *Yale Law Journal* 100, no. 8 (June): 2403–83. doi.org/10.2307/796898.

Zagor, M. 2015. 'The Struggle of Autonomy and Authenticity: Framing the Savage Refugee.' *Social Identities* 21, no. 4: 373–94. doi.org/10.1080/13504630.2015.1071702.

7

Drawing lines out of limbo: A critique of the European enthusiasm for 'safe, legal pathways'

Matthew Zagor[1]

The transformation of a route into a corridor sheds light not only on modes of governing migration but also on Europe writ large.

—Bernd Kasparek (2016: 2)

Most of the legal pathways to enter the Schengen-zone, especially from the formerly colonized countries in the 'Global South', have been blocked.

—Laura Sumari (2021: 200)

Although empires did lay claim to vast stretches of territory, the nature of such claims was tempered by control that was exercised mainly over narrow bands, or corridors, and over enclaves and irregular zones around them.

—Lauren Benton (2010: 2)

---

1   A significantly extended version of this chapter with a different emphasis can be found in Zagor (2023).

Introduction

This chapter unpacks a rising phenomenon in the field of European and international refugee law and policy: the enthusiasm for (if not necessarily the creation of) 'safe, legal' and 'complementary' pathways to protection.[2] Recent years have seen the pathway metaphor become a pervasive element in instruments, speeches, scholarly works and reports by politicians, policymakers, academics and advocates. Whether discussed at the local, regional or international level, there is a resounding call to save lives and combat human smuggling by establishing secure and legally sanctioned routes through resettlement programs and complementary migration initiatives. However, despite its widespread usage and its connection to extensively examined border methods and practices, the pathway's distinct function, structure and significance are yet to be thoroughly explored.[3]

My aim here is to provide a modest start to that analytical program. After presenting the background to 'pathways' as a contemporary phenomenon in the field of refugee policy, the analysis pulls out to look at pathways as part of a suite of policy instruments and initiatives that are both colonially derived and colonially productive, playing a key role in the extractive political economy, which, alongside a resurgence in Western military ventures and a renewed Orientalist reaction to Islam, govern the relationship between Europe and the geopolitical South. The peculiar spatiality of the 'pathway' is considered within the context of its complex legalities as something new and not easily reducible to the many manifestations of the 'border'. There is, of course, a rich literature on externalisation, extraterritoriality, outsourcing of sovereignty, jurisdiction shopping, (cr)immigration, securitisation, surveillance, policing and border violence—all of which assist in understanding today's pathway, as does the powerful presence of an often internally contradictory humanitarian narrative. In this sense, I find the 'pathway' provides an opportunity to revisit core assumptions and

---

2   Terminology differs. The Global Compact on Refugees uses, alongside 'resettlement', the term 'other legal pathways' (para. 16) and, more often, 'complementary pathways' (paras 10, 14, 18, 21, 23, 27, 47, 76, 85, 86, [3.3], 95). US policy discusses 'lawful, safe, and orderly' pathways, sometimes adding the word 'humane'. See *Circumvention of Lawful Pathways*, A Rule by the Homeland Security Department and the Executive Office for Immigration Review on 16 May 2023, 88 FR 31314, 8 CFR Part 208 (2023), www.federalregister.gov/documents/2023/05/16/2023-10146/circumvention-of-lawful-pathways#:~:text=Specifically%2C%20this%20rule%20establishes%20a,or%2C%20if%20stateless%2C%20%20last%20habitual.

3   Kasparek (2016) is an exception, although he deals exclusively with pathways created *within* Europe during the 2015 'crisis'.

expose theoretical frailties in various disciplines, not least in international legal scholarship. In this sense, the 'safe, legal' pathway, and the 'dangerous, illegal' route it conceptually calls into existence, link these disparate narratives, inviting new analytical avenues—spatial and cartographical, extractive and neo-colonial, metaphorical and performative—which shed light on this moment in the movement of people.

Background to pathways: The problematic of 'solutions' and coercive conditionalities

In the area of refugee policy, the creation of officially sanctioned and state-coordinated routes for those seeking protection from persecution has traditionally come under the broader rubric of 'solutions'—a term that has attracted critical attention of late for its potential to pathologise both the discipline and 'refugeehood' (see Hathaway 2007: 3, citing Johns 2004: 587), as well as deflect attention from the law's protective purpose and exilic nature (Chimni 1998: 350). The three traditional durable solution categories—voluntary repatriation, local integration and resettlement—have always operated as a matter of discretionary policy rather than legal obligation, with the last being found in the 1951 Refugee Convention and 1967 Protocol to which all EU states are party, as well as in the *European Convention on Human Rights*, which has been read as providing 'subsidiary protection' from forcible return. Instead of being codified in the convention,[4] solutions appear in UNHCR (1950) instruments as aspirational guides for states and operational goals for an agency whose normative influence and capacity to obtain protection for refugees depend, in part, on it providing some 'resolution' to this most international of 'problems' (Loescher and Milner 2011).[5]

---

4   The 1951 convention is almost entirely silent on 'solutions' beyond a preambular reference and a tacit understanding that solutions will lead to the cessation of status, in Article 1C. Note, however, James Hathaway's (2021: 1028–220) compelling reading of the convention as representing a human rights 'solution' in its own right.
5   The 'UNHCR's capacity to obtain protection and asylum for refugees is often closely linked to, if not contingent on, its success in promoting solutions' (Goodwin-Gill and McAdam 2021: 490).

Although relegated to the UNHCR's 'less preferred' solution for several decades (Troeller 2002: 85), resettlement of those considered most vulnerable (the concept of vulnerability now being the central selection criterion)[6] has been enjoying a renaissance in recent years, partly as a result of successful campaigning by civil society and partly because of its compatibility with a border-control narrative that denigrates and deters irregular arrivals while elevating sovereign decisionism over international obligation. The newfound enthusiasm for resettlement, moreover, has been accompanied by policy initiatives at the state, international governmental organisation (IGO) and NGO levels around the creation of other 'legal pathways' for the millions stuck in what is commonly referred to in quasi-theological terms as 'limbo' in countries of first asylum, awaiting a 'resolution' to their precarious situation and ambiguous legal status.

These imperatives informed the negotiations of the Global Compact on Refugees in 2017 and 2018. The final document, although disappointingly non-binding and sorely lacking in substantive burden-sharing and 'solidarity' initiatives (see Chimni 2018: 630; Hathaway 2018: 591), presented pathways—under the general heading of 'solutions'—as both incorporating and 'complementing' a beefed-up resettlement initiative.[7] The document suggested a number of types of 'complementary pathways', including 'humanitarian visas, humanitarian corridors and other humanitarian admission programmes' alongside student, academic and 'labour mobility opportunities for refugees, including through the identification of refugees with skills that are needed in third countries' (GCR 2022: 95).[8] Crucially, the mechanism created for implementing the compact would be pledges

---

6   See *Refugee Resettlement Handbook* (UNHCR 2011): 'Identification of Resettlement Needs' (p. 215) and the 'UNHCR Resettlement Submissions Categories' (p. 243). The term 'vulnerability' appears 105 times in the document.

7   Given their essentially non-legal status, one looks to policy documents rather than international instruments to find definitions of the various solutions. Here is the definition of 'resettlement' as it appears in the *Refugee Resettlement Handbook* (UNHCR 2011: 3): 'Resettlement involves the selection and transfer of refugees from a State in which they have sought protection to a third State which has agreed to admit them—as refugees—with permanent residence status. The status provided ensures protection against refoulement and provides a resettled refugee and his/her family or dependants with access to rights similar to those enjoyed by nationals. Resettlement also carries with it the opportunity to eventually become a naturalized citizen of the resettlement country.' The handbook was fully revised in 2022 and now appears online (www.unhcr.org/resettlement-handbook/).

8   Significant policy work has since been conducted into these initiatives. See, for instance, Fratzke et al. (2021). Not everyone has welcomed the additional less-than-durable solutions suggested in the instrument. James Hathaway (2021: 1130) is particularly critical of what he sees as 'interim' status categories, seeing the expansive non-legal list as 'likely reflect[ing] the desire of states unwilling to receive refugees but nonetheless determined to be seen to have "dealt with the problem"'.

and contributions made at the periodic Global Refugee Forum (GRF).[9] The expectation was and is that an increasing number of states would be brought into the fold through pledges and regular GRF reviews, gradually addressing what the UNHCR has identified as a growing gap between need (expected to tip 2 million people in 2023) and placements (addressing just 4 per cent of those identified as in need of resettlement in 2021) (see UNHCR 2022a: 9; 2023a: 13).

Although Europe was a space *from which* refugees and displaced persons were resettled in the immediate postwar and early Cold War period, it has historically played a very minor role in the resettlement of refugees *to* European states. Instead, the United States, Canada and Australia—settler colonies whose postwar economies have depended on large, controlled migration programs—have overwhelmingly dominated the field. With the global compact and related European initiatives, there was considerable hope among pathway proponents that Europe would pick up on promised policy initiatives that date back to the early 2000s to become a more global player. European Commission (EC 2004) proposals in 2003 for a 'community-wide resettlement scheme' (linked to targeted development assistance and burden-sharing programs), incorporation of resettlement objectives in regional protection and development and protection programs, the (underutilised) provision of financial incentives in the 2007 European Refugee Fund and, finally, the drafting of an EU Resettlement Regulation in 2016 (adopted in principle in late 2022) reflect 20 years of deliberation, delay and consolidation around a new pathways agenda (EC 2016: 468).

Despite there being a degree of optimism about these proposals and initiatives, there has long been a strain of scepticism that Europe's interest in resettlement is motivated more by migration management concerns and perceived abuses of the asylum system than by a broader interest in solidarity, burden-sharing and durable solutions.[10] Indeed, the earliest statements promoting the formation of EU resettlement policies illustrate the extent to which they were driven by a desire to decrease the number of claims being made in Europe (and thereby reduce 'the costs of the domestic system') and

---

9   See 'Introductory Note by the Office of the United Nations High Commissioner for Refugees' and paragraphs 16–19 and 92 on resettlement in Global Compact on Refugees (2022).

10   Indeed, Gary Troeller (2002) made these observations about resettlement moves in the EU as early as 2002.

to 'reinforce the credibility, integrity and efficiency' of the asylum system, which was depicted as riddled with 'deficiencies' (EC 2003). As Migreurop put it back in 2005, European resettlement initiatives

> must be analysed within the global context of the externalisation by the EU of a growing part of its asylum and migration policy. Being mainly worried about protecting its external borders, the EU has chosen to close its eyes to human rights violations perpetrated by Member States or third-party states, provided the resettlement procedures demonstrate their effectiveness.
>
> (Migreurop 2005)

One of the core theses of this chapter is that these concerns have become more acute over time. The myriad resettlement and 'new pathways' initiatives proposed by the EU and European states are now core components of their well-established externalisation, securitisation and deterrence regimes, as well as being central to the necropolitical and neo-colonial narratives dominating EU aid and foreign policies. In this sense, they are part of the shift away from territorial obligations involved in the exercise of 'making people illegal'. As Naoko Hashimoto (2018: 162) has noted, for instance, there is an empirically demonstrable discursive link between resettlement and restrictions on the right to claim asylum. European initiatives fall squarely into this dynamic.

The new pathways' most vocal supporters, such as the Churches Commission for Migrants and the umbrella European Resettlement Network (ERN+) group,[11] whose focus is on Canadian-style public–private partnerships, have largely failed to engage critically with this reality (see Lenard 2016: 300). While advocates, academics and think tanks have urged governments to not use resettlement and pathways as migration-control mechanisms, few have taken the necessary structural and theoretical steps to consider the entire pathways problematic in its broader context.

In a longer, related piece, I explore the contemporary pathway in a very specific geopolitical context: the European involvement in the Sahel—that band of sub-Saharan Africa including Mali, Niger and Chad with an unenviable place in the colonial imaginary, which has re-emerged as a site for European security

---

11   This is a joint initiative coordinated by the International Organization for Migration, the International Catholic Migration Commission and the UNHCR.

and siege anxieties to be expressed and addressed (Zagor 2023).[12] That paper traces the development of the interconnected policy areas of migration, aid and security, and sheds light on the weaponisation of EU-affiliated funding institutions as tools for pursuing strategic foreign policy goals (Venturi 2017; Barana 2017). Notably, aid instruments designed for the region have made the receipt of development funds conditional on the criminalisation of 'people smuggling' (using EU-drafted templates for legislation) as well as the introduction of surveillance technology and the adoption of coercive policing tactics to close off traditional routes across the Sahara.

Importantly for our purposes, these initiatives are invariably accompanied by aspirational statements about the creation of safe, regulated routes to Europe and alternative economic opportunities in the region to compensate for the impact on local economies that revolve around the movement of people. Thus, the seminal 2015 Valetta Declaration asserts that states must address 'the root causes of irregular migration and forced displacement' by creating employment opportunities, supporting basic services, enhancing stability and governance, and 'promoting legal migration and safe legal pathways to Europe'—objectives that also appear in the 2020 *New Pact on Migration and Asylum* and the 2021 *Renewed EU Action Plan Against Migrant Smuggling (2021–2025)* (EC 2020b, 2021).

These 'safe, legal pathways' *to Europe* have turned out in practice to be more imaginary than real. And the predictably perverse consequences of the EU's security-centred development policy—the destruction of livelihoods, increased economic and societal instability and the emergence of more dangerous, sophisticated and professionalised smuggling networks— have been met with a doubling down on the rhetoric and the further pursuance of coercive policing technologies as part of the West's 'forever wars' against 'terror' and 'people smuggling' (see Danner 2011). All this is reinforced by the dominant argumentative pattern based on the concept of 'civilisation' in international law,[13] assisted by the purported (in)applicability extraterritorially of European norms that makes checking such actions in European courts difficult if not impossible.

Pathways, in other words, while essential discursive entities, remain elusive in practice, and Europe remains, as discussed below, a bit player in the field.

---

12   On European neo-colonial engagement in the Sahel, see Idrissa (2017, 2021). On Europe's siege anxieties, see Hage (2016: 38).

13   The idea of international law as argumentative practice owes much to Koskenniemi (2005).

Bringing pathways together: Lines out of 'limbo'

> Can one truly come to presence in the world, inhabit the world, or cross it, on the basis of this impossibility of sharing it with others, of this unsurpassable distance?
>
> —Achille Mbembe (2019: 65)

As noted above, the 'safe, legal pathway' appears in almost every instrument, agreement and arrangement making up Europe's contemporary package of migration policies. It has become, as a matter of policy aspiration if not practical reality, an essential component for tackling the challenges faced in the movement of people along 'routes' into Europe. The fact that NGOs, IGOs, churches and leaders across the civil society spectrum are on board with the push to create safe, legal and complementary pathways—conceived almost exclusively as running from the geopolitical South to the North—only serves to secure their position in today's dominant policy paradigm and legal geography.

At the discursive level, pathways are central to the political narrative that marries so-called European values—its 'moral duty' towards the South and the value placed by Europeans on human life—with its constituent states' newfound muscular sovereignty over their borders. In this sense, it is unsurprising that the imperative of creating such pathways has a ubiquitous presence in the speeches of European politicians decrying deaths at sea and promising to shut 'illegal' routes as part of dismantling the 'people-smuggling business model'—terminology that originated in Australia and has now entered the global canonical lexicon of refugee policy.[14] Every report of human suffering is met by EU leaders with a steely reassertion of the imperative to 'fight smuggling' and close 'illegal routes' with the assistance of 'third countries',[15] without irony or embarrassment. The manifest contradiction of perverse humanitarian consequences of EU policy—not least the fact that such reductive reasoning predictably results

14 Then Australian prime minister Julia Gillard is first cited as using the term in her remarks during a press conference with Indonesian prime minister Susilo Bambang Yudhoyono on 2 November 2010 (see Gillard 2010). The words were subsequently adopted as part of the failed regional cooperation framework with Malaysia and would soon become ubiquitous in Australian refugee discourse, before being exported globally. See Barker (2013); Schloenhardt and Ezzy (2012: 120).
15 European Commissioner for Home Affairs Ylva Johansson's public statements follow this formula—for example, her tweets concerning the deaths of at least 59 people off the coast of Calabria on 26 February 2023.

in the opening of more dangerous routes managed by more sophisticated, professionalised and ruthless smuggling outfits—disappears seamlessly into a totalising, Manichean narrative. The 'legal' pathway thus operates rhetorically to smooth unreflective acceptance of the existence of the 'illegal' pathway, governed by shady entities who threaten 'our' sovereignty and security and whose currency is human misery. And, of course, this all feeds a justificatory discourse for the coercive policing of such pathways, whether in the Mediterranean through the bolstering since 2019 of Frontex's powers (see Gkliati 2019) or in the leveraging of European financial might through development and security assistance aimed primarily at arming third countries to close such routes at their source.[16]

'Legal' pathways are thus an essential component of 'making people illegal' (Dauvergne 2008). They semiotically call into being the 'illegal' routes, and taint those who take and regulate them, while consolidating a self-narrative of the European—both person and state—as capable of protecting borders and saving lives, here and overseas. They reclaim, in other words, the core elements of sovereignty as full agency over people, territory and life itself.

The regulatory theory underpinning the idea of the pathway relies on the orthodox notion that there are push and pull factors determining the movement of people that can be leveraged by states using the carrot-and-stick or command-and-control approach to public policy—elements of the widely critiqued deterrence paradigm that underpins so much refugee policy (Gammeltoft-Hansen and Tan 2017: 28).[17] If we provide safe ways to arrive and penalise those who take 'illegal' routes or use criminal networks, we will shift the pull factor in the preferred direction, normatively and politically. As President of the European Commission Jean-Claude Juncker put it in his 2017 State of the Union Address: 'Irregular migration will only stop if there is a real alternative to perilous journeys.'

---

16 For a critique of EU aid policy and the development–security–migration nexus, see Brachet (2018: 16); Venturi (2017); Lebovich (2018); Räty and Shilhav (2020); Zagor (2023).

17 Although this is not the place to flesh this out, it is worth considering the application of Ian Ayres and John Braithwaite's seminal arguments in *Responsive Regulation* (1992) as a starting point for critiquing the regulatory theory underpinning European approaches to migration management, which rely so heavily on deterrence.

A brief foray into the now quite abundant EU literature on resettlement exposes the policy paradigm at work. In their press release announcing the European Council's endorsement of a mandate to negotiate a regulation on resettlement in November 2017, then Estonian interior minister Andres Anvelt succinctly encapsulated the logic:[18]

> Resettlement is a strategic instrument to manage migration flows. At the same time, resettlement is an important legal pathway to offer protection to those in real need … It will help decrease flows to our own external borders, disrupt the business model of smugglers and balance the efforts done in other fields, for example in returns.
>
> (European Council 2017)

Resettlement, in other words, is first and foremost a migration management tool that provides 'legal pathways' to those in 'real need'—implying that those taking 'illegal' routes are less authentic (or 'genuine'), less 'needy', than those whom states are able to choose using their own unimpeded discretion through one of these pathways that they create and control. It is an exercise in both reclaiming state agency and denying refugee autonomy (see Zagor 2015: 373). The justification of protection is thus qualified by the notion of enhancing legal (and thus implicitly censuring 'illegal') movement, followed almost immediately by its consequent benefit of protecting Europe's external borders, disrupting the undefined and ill-theorised 'people-smuggling business model'. And, finally, all this is complemented by the return of failed asylum seekers. The humanitarian rationale is almost lost in the mix (European Council 2017).

Although its tendency to be coopted as a migration-control strategy has been widely condemned, the underlying logic that 'more safe paths reduce reliance on unsafe ones' has been uncritically adopted in the literature and the lobbying of civil society.[19] It remains orthodoxy for most NGOs that, as International Rescue (IRC 2018) put it, 'the creation of safe routes to protection is the missing piece in the EU's asylum and migration policy'.[20]

18 '[B]y promoting resettlement, humanitarian admission and other complementary pathways by offering safe and legal pathways for those in need of protection, *resettlement helps save lives, reduce irregular migration and counter the business model of smuggling networks*' (EC 2020a: L 317/13; emphasis added).

19 See analysis in Gatta (2018: 163, 165): '[L]egal mobility channels would contribute to the safeguard of asylum seekers' life and safety, reducing the need to resort to dangerous journeys and smuggling networks.' The European Council on Refugees and Exiles has perhaps been the most vocal in lobbying to ensure resettlement is not abused. The title of its 2016 analysis of the proposal for a regulation establishing an EU resettlement framework, for instance, included 'breaking the link with migration control and preserving the humanitarian focus of resettlement' (ECRE 2016).

20 For a more sophisticated agenda, see Bokshi (2013).

Legitimate concerns expressed about the EU's resettlement framework are therefore accompanied, understandably, by recommendations for ensuring such policies are non-discriminatory and shielded from being weaponised. For the most part, general support—especially from those organisations which would have a role in sponsorship arrangements—remains unwavering. For instance, the report of the massive churches conference held under the auspices of the umbrella ERN+ group in 2017, which focussed exclusively on the role of churches in community sponsorship (or what the report called 'public–private sponsorships'), is almost entirely devoid of a downside other than a couple of references to the need to ensure non-discrimination.[21]

While I appreciate and endorse these modest suggestions, the concern expressed in this chapter is more structural. The adoption of pathways should be understood contextually as a necessary and inevitable corollary to the logic of deterrence that has come under such withering critique. They cannot be analysed in isolation from the coercive mechanisms that characterise European refugee policy more broadly—from Europe's funding and outsourcing of oppressive policies to third states and private entities on its 'periphery' in an attempt to close off the various 'routes' taken by migrants (see, for instance, Andersson 2014; Akkerman 2022) to its weaponising of Frontex into what one commentator has described as 'a fully-fledged European Border Police Corps' (Gkliati 2019). They work with and alongside the pulling back from rescue missions on the Mediterranean with the consequent rise in mortality rates[22] and the criminalisation by many states of the activities of civil society (see Cusumano and Villa 2021: 23). Pathways, in other words, cannot be analysed as a *humanitarian* policy tool separately from the securitisation, externalisation, outsourcing and neo-colonial policing policies that otherwise characterise the current moment.

Moreover, a pathways narrative facilitates the natural nadir of deterrence: the denigration and, where feasible, elimination of the right to seek asylum itself (Moreno-Lax 2017). For if one holds that there are safe routes to protection that can and should be used but that will only work—and thus only save lives—if asylum seekers are deterred from irregular arrival, the

---

21 The publicity for the event noted that 'private sponsorship can be defined as a public–private partnership between governments who facilitate legal admission for refugees and private actors who provide financial, social and/or emotional support to receive and settle refugees into the community' (ERN+ 2017).

22 'There was one death for every seven arrivals in Europe from Libya in June … and one death for every 14 arrivals from Libya in 2018 as a whole (compared to one for every 38 arrivals from Libya in 2017) *as a result of the big reduction in overall search and rescue capacity*' (UNHCR 2019a; emphasis added). See also UN (2022); UNHCR (2022b).

time-honoured mode of seeking asylum on a territory to which one has fled without authorisation must be part of the problem. Better policing of the 'bad' routes (at each end) and criminalising those who facilitate movement along them will only take you so far. Eventually, as has happened in Australia (Hirsch 2017: 48)—and, with its *Illegal Migration Act 2023*, is on the cards for the United Kingdom—claiming asylum on a European state's territory becomes a legitimate target for policymakers. This can be seen in the way international legal obligations of non-refoulement and the prohibition of the penalisation of unauthorised arrivals are treated as vestigial inconveniences, skirted by legislative and interpretative devices to take advantage of the Refugee Convention's inbuilt ambiguities or presented as proof of the convention's outdatedness (Nicholson 2023). This is the ultimate juridical logic of extraterritoriality and the pathway. It should come as little surprise, for instance, that former UK home secretary Suella Braverman would assert on introducing the Illegal Migration Bill to the House of Commons on 7 March 2023 that she could not guarantee that the statute would be compatible with the UK's human rights obligations because, as she put it, 'yesterday's laws are simply not fit for purpose'.[23]

This is not to say that the pathways' push–pull logic is incoherent on its own terms. Leaving aside what 'legal' pathways mean for 'illegal' routes, the logic requires at the very least that such new pathways be created. At the empirical level, however, they remain non-existent, dysfunctional, corrupted or so numerically paltry as to be effectively worthless in the face of overwhelming global need.[24] Despite almost two decades of lobbying and the aforementioned centrality of their position in the global compact, the GRF pledging mechanism and various UNHCR planning initiatives,[25] as well as the motherhood statements in the EU's 2020 *New Pact on Migration and Asylum*,[26] EU and European states remain bit players on the international 'pathways' scene.[27] For two years, the EU failed to fill even the modest pledge of 30,000 places at the first GRF in 2019[28]—a figure

23 See the statement made by former home secretary Suella Braverman in House of Commons (2023); UNHCR (2023b); see also Nicholson (2023).
24 For an analysis of the situation up to 2018, see Gatta (2018: 163).
25 See UNHCR (2019b: 4): 'The imperative to realise expanded access to third country solutions for refugees, including through resettlement and complementary pathways, is a cornerstone of the [Global Compact on Refugees].' See also GCR (2022).
26 'It aims to reduce unsafe and irregular routes and promote sustainable and safe legal pathways for those in need of protection' (EC 2020b).
27 For up-to-date data, see UNHCR (2001–23).
28 This pledge originally included the UK. The total number resettled in EU28 in 2019 was 25,651, in 2020 it was 9,143 and 17,255 in 2021 (noting the impact of Covid-19).

far below both capacity and global need, which UNHCR projected to increase to more than two million persons in 2023.[29] And while the past two years have seen resettlement and complementary pathway numbers climb in Europe, a significant proportion of this can be linked to temporary 'corridors', such as the evacuation program for Afghans after the Taliban's takeover in August 2021 (see EUAA 2022). Others can be linked to regressive, ad hoc 'contained mobility' programs such as the (non–legally binding) 2016 EU–Turkey Statement under which restrictive admission arrangements are used in exchange for third-country commitments to EU readmission and expulsion policies (see Carrera and Cortinovis 2019).[30] The contrast between humanitarian rhetoric and numerical reality has not gone unnoticed in civil society, with a robust call in mid-2022 from seven peak NGOs for EU states to 'urgently reaffirm their commitment to refugee resettlement and prevent programmes from shrinking further' (IRC et al. 2022).

Meanwhile, the numbers coming to Europe along 'safe' pathways from areas identified as critical to Europe's migration program remain pitiably low. For instance, the number of refugees stuck in or returned to states in the Sahel such as Niger, where so much effort and money have been expended as part of the externalisation of the EU's border-control regime (see Planck and Bergman 2021: 382, 389), has only grown over recent years (OCHA 2023). Augmented in part by internal pathways moving refugees back from Libya (where many have languished in EU-funded camps), this has only created more frustration, more hostility and more determination among those caught in Europe's externalised migration-control web.[31]

Internal European politics also plays an important role in determining the direction and implementation of policy. Notably, there has been strong resistance from the Visegrád Group of states to the implementation of any regionally designed program. Poland, Slovakia and Hungary, for instance, effectively froze negotiations over a draft regulation to establish an EU resettlement framework for six years, with agreement only reached on the framework in December 2022 (EC 2016). These states have also expressed a preference for programs aimed at 'rescuing' Christians facing persecution

---

29 'In 2023, UNHCR estimates that global resettlement needs will significantly increase to 2,003,982 persons, as compared to 2022 when 1,473,156 were estimated to be in need of resettlement' (UNHCR 2023a: 12).

30 Eisele et al. (2020: 19) identify four main types of agreements: 1) formal EU readmission agreements, 2) informal agreements, 3) Frontex working arrangements, and 4) Frontex status agreements.

31 See, for instance, figures cited in Brachet (2018).

in Muslim lands—a rhetorical trope that found favour in their opposition to the 2015 internal relocation scheme (see Zagor 2019: 387). This in turn reflects the influence of a revived European Christian nationalism as well as a worrying sacralisation of border politics—seen, for instance, in Poland's government-endorsed prayer day at the border to commemorate the Christian victory over Ottoman Turks at the sea battle of Lepanto in 1571 (BBC News 2017). Cognisant of the power this bloc demonstrated to generate constitutional crises through their approach to migration and their failure to adopt the internal relocation mechanism for Syrian refugees in 2015, the EU now walks very cautiously in this field (see Byrne et al. 2020: 871; Chapter 6, this volume).

Given this context, it is perhaps unsurprising that the new EU Resettlement Framework—which falls, after all, within the mega-portfolio covering migration, border security, integration and culture under the revealing title of 'Protection of our European Way of Life'—retains so many problematic elements. Notably, it includes conditionalities aimed at third countries that have a distinctly neo-colonial hue—similar to those that characterise the EU's development, security and migration policies in third countries where the receipt of funds is made dependent on the implementation of coercive border-control regimes (see Brachet 2018; Venturi 2017; Lebovich 2018; Räty and Shilhav 2020; Zagor 2023; Akkerman 2022).[32] Thus, the European Commission's proposal prioritises the resettlement of refugees from countries that demonstrate 'effective cooperation' with EU migration-control imperatives, allowing the inclusion of restrictive criteria such as 'integration potential' and the exclusion of anyone who tried previously to enter the EU irregularly (HRW 2018). As the European Council on Refugees and Exiles (ECRE) pointed out in 2016:

> Instead of being a humanitarian programme that provides durable solutions for the most vulnerable, resettlement is 'a partnership' activity ... Inspired by the EU–Turkey deal that offers resettlement as a quid pro quo, the Framework risks instrumentalizing resettlement to exert leverage on these 'partner' countries.
>
> (ECRE 2016)[33]

---

32 Homi Bhabha (2004: xvi) describes 'coercive conditionality' as a mechanism for turning the granting of loans 'into the peremptory enforcement of policy'.

33 One of the legal grounds of the framework agreed to in December 2022 is 'partnership and cooperation with third countries' (based on art. 78(2)g of the *Treaty on the Functioning of the European Union*).

This concern remains with respect to the now agreed 2022 EU Resettlement Framework.

The global picture also remains rather bleak, not helped by the impact of the Covid-19 pandemic and the continuing repercussions of the Trump administration's decimation of the flagship US program. Despite the initial successes of the global compact and its mechanisms, UNHCR has ruefully noted in lowering its ambitious targets in 2022 that the number of countries receiving UNHCR resettlement submissions by the end of 2021 had declined to 23 from a high of 35 in 2016, while those implementing 'skill based complementary pathways programmes' had increased by 12 (UNHCR 2022a: 12).

This points to another inherent problem: even should such safe routes be created and properly resourced, there is a very real risk that they will be used to cherry-pick migrants based on their economic, cultural or religious compatibility or ideological value. This is, after all, how resettlement operated for decades. And while these pitfalls were partly ameliorated by the UNHCR's adoption in the 1990s of categories of vulnerability in resettlement policies for the selection of the most needy (see de Boer and Zieck 2020: 54; Zagor 2019), the scarcity of places in the context of overwhelming demand ensures that selectivity, even within broadly non-discriminatory categories, is structurally hardwired into what is a highly discretionary system. Moreover, as the Australian experience demonstrates, the inherent ambiguity of 'vulnerability' as a principle allows states to implement selective resettlement programs within the UNHCR's objective categories (Zagor 2019: 393–96). Combine this with the privatisation of schemes, such as Canadian-inspired sponsorship models, and the increasing tendency for programs to operate outside the UNHCR's programmatic oversight. When you add the creation of 'complementary pathways' built around labour needs and skill sets, the accusation that the 'pathway' has become a vehicle for the neo-colonial extraction and exploitation of Third-World labour power—a new form of primitive accumulation—becomes tempting, if not irresistible (see Walia 2021: 157).

The connection between pathways, borders and exploitation has not escaped critical attention. In her review of three recent monographs on international migration in the *London Review of International Law*, Sara Dehm (2015: 133) connects the narrative of 'safe, orderly and regular' forms of migration to the 'managed migration' designed to meet the needs of the global economy—what she calls the 'mobilisation of migrants as participatory subjects of global development'. Dehm (2015: 135) cites the conclusions of the fourth International Assembly on Migrants and Refugees, which rejected the managed migration paradigm's attempt 'to shape life through the commodification of human mobility and the unequal distribution of rights, capital, exploitation and vulnerability'. As she points out in her conclusion, there is a sense arising from the literature that the illusive project of 'safe and orderly migration' is

> framed not only as an administrative fantasy but—more sinisterly perhaps—as a proxy for the increased securitization of migration and hardening of borders against impoverished people of the 'poor' world.
>
> (Dehm 2015: 159)

As noted, the critique in this chapter is structural rather than conspiratorial. In this sense, just as the 'safe, legal pathway' necessarily calls into being the dangerous, illegal pathway, it also relies on the latter's survival and continuance to maintain its rhetorical power. From this perspective, the perverse consequences of extraterritorial policing and criminalisation strategies—notably, the well-documented fact that coercive policies to close 'routes' merely ensure the creation of new, more dangerous ones, augmenting the very 'business model' that such policies purportedly aim to 'break'—seem less a policy failure than part of a self-sustaining ideational structure. This observation is consistent with what might be necropolitical critique—what Antonio Pele (2020) neatly summarises as 'the economic and political management of human populations through their exposure to death'. It also speaks to conjoined political and economic imperatives.[34] The economies of several states around the globe, after all, rely heavily on irregular migration while their politicians thrive on the marginalisation and demonisation of 'illegals'. That 'illegal' routes remain a reality, in other words, is not necessarily problematic for Europe's diverse economies.

These observations lend themselves neatly to the final piece in the neo-colonial critique of the current pathway enthusiasm: the role of the law in leveraging the pathway to facilitate today's version of 'primitive

---

34   For an analysis of how the Euro-Mediterranean migration regime is shaped by a multitude of actors (institutions, NGOs, individuals, etcetera) and material structures, including not just economic and political push and pull factors but also the legal settings of EU treaties and repatriation agreements between the EU and the Middle East and North Africa, see Jünemann et al. (2017).

accumulation'. One common view, derived indirectly from Carl Schmitt, is found in Amedeo Policante's observation that colonialism required the suspension of the law for such accumulation to be realised:[35]

> Plunder in the colonial world took place in a state of exception that negated, once and for all, the Universality of Christian international law; however, the wealth arriving in the ports of Europe would be soon registered and recognized as legitimate property. Plunder, piracy, theft—what originally had been a violent rupture—systematically becomes legal property ... The stronger freebooter 'beyond the line' becomes the legitimate holder of property on this side of the line.
>
> (Policante 2015: 60, cited in Hage 2016: 43)

The 'plunder' here can be considered to comprise those bodies warehoused in camps—which Betts and Collier call 'humanitarian silos'[36]—or waiting in states of coerced precarity carved out of the European legal order on the 'other' side of an amorphous territorial imaginary in the geopolitical South, where local state law is implicitly considered too 'thin' to merit the designation of the territory as a fully sovereign 'state', which is one of the many ways the 'standard of civilisation' continues to resonate in contemporary international legal argument.[37] Processed using unreviewable discretionary powers and selected for transfer by European states vying for extraterritorial influence, migrants are transformed by their passage along the 'legal' pathway into legitimate property—both *in* themselves as legal persons subject to (and protected by) the rule of law and *of* others as workers in the European economic order (see Zagor 2014: 345–47).

In this sense, the pathway operates much like the way the 'border' has been envisaged to work by critical scholars who have reformulated it as less a site than a *method*, or set of contingent, performative practices (Vaughan-Williams 2015: 6), for producing new subjects of state power, not least in the context of European strategies of externalisation (Mezzadra and Neilson 2013: 170–73; see also the overview of the literature in Novak 2022: 1). The law merely facilitates this transformation: it excludes, coopts, coerces and creates before it provides protection and legal personality.

---

35   The reference to Schmitt takes us not just to his famous formula that it is the sovereign who decides on the exception, but also to his early elaboration on the Euro-centricity and instrumentalisation of international law in *The Nomos of the Earth* (2006).

36   Betts and Collier (2019: 127) depict camps as 'humanitarian silos' that undermine autonomy and dignity and erode human potential by focussing almost exclusively on people's vulnerabilities rather than their capacities.

37   For a full exegesis of this argument, see Tzouvala (2020).

The use of 'pathways' instead of 'borders' in this analysis inevitably raises the question of whether it holds any separate analytical value.

The concern here is that, like many terms that once had a presumptively understood meaning, the 'border' has become something of a floating signifier in the social sciences, capable in the wrong hands of absorbing rather than emitting meaning. Coopting the pathway as another manifestation of the contemporary border thereby risks further taxological confusion, telling us little more than the fact that the border has many manifestations. This is not to say that the pathway does not have clear border-like properties, or that border studies throw no light on the phenomenon. For instance, the collaboration of third states in the creation and guarding of pathways—evident in both the 'partnership' model underpinning the EU Resettlement Framework and the 'outsourcing' of border control more generally—can be usefully understood as part of the trend towards technology-driven multistate 'co-bordering' practices documented by Matthew Longo (2017: Ch. 4). Their policing, their connection physically and semantically to the refugee camp, the 'processing centre', the disembarkation 'platform' and 'hotspot'—all manifestations of Agamben's 'state of exception' and a permanent spatial arrangement outside law's normal state—speaks to the disciplinary nature of the 'border-plus-pathway' as a practice of control, representation and production of the non-European other.

However, there are important ways to distinguish the pathway from the border. For instance, in its legal and illegal, life-affirming and life-denying guises, the pathway in part answers the problem of anarchic chaos and the crumbling of 'colonially traced borders', which, as Hage (2016: 43–45) points out, characterise the drive towards primitive (or what he prefers to call 'savage') accumulation in the contemporary scramble for African resources. As borders once did, pathways operate as a means for European neo-colonial society to disavow 'the savage grounds on which it rejuvenates itself by distancing itself from those who have to be more openly savage than they are' (Hage 2016: 43). The adoption of the pathway thus helps create and consolidate certain areas outside Europe such as the unstable states of the Sahel or the inhospitable Sahara as distant—and unsurpassable—realms of savagery and death, beyond even the camp in their lawless exceptionality, connected to Europe through the one-way traffic of persons defined normatively and politically by reference to the path they took. The nature of their specific and peculiar spatiality is thus crucial to the pathway's function in heightening and entrenching the 'periphery' in the European imaginary. As Hage (2016: 42) puts it in another context, they operate here as tools of 'colonial spatial politics', managing relations between 'the spaces of the colonial good life … and the spaces of war and colonization' and providing in their legal/illegal guises a way for capitalist nations to recategorise as lawful accumulation 'the plunder that generate[s] their accumulated wealth'.

The pathway also connects differently to the law, operating to bridge the geopolitical gap between nominally equal but substantively hierarchical legal orders, spanning the legally ambiguous death zones where lives are at risk (the Sahara, the high seas), and reliant for its efficacy on the deflection and reinterpretation of 'universal' legal principles. The pathway, in other words, is generative not just of new legal statuses—producing the migrant as both a full legal person and an economic commodity—but of new ways of thinking about the nature and function of international law itself.

The conceptual challenge that arises when confronted with the legally amorphous, unstable and disruptive nature of the 'pathway' presents an opportunity to critically reassess our assumptions about international law and its relationship to space. The 'historical' and 'spatial' turns within the discipline offer valuable starting points. Lauren Benton's research illustrates how the formation of the contemporary international legal order emerged gradually within the 'narrow bands', 'passageways', 'corridors', 'enclaves' and 'anomalous legal zones' within which imperial sovereignty and control were expanded and consolidated (Benton 2010: 2). Her analysis delves into the legal qualities of these interconnected webs and corridors, encompassing the movement of goods, norms and people. It contributes to a more nuanced spatial understanding of the construction and perception of contemporary sovereignty as an outcome of the empire currently so prominent in the new historiography of the discipline (see Anghie 2005; Ward 2008); Pitts 2018). This challenges a dominant historical-theoretical narrative that has prevailed for more than a century: that international law consists of universal principles originating in Europe and gradually spreading as part of a 'progressive rationalization of space in an increasingly interconnected world', which Benton labels the 'Eurocentric rationalization thesis' (2010: 9; see also Pitts 2018: 93). In contrast, Benton's work reveals that international law was—and, for my purposes, still is—lumpier, contingent and more interconnected in its operation, dissemination and orientation. Crucially, her thesis highlights how European empires benefited from the activities of both official and unofficial agents who traversed and managed these diverse passageways and actions that often incurred little or no cost for imperial governments but promised to extend their influence and generate future revenue (Benton 2010: 31). These subjects, as they moved, engaged in legal rituals and assumed the roles of self-appointed representatives of European powers, thereby tracing pathways that became conduits for the application of law and corridors of jurisdiction.

In many respects, pathways are similarly better conceptualised as a web, or network, of intersecting corridors along which people, norms, ideologies, technologies and resources flow in both regulated and anarchic (that is, non–state-regulated, but not arbitrary) ways. Nor are they unidirectional. The dominant image of the 'legal migration pathway' as a regulated corridor carrying state-approved non-citizens from the South to the North, or the illicit people-smuggling 'route' breaching the barricades of fortress Europe, strategically ignores those paths that have long run in the other direction. Just as imperial corridors brought settlers, goods and militaries to colonies during the height of European imperialism, so should today's pathways be understood as moving 'experts', surveillance technology, anti-smuggling laws, funding and policing techniques to Europe's 'periphery' as part of the broader development–security–migration nexus. More specifically, 'safe, legal pathways' facilitate the 'return and readmission' of failed asylum seekers[38] and the implementation of the 2008 'Return Directive',[39] as well as the formal and informal return agreements.[40] The fact that the last arrangements fall outside the EU's integrity mechanisms (Eisele et al. 2020: 20) makes the line between 'legal' and 'illegal' EU-facilitated pathways moving to the Global South increasingly grey—a fact ignored in the 'illegality' narrative.

Put in these broader historical and spatial contexts, passageways and pathways can be envisaged once again as 'differentiated', 'suspended' and 'anomalous legal zones' for the management and extraction of resources and people, albeit this time as part of a neo-colonial global order. One can also think of bodies such as Frontex, the semi-governmental EU Trust Fund for Africa, domestic aid organisations, enthusiastic church groups keen to sponsor refugees for resettlement, the UNHCR and the International Organization for Migration, and even co-opted local police forces and militia in places

---

38   This has been an integral part of the EU's immigration and asylum policy since the 1999 Tampere Council Conclusions and the Treaty of Amsterdam.

39   *Directive 2008/115/EC on Common Standards and Procedures in Member States for Returning Illegally Staying Third-Country Nationals* (known as the 'Return Directive'). The European Parliament recognised in its June 2020 implementation assessment that the directive has significant protection gaps and shortcomings. See Eisele et al. (2020: 7).

40   Eisele et al. (2020: 10) note that 18 formal agreements existed as of March 2022; the difficulty in negotiating them, however, has resulted in a proliferation of 'informal' arrangements. See Cassarino (2018).

like Libya and Niger as the unofficial agents or, as Sverre Moland (2022) puts it, brokers of the pathways 'business model'. As at the height of the empire, the activities of such semi-official entities extend European de facto sovereign power as well as, where convenient and appropriate, European law and—less often and more contentiously—jurisdiction. Indeed, as European jurists struggle with the applicability of universalised European rights in this legally striated space,[41] we are challenged to reimagine the spatiality and rationality of both international and European refugee law. European pathways provide such an opportunity.

References

Akkerman, M. 2022. *Outsourcing Oppression: How Europe Externalises Migrant Detention Beyond Its Shores*. Policy Briefing. Amsterdam: Transnational Institute and Stop Wapenhandel.

Andersson, R. 2014. *Illegality, Inc.: Clandestine Migration and the Business of Bordering*. Berkeley: University of California Press.

Anghie, A. 2005. *Imperialism, Sovereignty and the Making of International Law*. Cambridge: Cambridge University Press. doi.org/10.1017/CBO9780511614262.

Ayres, I., and J. Braithwaite. 1992. *Responsive Regulation*. Oxford: Oxford University Press. doi.org/10.1093/oso/9780195070705.001.0001.

Barana, L. 2017. 'The EU Trust Fund for Africa and the Perils of a Securitized Migration Policy.' *Istituto Affari Internazionali (IAI) Commentaries* 17, no. 31.

Barker, C. 2013. *The People Smugglers' Business Model*. Parliamentary Library Research Paper No. 2. Canberra: Parliament of Australia.

BBC News. 2017. 'Poland Catholics Hold Controversial Prayer Day on Borders.' *BBC News*, 7 October. www.bbc.com/news/world-europe-41538260.

Benton, L. 2010. *A Search for Sovereignty: Law and Geography in European Empires, 1400–1900*. Cambridge: Cambridge University Press. doi.org/10.1017/CBO9780511988905.

Betts, A., and B. Collier. 2019. *Refuge: Transforming a Broken Refugee System*. London: Penguin Random House.

---

41 I am borrowing from Deleuze and Guattari (1988). I am unaware of Benton drawing on their work, but the synergies are too apparent to ignore.

Bhabha, H. 2004 [1994]. *The Location of Culture*. London: Routledge.

Bokshi, E. 2013. *Refugee Resettlement in the EU: The Capacity to Do It Better and To Do It More*. KNOW RESET Research Report 2013/04, EU Comparative Report. Florence: Robert Schuman Centre for Advanced Studies, European University Institute. ecre.org/wp-content/uploads/2016/03/00013_20140108 160733_knowresetrr-2013-04.pdf.

Brachet, J. 2018. 'Manufacturing Smugglers: From Irregular to Clandestine Mobility in the Sahara.' *The Annals of the American Academy of Political and Social Science* 676: 16–35. doi.org/10.1177/0002716217744529.

Byrne, R., G. Noll, and J. Vedsted-Hansen. 2020. 'Understanding the Crisis of Refugee Law: Legal Scholarship and the EU Asylum System.' *Leiden Journal of International Law* 33, no. 4: 871–92. doi.org/10.1017/S0922156520000382.

Carrera, S., and R. Cortinovis. 2019. *The EU's Role in Implementing the UN Global Compact on Refugees: Contained Mobility vs. International Protection*. CEPS Papers in Liberty and Security in Europe, No. 2018-04, April. Brussels: Centre for European Policy Studies.

Cassarino, J.P. 2018. 'Informalising EU Readmission Policy.' In *The Routledge Handbook of Justice and Home Affairs Research*, edited by A.R. Servent and F. Trauner. London: Routledge. doi.org/10.4324/9781315645629-7.

Chimni, B.S. 1998. 'The Geopolitics of Refugee Studies: A View from the South.' *Journal of Refugee Studies* 11, no. 4: 350–37. doi.org/10.1093/jrs/11.4.350-a.

Chimni, B.S. 2018. 'Global Compact on Refugees: One Step Forward, Two Steps Back.' *International Journal of Refugee Law* 30, no. 4: 630–34. doi.org/10.1093/ijrl/eey067.

Cusumano, E., and M. Villa. 2021. 'From "Angels" to "Vice Smugglers": The Criminalization of Sea Rescue NGOs in Italy.' *European Journal on Criminal Policy and Research* 27 (September): 23–40. doi.org/10.1007/s10610-020-09464-1.

Danner, M. 2011. 'Torture and the Forever War: The Tanner Lectures on Human Values.' Delivered at Stanford University, Stanford, CA, 14–16 April. tannerlectures.utah.edu/_resources/documents/a-to-z/d/Danner_10.pdf.

Dauvergne, C. 2008. *Making People Illegal*. Cambridge: Cambridge University Press. doi.org/10.1017/CBO9780511810473.

de Boer, T., and M. Zieck. 2020. 'The Legal Abyss of Discretion in the Resettlement of Refugees: Cherry-Picking and the Lack of Due Process in the EU.' *International Journal of Refugee Law* 32, no. 1: 54–85. doi.org/10.1093/ijrl/eeaa005.

Dehm, S. 2015. 'Framing International Migration.' *London Review of International Law* 3, no. 1 (March): 133–68. doi.org/10.1093/lril/lrv004.

Deleuze, G., and F. Guattari. 1988. *A Thousand Plateaus: Capitalism and Schizophrenia*. Translated by Brian Massumi. London: Athlone Press.

Eisele, K., I. Majcher, and M. Provera. 2020. *The Return Directive 2008/115/EC: European Implementation Assessment*. European Parliamentary Research Service report, June. Strasbourg: European Parliament.

European Commission (EC). 2003. *Communication from the Commission to the Council and the European Parliament: Towards More Accessible, Equitable and Managed Asylum Systems*. COM/2003/0315 final. Brussels: EC. eur-lex.europa. eu/legal-content/EN/TXT/HTML/?uri=CELEX:52003DC0315&from=FR.

European Commission (EC). 2004. *Communication from the Commission to the Council and the European Parliament on the Managed Entry in the EU of Persons in Need of International Protection and the Enhancement of the Protection Capacity of the Regions of Origin 'Improving Access to Durable Solutions'*. COM/2004/0410 final. Brussels: EC. eur-lex.europa.eu/legal-content/PL/TXT/?uri=CELEX%3A5 2004DC0410.

European Commission (EC). 2016. *Proposal for a Regulation of the European Parliament and of the Council Establishing a Union Resettlement Framework and Amending Regulation (EU) No 516/2014 of the European Parliament and the Council*. COM/2016/0468 final, 2016/0225 (COD). Brussels: EC. eur-lex. europa.eu/legal-content/EN/TXT/?uri=COM:2016:0468:FIN.

European Commission (EC). 2020a. *Commission Recommendation (EU) 2020/1364 of 23 September 2020 on Legal Pathways to Protection in the EU: Promoting Resettlement, Humanitarian Admission and Other Complementary Pathways*. C/2020/6467. Brussels: EC. eur-lex.europa.eu/legal-content/en/TXT/?uri= CELEX%3A32020H1364.

European Commission (EC). 2020b. *Communication from the Commission to the European Parliament, the Council, the European Economic and Social Committee and the Committee of the Regions on a New Pact on Migration and Asylum*. 23 September, COM/2020/609 final. Brussels: EC. eur-lex.europa.eu/legal-content/EN/TXT/?uri=CELEX:52020DC0609.

European Commission (EC). 2021. *Communication from the Commission to the European Parliament, the Council, the European Economic and Social Committee and the Committee of the Regions: A Renewed EU Action Plan Against Migrant Smuggling (2021–2025)*. 29 September, COM/2021/591 final. Brussels: EC. eur-lex.europa.eu/legal-content/EN/TXT/?uri=CELEX%3A52021DC0591.

European Council. 2017. 'EU Resettlement Framework: Council Ready to Start Negotiations.' Press release, 15 November. Brussels: Council of the European Union. www.consilium.europa.eu/en/press/press-releases/2017/11/15/eu-resettlement-framework-council-ready-to-start-negotiations/.

European Council on Refugees and Exiles (ECRE). 2016. *Untying the EU Resettlement Framework: ECRC's Recommendations on Breaking the Link with Migration Control and Preserving the Humanitarian Focus of Resettlement.* Policy Note #1. Brussels: ECRE. ecre.org/wp-content/uploads/2016/10/Policy-Note-01.pdf.

European Resettlement Network (ERN+). 2017. *Conference Report: The Role of Churches and Christian Organisations in Community-Based Sponsorship Programmes of Refugees in Europe—Challenges, Opportunities and Next Steps, 18 and 19 September 2017, Brussels.* International Catholic Migration Commission and ERN+. static1.squarespace.com/static/61701919c9cd9200cd8e6ccc/t/61b88d0e0709ac5a9ff35147/1639484703278/ERN%2B+ICMC+Churches+Conference+Report.pdf.

European Union Agency for Asylum (EUAA). 2022. *Data on Resettlement Activities in 2021.* Fact Sheet, EUAA/2022/15, November. Valletta: EUAA. euaa.europa.eu/sites/default/files/publications/2022-12/AR2022_data_resettlement_factsheet15_EN.pdf.

Fratzke, S., M.B. Zanzuchi, K. Hooper, H. Beirens, L. Kainz, N. Benson, E. Bateman, and J. Bolter. 2021. *Refugee Resettlement and Complementary Pathways: Opportunities for Growth.* MPI Report, September. Washington, DC: Migration Policy Institute. www.migrationpolicy.org/research/refugee-resettlement-complementary-pathways.

Gammeltoft-Hansen, T., and N. Tan 2017. 'The End of the Deterrence Paradigm? Future Directions for Global Refugee Policy.' *Journal on Migration and Human Security* 5: 28–56. doi.org/10.1177/233150241700500103.

Gatta, F.L. 2018. 'Legal Avenues to Access International Protection in the European Union: Past Actions and Future Perspectives.' *European Journal of Human Rights* 3.

Gillard, J. 2010. 'Prime Minister: Transcript of Joint Press Conference.' Jakarta, 2 November. Jakarta: Australian Embassy Indonesia. indonesia.embassy.gov.au/jakt/TRANSC10_002.html.

Gkliati, M. 2019. 'The New European Border and Coast Guard: Do Increased Powers Come with Enhanced Accountability?' *EU Law Analysis* blog, 17 April. eulawanalysis.blogspot.com/2019/04/the-new-european-border-and-coast-guard.html.

Global Compact on Refugees (GCR). 2022. *Third Country Solutions for Refugees: Roadmap 2030—The Next Phase of the Three Year Strategy on Resettlement and Complementary Pathways (2019–2021)*. June. Geneva: Global Compact on Refugees. globalcompactrefugees.org/sites/default/files/2022-08/Third%20 Country%20Solutions%20for%20Refugees%20-%20Roadmap%202030.pdf.

Goodwin-Gill, G.S., and J. McAdam. 2021. *The Refugee in International Law*. Oxford: Oxford University Press.

Hage, G. 2016. 'État de siège: A Dying Domesticating Colonialism?' *American Ethnologist* 43, no. 1 (February): 38–49. doi.org/10.1111/amet.12261.

Hashimoto, N. 2018. 'Refugee Resettlement as an Alternative to Asylum.' *Refugee Survey Quarterly* 37, no. 2 (June): 162–86. doi.org/10.1093/rsq/hdy004.

Hathaway, J. 2007. 'Refugee Solutions, or Solutions to Refugeehood?' *Refuge: Canada's Journal on Refugees* 24, no. 2: 3–10. doi.org/10.25071/1920-7336.21378.

Hathaway, J. 2018. 'The Global Cop-Out on Refugees.' *International Journal of Refugee Law* 30, no. 4 (December): 591–604. doi.org/10.1093/ijrl/eey062.

Hathaway, J. 2021. *The Rights of Refugees under International Law*. 2nd edn. Cambridge: Cambridge University Press. doi.org/10.1017/9781108863537.

Hirsch, A.L. 2017. 'The Borders beyond the Border: Australia's Extraterritorial Migration Controls.' *Refugee Survey Quarterly* 36, no. 3 (September): 48–80. doi.org/10.1093/rsq/hdx008.

House of Commons. 2023. *Illegal Migration Bill: Explanatory Notes*. Bill 262-EN, 7 March. London: UK Parliament. publications.parliament.uk/pa/bills/cbill/ 58-03/0262/en/220262en.pdf.

Human Rights Watch (HRW). 2018. *Towards an Effective and Principled EU Migration Policy: Recommendations for Reform*. Report, 18 June. New York: Human Rights Watch. www.hrw.org/news/2018/06/18/towards-effective-and-principled-eu-migration-policy.

Idrissa, R. 2017. *The Politics of Islam in the Sahel: Between Persuasion and Violence*. London: Routledge. doi.org/10.4324/9781315270401.

Idrissa, R. 2021. 'Mapping the Sahel.' *New Left Review* 132.

International Rescue Committee (IRC). 2018. *Unlocking Frozen Futures: Recommendations for an Ambitious, Humanitarian and Sustainable Union Resettlement Framework*. IRC Briefing, January. New York: IRC. www.rescue-uk.org/sites/default/files/document/1446/internationalrescuecommittee-union resettlementframeworkbriefing-january2018final.pdf.

International Rescue Committee (IRC), Amnesty International, Caritas Europa, Churches' Commission for Migrants in Europe, European Council on Refugees and Exiles, International Catholic Migration Commission Europe/SHARE Network, and Red Cross EU. 2022. 'Mounting Global Needs Call for Renewed European Leadership on Resettlement.' Joint NGO Statement, 13 June. www. rescue.org/sites/default/files/2022-06/Joint%20Resettlement%20Statement% 202022.pdf.

Johns, F. 2004. 'The Madness of Migration: Disquiet in the International Law Relating to Refugees.' *International Journal of Law and Psychiatry* 27, no. 6 (November–December): 587–607. doi.org/10.1016/j.ijlp.2004.08.003.

Jünemann, A., N. Fromm, and N. Schere, eds. 2017. *Fortress Europe? Challenges and Failures of Migration and Asylum Policies.* Cham, Switzerland: Springer. doi.org/ 10.1007/978-3-658-17011-0.

Kasparek, B. 2016. 'Routes, Corridors, and Spaces of Exception: Governing Migration and Europe.' In *Europe at a Crossroads: Managed Inhospitality*, edited by M. Feher, W. Callison, M. Odabaei, and A. Windels. New York: Zone Books.

Koskenniemi, M. 2005. *From Apology to Utopia: The Structure of International Legal Argument.* Cambridge: Cambridge University Press. doi.org/10.1017/CBO978 0511493713.

Lebovich, A. 2018. *Halting Ambition: EU Migration and Security Policy in the Sahel.* ECFR Policy Brief, 25 September. Berlin: European Council on Foreign Relations.

Lenard, P.T. 2016. 'Resettling Refugees: Is Private Sponsorship a Just Way Forward?' *Journal of Global Ethics* 12, no. 3: 300–10. doi.org/10.1080/17449626.2016. 1247290.

Loescher, G., and J. Milner. 2011. 'UNHCR and the Global Governance of Refugees.' In *Global Migration Governance*, edited by A. Betts. Oxford: Oxford University Press. doi.org/10.1093/acprof:oso/9780199600458.003.0008.

Longo, M. 2017. *The Politics of Borders: Sovereignty, Security, and the Citizen after 9/11.* Cambridge: Cambridge University Press. doi.org/10.1017/9781316761663.

Mbembe, A. 2019. *Necropolitics.* Durham: Duke University Press. doi.org/10.1215/ 9781478007227.

Mezzadra, S., and B. Neilson. 2013. *Border as Method, or, the Multiplication of Labor.* Durham: Duke University Press. doi.org/10.2307/j.ctv1131cvw.

Migreurop. 2005. *Resettling Refugees, The European Instrument for the Externalisation of Asylum Procedures*. Report, November. Paris: Migreurop. migreurop.org/article 978.html.

Moland, S. 2022. *Safe Migration and the Politics of Brokered Safety in Southeast Asia*. London: Routledge. doi.org/10.4324/9781003185734.

Moreno-Lax, V. 2017. *Accessing Asylum in Europe: Extraterritorial Border Controls and Refugee Rights Under EU Law*. Oxford: Oxford University Press. doi.org/10.1093/oso/9780198701002.001.0001.

Nicholson, R. 2023. 'Rishi Sunak's Illegal Migration Bill: What Happens When Violating International Law is the Point?' *Australian Outlook*, 4 April. Canberra: Australian Institute of International Affairs. www.internationalaffairs.org.au/australianoutlook/rishi-sunaks-illegal-migration-bill-what-happens-when-violating-international-law-is-the-point/.

Novak, P. 2022. 'Re-Producing the Humanitarian Border.' *Geopolitics*. doi.org/10.1080/14650045.2022.2105699.

Pele, A. 2020. 'Achille Mbembe: Necropolitics.' [Book review.] *Critical Legal Thinking*, 2 March. criticallegalthinking.com/2020/03/02/achille-mbembe-necropolitics/.

Pitts, J. 2018. *Boundaries of the International: Law and Empire*. Cambridge: Harvard University Press. doi.org/10.4159/9780674986275.

Plank, F., and J. Bergman. 2021. 'The European Union as a Security Actor in the Sahel: Policy Entrapment in EU Foreign Policy.' *European Review of International Studies* 8, no. 3: 382–412. doi.org/10.1163/21967415-08030006.

Policante, A. 2015. *The Pirate Myth: Genealogies of an Imperial Concept*. London: Routledge. doi.org/10.4324/9781315757223.

Räty, T., and R. Shilhav. 2020. *The EU Trust Fund for Africa: Trapped Between Aid Policy and Migration Politics*. Oxfam Briefing Paper, January. Oxford: Oxfam International. oxfamilibrary.openrepository.com/bitstream/handle/10546/6209 36/bp-eu-trust-fund-africa-migration-politics-300120-en.pdf. doi.org/10.21201/2020.5532.

Schloenhardt, A., and L. Ezzy. 2012. 'Hadi Ahmadi—And the Myth of the "People Smugglers' Business Model".' *Monash University Law Review* 38, no. 3.

Schmitt, C. 2006 [1950]. *The Nomos of the Earth in the International Law of the Jus Publicum Europaeum*. Translated by G.L. Ulmen. Candor: Telos Press Publishing.

Sumari, L. 2021. 'Re-Imagining the "Area of Freedom, Security and Justice": Europe's Security Measures Experienced by African Migrants.' In *Expanding Boundaries: Borders, Mobilities and the Future of Europe–Africa Relations*, edited by J.P. Laine, I. Moyo, and C. Changwe Nshimbi. London: Routledge. doi.org/10.4324/9781003083726.

Troeller, G. 2002. 'UNHCR Resettlement: Evolution and Future Direction.' *International Journal of Refugee Law* 14, no. 1 (January): 85–95. doi.org/10.1093/ijrl/14.1.85.

Tzouvala, N. 2020. *Capitalism as Civilisation: A History of International Law.* Cambridge: Cambridge University Press. doi.org/10.1017/9781108684415.

United Nations (UN). 2022. 'Deaths at Sea on Migrant Routes to Europe Almost Double, Year on Year.' *UN News*, 29 April. New York: UN. news.un.org/en/story/2022/04/1117292.

United Nations General Assembly (UNGA). 2018. *Global Compact on Refugees.* GA Res. 12107, UN GAOR, 53 Comm, 73rd Session, 55th & 56th Meetings, Agenda Item 1, UN DOC A/73/12 (Part II), 2 August. New York: UNGA.

United Nations High Commissioner for Refugees (UNHCR). 1950. *Statute of the Office of the United Nations High Commissioner for Refugees, General Assembly Resolution 428 (V) of 14 December 1950.* Geneva: UNHCR. www.unhcr.org/sites/default/files/legacy-pdf/3b66c39e1.pdf.

United Nations High Commissioner for Refugees (UNHCR). 2001–23. *Resettlement Data Finder.* [Online.] Geneva: UNHCR. rsq.unhcr.org/.

United Nations High Commissioner for Refugees (UNHCR). 2011. *Refugee Resettlement Handbook.* Geneva: UNHCR. www.unhcr.org/in/sites/en-in/files/legacy-pdf/46f7c0ee2.pdf.

United Nations High Commissioner for Refugees (UNHCR). 2019a. *Desperate Journeys: Refugees and Migrants Arriving in Europe and at Europe's Borders. January–December 2018.* Geneva: UNHCR. www.unhcr.org/desperatejourneys/.

United Nations High Commissioner for Refugees (UNHCR). 2019b. *The Three-Year Strategy (2019–2021) on Resettlement and Complementary Pathways.* Report, June. Geneva: UNHCR. www.unhcr.org/au/media/three-year-strategy-resettlement-and-complementary-pathways.

United Nations High Commissioner for Refugees (UNHCR). 2022a. *Global Trends: Forced Displacement in 2022.* Geneva: UNHCR. www.unhcr.org/global-trends-report-2022.

United Nations High Commissioner for Refugees (UNHCR). 2022b. 'UNHCR Data Visualization on Mediterranean Crossings Charts Rising Death Toll and Tragedy at Sea.' *Briefing Notes*, 10 June. Geneva: UNHCR. www.unhcr.org/news/briefing/2022/6/62a2f90a1a/unhcr-data-visualization-mediterranean-crossings-charts-rising-death-toll.html.

United Nations High Commissioner for Refugees (UNHCR). 2023a. *Projected Global Resettlement Needs 2023*. Geneva: UNHCR. www.unhcr.org/au/media/2023-projected-global-resettlement-needs.

United Nations High Commissioner for Refugees (UNHCR). 2023b. 'Statement on UK Asylum Bill.' 7 March. Geneva: UNHCR. www.unhcr.org/uk/news/statement-uk-asylum-bill.

United Nations Office for the Coordination of Humanitarian Affairs (OCHA). 2023. 'Needs of Stranded Migrants in Northern Niger Rise as Numbers Soar.' News and press release, 5 April. New York: ReliefWeb. reliefweb.int/report/niger/needs-stranded-migrants-northern-niger-rise-numbers-soar.

Vaughan-Williams, N. 2015. *Europe's Border Crisis: Biopolitical Security and Beyond*. Oxford: Oxford University Press. doi.org/10.1093/acprof:oso/9780198747024.001.0001.

Venturi, B. 2017. *The EU and the Sahel: A Laboratory of Experimentation for the Security–Migration–Development Nexus*. IAI Working Papers 38. Rome: Istituto Affari Internazionali.

Walia, H. 2021. *Border and Rule: Global Migration, Capitalism, and the Rise of Racist Nationalism*. London: Haymarket.

Ward, K. 2008. *Networks of Empire: Forced Migration in the Dutch East India Company*. Cambridge: Cambridge University Press. doi.org/10.1017/CBO9780511551628.

Zagor, M. 2014. 'Recognition and Narrative Identities: Is Refugee Law Redeemable?' In *Allegiance and Identity in a Globalised World*, edited by F. Jenkins, M. Nolan, and K. Rubenstein. Cambridge: Cambridge University Press. doi.org/10.1017/CBO9781139696654.021.

Zagor, M. 2015. 'The Struggle of Autonomy and Authenticity: Framing the Savage Refugee.' *Social Identities* 21, no. 4: 373–94. doi.org/10.1080/13504630.2015.1071702.

Zagor, M. 2019. 'Martyrdom, Antinomianism, and the Prioritising of Christians: Towards a Political Theology of Refugee Resettlement.' *Refugee Survey Quarterly* 38, no. 4 (December): 387–424. doi.org/10.1093/rsq/hdz011.

Zagor, M. 2023. '"Safe Legal Pathways" or New Colonial Frontiers? A Critical Analysis of European Intervention in the Sahel and the Creation of Anomalous Legal Zones.' *Refugee Survey Quarterly* 43, no. 1: 22–52. doi.org/10.1093/rsq/hdad021.